THE
FABULOUS
FIBER
COOKBOOK

GREAT RECIPES YOU
CAN'T LIVE WITHOUT

SANDRA WOODRUFF, MS, RD

SQUAREONE
PUBLISHERS

COVER DESIGNER: Jeannie Tudor
EDITOR: Michael Weatherhead
TYPESETTER: Gary A. Rosenberg

Square One Publishers
115 Herricks Road • Garden City Park, NY 11040
516-535-2010 • 877-900-BOOK • www.squareonepublishers.com

Library of Congress Cataloging-in-Publication Data
Names: Woodruff, Sandra L., author.
Title: The fabulous fiber cookbook : great recipes you can't live without / Sandra Woodruff.
Description: Garden City Park, NY : Square One Publishers, 2017. | Includes bibliographical references and index.
Identifiers: LCCN 2017003999 (print) | LCCN 2017007183 (ebook) | ISBN 9780757004216 (pbk. : alk. paper) | ISBN 9780757054211 (epub)
Subjects: LCSH: High-fiber diet—Recipes. | Cooking. | Fiber in human nutrition. | LCGFT: Cookbooks.
Classification: LCC RM237.6 .W66 2017 (print) | LCC RM237.6 (ebook) | DDC 641.5/63—dc23
LC record available at https://lccn.loc.gov/2017003999

Printed in the United States of America

10   9   8   7   6   5   4   3   2   1

Contents

Preface

As a registered dietitian and nutritionist, I have seen countless diets come and go, each touted as a miracle cure or fountain of youth. From low-fat to low-carb, vegetarian to omnivore, Mediterranean to Paleo, and everything in between, there is no shortage of diets to choose from. Yet we aren't getting any healthier. This may be why the most frequent question I get from clients and acquaintences alike is, "What is the best diet?"

The truth is that many different diets or eating patterns can promote good health—but they all have one thing in common: a foundation of fiber-rich foods. Vegetables, fruits, whole grains, legumes, nuts, and seeds—these are the cornerstones of the tastiest and most healthful cuisines in the world. These are also the very same foods that are profoundly lacking in the Standard American Diet (SAD). That's why *The Fabulous Fiber Cookbook* was written. This is not a book about dieting, although fiber-rich foods have been found to promote weight loss naturally. Rather, it is about enjoying wholesome and delicious fiber-rich foods and reaping the many benefits these foods have to offer.

I have long been inspired not only by the power of food as medicine but also by the power of food to satisfy the senses, bring people together, and create lasting memories. Delicious food is surely one of life's simplest and greatest pleasures. With this in mind, my goal in writing this book was to translate the latest scientific findings about food and nutrition into simple and tasty meals to nourish both body and soul. It is my hope that this book will inspire many wonderful meals and also help you achieve excellent health for many years to come.

Introduction

Although the term "dietary fiber" did not exist before 1953, the health benefits of high-fiber foods have been recognized for over 2,000 years. In ancient Greece, Hippocrates noted the laxative effect of bread made from coarse whole wheat instead of refined wheat flour. Throughout the ensuing centuries, many others have attributed digestive health benefits to the fibrous residue, or "roughage," found in whole plant foods.

It wasn't until the 1970s, however, that scientists began to unravel the science behind fiber and understand that fiber's benefits extend far beyond digestive health.

British researchers Drs. Hugh Trowell and Denis Burkitt observed that a number of diseases seen in affluent Western societies were extremely rare or absent in rural African populations. They proposed that the fiber-rich diet of these groups protected them against a range of diseases, including diverticular disease, constipation, colon cancer, heart disease, diabetes, and obesity. The pair strongly criticized the modern habit of eating refined sugars and starches, which have been stripped of their fibrous, chewy coverings. They warned of the dangers of a fiber-depleted food supply, in which white flour, sugar, and meat crowded out whole grains, vegetables, and fruits.

Dr. Burkitt and Dr. Trowell's fiber hypothesis was soon extended by others who confirmed that people who ate fiber-rich diets, indeed, suffered far less from the diseases that plague the modern world. The question was: How could dietary fiber—a substance that does not leave the gastrointestinal tract and is not absorbed—confer these benefits?

Research over the past fifty years has shown that although fiber is not absorbed, it is far from inert. It is now clear that there are many mechanisms by which fiber protects health. For instance, fiber can lower blood cholesterol levels, modulate blood sugar levels, and increase feelings of fullness. Fiber is also a key food source for the "good bacteria" that reside in the colon. These bacteria produce substances that boost the immune system, fight inflammation, thwart cancer cells, and much more. As well, fiber-rich plant foods are loaded with nutrients and antioxidants that fight diseases in their own right.

Unfortunately, fiber is one of the most under-consumed nutrients in the modern diet. Most people get only half of what is considered to be an adequate daily amount—a situation referred to as the "fiber gap." Because fiber-depleted diets are so strongly linked to poor health, the committee tasked with updating the 2015 Dietary Guidelines classified fiber as a "nutrient of public health concern."

Why are so many people deficient in fiber? Simply because we eat too few plant foods. Vegetables, fruits, whole grains, legumes, nuts, and seeds provide fiber in abundance. Adding to the problem, many people find the topic of fiber to be way more confusing than it needs to be. What exactly is fiber? Why do we need it? How much do we need? What are the best sources? This confusion is, in part, due to a myriad of ways to define and classify fiber, not to mention a marketplace flooded with ultra-processed fiber-fortified foods. On top of that, the perception that high-fiber foods are boring or tasteless keeps some people stuck in a low-fiber rut.

The good news is that you can easily fill the fiber gap by including plenty of wholesome plant foods in your daily meals. A good place to start is to fill at least half your plate with vegetables and fruits. You can also expand your repertoire of vegetables and fruits, try new ways to use whole grains, enjoy creative bean dishes, add a sprinkling of nuts or seeds to dishes, and so much more. You may be surprised to discover that you can improve your health by eating more of something instead of solely cutting things out. You may also find that filling up on fiber helps you achieve a healthier body weight without actually "dieting." A 2015 study in the *Annals of Internal Medicine* found that people who simply aimed to eat at least 30 grams of fiber per day lost nearly

five pounds over the course of a year. This was about the same amount of weight that another group lost while following the more complex American Heart Association diet, which requires measuring foods, cutting fat intake, and other dietary restrictions.

Keep in mind that there are some caveats to adopting a high-fiber diet, so it's vitally important to do it right. It may be tempting to take a fiber supplement and be done with it or to rely on foods pumped up with added fiber. The problem is that products are not always what they seem to be. Moreover, the best evidence to date points to fiber from real foods, rather than isolated or synthetic fibers, as being protective against disease. This is likely due to the synergy of fiber, vitamins, minerals, antioxidants, and other components in whole plant foods.

The intention of this book is to simplify the science, sidestep the marketing gimmicks, and enable you to reap the benefits of a fiber-rich diet. Here you will find many delicious ways to boost fiber intake naturally with a goal of maximizing health and wellness for years to come.

Chapter 1 takes a fresh look at fiber, explains what it is, why we need it, and where to find it. You will find that fiber-rich food protects against virtually every aspect of chronic disease. Chapter 2 highlights foods that can fit into a healthy high-fiber eating plan, offers smart substitutions for low-fiber foods and ingredients, and provides additional tips for preparing and selecting foods. The remainder of the book offers over 170 recipes that emphasize nutritious fiber-rich foods. From breakfast to dessert, main courses to sides, these dishes are not only easy to make but also easy to love. Each recipe includes Nutrition Facts—calorie, carbohydrate, fiber, protein, fat, saturated fat, cholesterol, sodium, and calcium counts—so you can be sure your meals meet your individual nutritional needs and goals.

Beyond any doubt, research shows that a fiber-rich diet provides a myriad of health benefits, from reducing the risk of chronic disease to better weight management to fostering a diverse and robust microbiome. Moreover, a fiber-rich diet—with more plant foods, less meat, and fewer processed foods—will move you toward a cleaner way of eating and a more ecologically sustainable lifestyle. All things considered, the recommendation to consume a healthy amount of dietary fiber may turn out to be the most important nutritional recommendation of all.

It is my hope that the information provided in this book introduces you to some simple but important changes that can make a real difference to your well-being and the well-being of your loved ones. I wish you many satisfying meals to come.

1

A Fresh Look at Fiber

Just about everyone knows fiber is good for you. While fiber is best known for its beneficial role in promoting "regularity," a high-fiber diet may also protect against diabetes, cardiovascular disease, some types of cancer, and a number of other health problems. In addition, fiber has come to be known as a powerful tool in weight control. More recently, fiber's ability to nourish beneficial bacteria in the gut has added a whole new dimension to the conversation.

This chapter explains what fiber is, where to find it, and how a fiber-rich diet can help fill you up, slim you down, and improve your overall health. You will also find important tips on how to follow a high-fiber diet correctly, as things are not always what they seem when it comes to high-fiber foods.

WHAT IS FIBER?

Generally speaking, fiber is a type of carbohydrate that cannot be digested. While this may not sound very impressive, fiber actually has a significant impact on the body as it makes its way through the digestive tract. Plant foods such as vegetables, fruits, whole grains, legumes, nuts, and seeds naturally contain fiber. Technology has also made it possible to isolate various types of fiber from plants or even manufacture it for use in packaged foods or supplements. There is now a dizzying assortment of fibers touting a wide variety of potential health benefits. Unfortunately, this fact seems to have resulted in an information overload that has left many people confused and frustrated.

The good news is that a well-balanced diet built around whole foods can provide plenty of fiber and offer a bounty of health benefits without asking you to dwell on specifics. The tips and recipes in this book will guide the way, but for those who do like details, this chapter sheds some light on the facts.

DEFINITION DILEMMA AND CLASSIFICATION CONFUSION

One reason why people find fiber so confusing is that it is has been defined differently throughout the world and classified in a variety of different ways over the years. In an effort to clear up the confusion, let's take a look at some fiber-related terms. Here are the most common classifications of fiber.

Dietary Fiber, Isolated Fiber, and Synthetic Fiber

Fiber that occurs naturally in plants has long been referred to as dietary fiber, or intact fiber. Vegetables, fruits, legumes, whole grains, nuts, and seeds naturally contain fiber, which lends structure to these foods. The strings found in celery, the woody coatings of seeds and grains, and the crunch of carrots and apples all come from natural fiber. This intact variety also lends a thick, gummy quality to foods such as oatmeal and barley.

In 2002 and again in 2005, the Institute of Medicine (IOM) reinforced the idea that the term "dietary fiber" should be reserved for fiber that is "intrinsic and intact" in plants. According to the IOM, fiber-containing foods should be set apart from isolated or synthetic fibers because they contain beneficial nutrients. (Moreover, it is difficult to tease out the effects of fiber on its own from the effects of fiber in combination with all the other components of a food.) The IOM also recommended that isolated or synthetic fiber that has beneficial health effects should be referred to as "functional fiber." In 2016, the US Food and Drug Administration (FDA) changed course and created a legal definition of dietary fiber that includes both the natural fiber found in plants and any isolated fiber or synthetic fiber that has been deemed to have a "beneficial physiological effect in humans."

Isolated fiber is fiber that has been extracted from its natural source in order to be added to food products or used in dietary supplements. Examples of isolated fiber include inulin (from chicory root), cellulose (from wood or cotton), pectin (from fruit), beta-glucan (from oats or barley), oat fiber (from oat hulls), soy fiber (from soybean hulls or defatted soybeans), and various gums, including guar and xanthan gums.

As its name implies, synthetic fiber has been chemically synthesized. Starches, such as cornstarch and wheat starch, and sugars, such as glucose, are used to make additives that include resistant starch, polydextrose, and maltodextrin. These substances are not natural fibers but rather carbohydrates that have been doctored to act as fiber.

Food labeling regulations adopted in May of 2016 allow isolated and synthetic fibers that have been shown to have beneficial health effects to be included in the dietary fiber counts on food labels. In order to classify their isolated or synthetic fibers under the umbrella of dietary fiber, manufacturers must provide evidence of their benefits to the FDA. A common example of an approved fiber is beta-glucan soluble fiber isolated from barley or oats, which has been found to lower blood cholesterol levels. It is not yet known, however, if isolated or synthetic fibers produce the same positive outcomes—such as less heart disease, diabetes, and cancer—typically associated with a diet that is made up of naturally high-fiber whole foods.

Isolated and synthetic fibers are often used as low-calorie bulking agents, replacing some of the flour, sugar, or fat in food products. They are also used as thickeners and stabilizers, and to provide a rich and creamy mouth-feel. In some cases, fiber is added mainly for marketing appeal, as increasing a product's fiber count tends to give that product a "health halo," leading people to believe it is more healthful than it really is.

In recent years, isolated and synthetic fibers have been added to breads, pastas, breakfast cereals, yogurts, ice creams, snack foods, and juices. Many fiber-fortified foods are decent choices, but others are just high-fiber junk. On the other hand, unprocessed foods supply many health-promoting nutrients in addition to fiber. Eating fiber in its most natural state simply makes the most sense if you're looking to improve your health.

Soluble Fiber and Insoluble Fiber

Historically, fiber has been classified as either soluble or insoluble based on its physical properties and related health effects. *Soluble fiber* absorbs water as it passes through the digestive tract. It forms a sticky gel when mixed with water, which slows digestion and, in turn, stabilizes blood sugar levels and increases feelings of fullness. Soluble fiber also helps reduce blood cholesterol levels and supports the growth of "good" bacteria in the colon. It is associated with foods such as oats, barley, and legumes. *Insoluble fiber* does not absorb water in the digestive tract and thus does not form a gel. It helps food pass more quickly through the digestive system, promoting regularity. Food sources of insoluble fiber include wheat bran, the seeds and skin of fruits and vegetables, whole wheat, and brown rice. Most foods contain a mixture of soluble and insoluble fibers.

According to experts, one problem with viewing fiber strictly in terms of soluble or insoluble is that generalizations about their health effects do not always fit. For instance, oat bran and psyllium, which are rich in soluble fiber, have a laxative effect—a trait generally attributed to insoluble fiber. Moreover, soluble fiber can be synthesized to occur without its characteristic thickness and stickiness, eliminating some of the health benefits associated with soluble fiber. In addition, certain manufactured insoluble fibers support the growth of gut bacteria, a trait previously attributed only to soluble fiber.

Viscous Fiber, Fermentable Fiber, and Bulk-Forming Fiber

The IOM has recommended that instead of classifying fiber as soluble or insoluble, we should describe fiber according to its viscosity, fermentability, and bulk-forming properties.

Viscosity refers to the thickness of a liquid. As mentioned, viscous fiber forms a gel-like substance when mixed with water. Foods high in viscous fiber are the same as those associated with soluble fiber, which include oats, barley, legumes, flaxseed, and chia. Psyllium husk is also a rich in viscous fiber. The flesh of many fruits and vegetables contains viscous fiber as well. By slowing digestion and absorption, viscous fiber lowers blood sugar levels, makes you feel fuller longer, and may promote weight control. Viscous fiber also helps to lower blood cholesterol levels. One way it does this is by binding with bile in the small intestine, causing it to be excreted in the stool. Since the liver needs cholesterol to make new bile, it may remove some from the blood in order to do so. In addition, the short-chain fatty acids that form when soluble fiber ferments in the colon may reduce the amount of cholesterol produced by the liver, resulting in less cholesterol circulating in the bloodstream.

Fermentable fiber is so called because it is fermented and used as a source of nourishment by "good" bacteria in the colon. Throughout history, fermentable fiber has been a key food source for these beneficial microbes. Fermentable fibers are also referred to as prebiotics. This is not to be confused with probiotics, the beneficial microbes that may be taken as dietary supplements or consumed in foods such as yogurt, which contains live active cultures. A healthy population of microbes in the gut enhances gastrointestinal health, bolsters the immune system, and impacts weight control, chronic disease risk, and much more. (See "Feeding Your Gut Flora," below.) Many foods, including fruits, vegetables, legumes, oats, barley, and garlic, naturally contain fermentable fibers. Inulin and oligosaccharide are examples of fermentable fiber that is sometimes added to foods such as yogurt, snack bars, and cereals, or sold as a dietary supplement. The downside of fermentable fiber is that gas is a by-product of the fermentation process. Some people are more susceptible to this uncomfortable side effect than others. Fortunately, this gastrointestinal problem may subside over time as your body adapts to a high-fiber intake.

Bulk-forming fiber increases stool bulk, speeds movement of material through the intestines, and promotes regularity. Wheat bran is high in the bulk-forming fiber known as cellulose, which makes it very effective at preventing constipation.

Feeding Your Gut Flora

It has been said that we are what we eat, but we are also very much what our gut microbes eat. The gut is home to trillions of microbes, most of which reside in the colon. These microbes, which include large numbers of bacteria but also some fungi, viruses, and other organisms, are collectively known as the gut microbiota, or gut flora. Emerging research suggests that gut flora functions as its own distinct organ; so much so, in fact, that some experts describe gut flora as the "control center" of the body.

Gut microbes carry out countless activities that support health. They maintain the structure and function of the GI tract, strengthen the immune system, break down toxins, synthesize nutrients, produce anti-inflammatory compounds, and aid in the breakdown of fat. They even produce neurotransmitters that are taken up by the brain. Altered microbiota may be linked to a wide range of health problems, including obesity, diabetes, metabolic syndrome, bowel disease, autoimmune problems, cancer, and depression.

A key food source for gut microbes is fermentable fiber. (See page 7.) It follows that a processed, fiber-depleted diet could be causing your microbial self to starve. Without a proper food supply, your beneficial microbes can weaken and die off, allowing harmful ones to take over, a condition known as dysbiosis. The good news is you can start to change the makeup of your gut microbes in a matter of days simply by following a diet of fiber-rich vegetables, fruits, whole grains, legumes, nuts, and seeds. Many people also enjoy fermented foods, such as yogurt, keifer, miso, and sauerkraut, which provide probiotics (live beneficial bacteria) that can help replenish the gut.

Of course, good health habits, in general, will help maintain a healthy gut and a healthy community of microbes. These include avoiding unnecessary use of antibiotics and other medications that may harm gut flora, not smoking, getting enough sleep, being physically active, and managing stress. How well you care for your microbes largely determines how well they care for you.

Likewise, psyllium contains bulk-forming fiber, which enhances its effect on regularity.

As you can see, there are many different types of fiber, each with its own special characteristics. Some fibers help lower cholesterol or blood sugar, some promote regularity, some nourish good bacteria in the gut, and some may help you feel fuller for a longer period of time. Foods contain a mixture of various types of fiber, although certain foods are particularly high in one kind of fiber or another. By eating a variety of fiber-rich foods, you can enjoy a wide range of health benefits.

GLOSSARY OF FIBERS

As you now know, there is a wide array of fibers. Some are naturally present in foods. Some are isolated or manufactured and added to foods. Certain types of fiber are available as supplements. Here are some examples of fiber types that exist naturally in foods or are added to foods or supplements.

Beta-Glucan

Beta-glucan is a viscous fiber naturally found in foods such as oats and barley. Beta-glucan has been found to help lower blood cholesterol and blood sugar levels, and may also increase feelings of fullness. The Food and Drug Administration (FDA) allows the packaging of certain products made with oats, barley, or isolated beta-glucan to state that they may help reduce the risk of heart disease.

Cellulose

This non-viscous fiber is naturally present in plant foods, where it lends structure to cell walls.

Cellulose is very effective at increasing the bulk of stool. Wheat bran, which is especially high in cellulose, is one of the very best foods for promoting regularity. Powdered cellulose, which may be extracted from wood or cotton, is used as an anticaking, thickening, and texturizing ingredient in foods. Cellulose may be used as a low-calorie bulking agent in products such as low-carb tortillas. Methylcellulose is a viscous fiber made from cellulose. It is the active ingredient in the laxative Citrucel, and is also used by the food industry to thicken, emulsify, and stabilize foods.

Chitin and Chitosan

Although fiber is typically defined as a substance that is present only in plants, chitin and its derivative, chitosan, are exceptions to this rule. Both are fibrous substances found in exoskeletons of insects and crustaceans (such as crab, shrimp, or lobster) and in cell walls of most fungi. Chitosan is often sold as a weight-loss supplement, purporting to bind and trap dietary fat in the intestines. Most studies, however, have shown little evidence to support such a claim.

Gum

Rich in viscous fiber, gum—including guar gum, locust bean gum, gum arabic, xanthan gum, alginate, and carrageenan—is used to thicken and stabilize foods such as ice cream, yogurt, and salad dressings. Guar and xanthan gums are also used as binding agents in gluten-free foods. Guar gum is extracted from the cluster bean plant, and gum arabic is extracted from the sap of the acacia tree. Locust bean gum is extracted from the seeds of the carob tree. Xanthan gum is produced by fermentation of sugar by the bacteria *Xanthomonas campestris.* Alginate and carrageenan are extracted from seaweed. Due to their thick, sticky nature, some gums have been shown to lower blood cholesterol and blood sugar levels. Gums may also increase feelings of fullness.

Inulin

Inulin is composed of chains of fructose molecules bound together in a way that makes it resist digestion. Inulin occurs naturally in a variety of plant foods, including onions, leeks, garlic, asparagus, chicory root, dandelion greens, Jerusalem artichokes, and wheat. Commercially made inulin may be extracted from chicory roots or Jerusalem artichokes, or synthesized from sucrose.

Inulin is highly fermentable and functions as a prebiotic. It is one of the most frequently added fibers to processed foods, in which it is used to improve texture and mouth-feel, or as a low-calorie, low-glycemic replacement for part of the flour, sugar, or fat. In fact, some snack bars list inulin (or chicory root extract) as the main ingredient. Inulin is also sold as a powdery white fiber supplement to mix into food or a beverage. Be aware that too much can cause gas, bloating, or diarrhea in some people. Those who eat a lot of processed foods with added fiber may be vulnerable to these side effects.

Oligosaccharide

Oligosaccharide is composed of three to ten linked simple sugars that resist digestion. Oligosaccharides occur naturally in foods such as beans, peas, onions, and breast milk. They may also be manufactured from various sugars and starches. Oligosaccharides are used by the food industry to improve the texture and mouth-feel of a product, or as a low-calorie, low-glycemic bulking agent. Examples of oligosaccharides added to foods or supplements include oligofructose, galacto-oligosaccharides, and isomalto-oligosaccharides. Oligosaccharides also function as prebiotics. They may help promote regularity, although too much can cause gas, bloating, or diarrhea in some people.

Pectin

Pectin is a type of viscous fiber found in the cell walls and tissues of many fruits, including apples, citrus, and berries. Commercially made pectin is extracted from citrus peels and apples. Isolated pectin is mainly used to thicken jams and some other foods such as yogurt. Pectin has been found to help reduce blood cholesterol and blood sugar levels.

Polydextrose

Polydextrose is synthesized from glucose and sorbitol, which is often sourced from corn. It is used as a low-calorie, low-glycemic bulking agent in foods such as baked goods, cereals, low-sugar fruit spreads, ice cream, and snack foods. Polydextrose has been found to have a prebiotic effect and may also have a mild laxative effect.

Psyllium

Psyllium refers to the outer husk of seeds from the shrub-like herb *Plantago ovata.* It has a long history of medicinal use. Psyllium is very effective at promoting regularity and is the active ingredient in bulk-forming laxatives such as Metamucil and Konsyl. Ground or whole psyllium is also available in its pure form without any added sweeteners or flavorings. Psyllium is one of the richest sources of naturally occurring viscous fiber. Numerous studies have shown that psyllium can help reduce levels of blood cholesterol and glucose, sometimes reducing the need for medications to treat high cholesterol or blood sugar. The Food and Drug Administration allows certain products, including psyllium husk and healthy foods made with psyllium, to bear claims that they may help reduce the risk of heart disease. Due to its viscous nature, psyllium may also help increase feelings of fullness. It may also, however, cause an allergic reaction in some people.

Resistant Dextrin

Resistant dextrin is a short chain of low-digestible glucose, often made from corn or wheat starch. Maltodextrin and wheat dextrin are examples of resistant dextrin and may be added to products such as yogurt, ice cream, beverages, and other processed foods to enhance texture. Resistant dextrin is also included in some fiber supplements. Some types of resistant dextrin have been found to have a prebiotic effect.

Resistant Starch

As the name implies, resistant starch is a type of starch that resists digestion in the small intestine. Resistant starch naturally occurs in legumes, grains, seeds, fruits, and vegetables. Underripe bananas, corn tortillas, rye bread, white beans, lentils, and uncooked oats are examples of foods that are especially high in this type of fiber. The amount of resistant starch in a food increases after it has been cooked and cooled. Therefore, chilled potato salad has more resistant starch than a hot baked potato, and sushi has more resistant starch than hot cooked rice. Resistant starch is fermented by bacteria in the large intestine and is therefore classified as a prebiotic.

Resistant starch is also manufactured from cornstarch into a white powder that is used as a low-calorie, low-glycemic bulking agent to replace part of the flour in foods such as pasta and baked goods. This type of resistant starch also has a prebiotic effect. It may be listed as "resistant cornstarch" or "cornstarch" on product labels.

Soluble Corn Fiber

Soluble corn fiber is a non-viscous fiber manufactured from cornstarch. It is mainly used as a low-calorie, low-glycemic bulking agent in baked goods and cereals, but may also be found in dairy products, candy, soups, salad dressings, meal replacement drinks, flavored water, and other processed foods. It may be labeled as "soluble corn fiber," "maltodextrin," "corn syrup," or "corn syrup solids." Like most soluble fibers, soluble corn fiber has prebiotic properties.

WHY CHOOSE A HIGH-FIBER DIET?

Fiber is a common thread that links the world's healthiest diets. In the Mediterranean diet, numerous Asian diets, many African diets, vegetarian diets, and more, fiber-rich foods are mainstays. A fiber-rich diet offers many, many health benefits—both short-term and long-term ones. Here are six good reasons to add more of it to your diet.

Fiber Promotes Healthy Weight

Bulking up with fiber is crucial when you are trying to slim down. People who eat fiber-rich diets tend to experience healthier body weights, less belly fat, and less weight gain over time than people who eat low-fiber diets. And there are many reasons for this fact. Fiber-rich foods are slowly digested and absorbed, so they help you feel fuller longer and reduce the urge to graze between meals. High-fiber foods such as vegetables, fruits, and whole grains have a hearty texture, require more chewing, and take longer to eat, which enhances their ability to satisfy. And many foods that are naturally rich in fiber are also low in calories. Moreover, fiber may encourage weight loss by reducing the number of calories digested and absorbed from food. This is because high-fiber foods are less digestible and move more quickly through the intestines compared with refined and processed foods.

A 1997 United States Department of Agriculture study estimated that doubling fiber intake from 18 grams per day to 36 grams per day would result in about 130 fewer calories per day being absorbed. Over time, this reduction can lead to significant weight loss. Still another way that fiber may promote weight loss is through its prebiotic effect. As bacteria in the colon ferment different fibers, they produce short-chain fatty acids, including butyrate, propionate, and acetate, which may suppress appetite. Dietary fiber may also favor a healthy body weight by triggering a shift in the types of bacteria that populate the colon, affecting how the body stores fat.

The fat-fighting benefit of fiber is a big reason why so many fiber-fortified foods have flooded the marketplace. Ice cream, yogurt, baked goods, snack foods, beverages, and other products can have extraordinarily high fiber counts. Will fiber-fortified foods or supplements help with weight loss? Maybe. But ultimately, losing weight still requires eating fewer calories than you burn. Viscous fiber has been found to be more effective for satiety and weight loss than non-viscous fiber, but so far, studies have found the effects of added fiber on food intake and body weight to be relatively small. This is probably because there is more to satiety than just fiber. It is the total eating experience that makes people feel satisfied—the chewing, the visual appeal of food, the taste of the food, and any other factors that make eating pleasurable. Always keep in mind that foods that naturally contain fiber, such as fruits, vegetables, legumes, and whole grains, tend to be very filling and thus are self-limiting. The same cannot be said for fiber-fortified ice cream, chips, or cookies.

Fiber Improves Digestive Health and Regularity

A sluggish, constipated digestive system is perhaps the most common problem related to a low-fiber diet. Fiber is a natural colon cleanser, helping to sweep food quickly and efficiently through the intestines. Fiber works by adding bulk and water to stools, making bowel movements softer and easier to pass. This natural cleansing action is key not just to staying regular but also to avoiding other gastrointestinal problems, or GI problems, such as hemorrhoids or diverticular disease. The fiber in wheat bran and psyllium is especially good for regularity. Of course, adequate water intake is needed for fiber to do its job. Eating high amounts of fiber without enough water may actually make matters worse. You may be surprised to know that fiber can also be helpful for diarrhea. Diarrhea can occur when there is too much water in the colon. Soluble (viscous) fiber can absorb this excess fluid, helping firm up loose stool, much like a sponge. Items with soluble fiber such as oatmeal, bananas, and applesauce are sometimes recommended for diarrhea, as is psyllium.

Another way that fiber promotes digestive health, and overall health, is through its ability to nourish "good bacteria" in the gut. As mentioned earlier, fermentable or "prebiotic" fibers, in particular, support the growth of beneficial bacteria in the colon. As numerous bacteria ferment these fibers, they produce short-chain fatty acids such as acetate, propionate, and butyrate. These substances directly influence the environment of the large intestine. For instance, by making the intestine more acidic, they inhibit the growth of harmful bacteria and enhance the absorption of minerals such as calcium and magnesium. Butyrate is the preferred energy source for cells that line the colon and may also protect against colon cancer.

Natural food sources of prebiotic fiber include oats, barley, wheat, dried beans, onions, leeks, garlic, asparagus, bananas, apples, and chia and flax seeds. All plants, however, contain a mixture of fibers that includes prebiotic fiber, so eating a variety of fiber-rich plant foods will supply plenty of prebiotics. Inulin, oligosaccharide, and resistant starch are examples of prebiotics that are added to foods or sold as supplements. Prebiotics is an active field of research with great potential in areas of study that include immune function, bone health, colon cancer, obesity, and much more. There is still much to be learned about the long-term benefits and potential side effects of consuming large amounts of isolated or manufactured prebiotic fibers.

Fiber Fights Diabetes

It has been estimated that approximately 40 percent of Americans will develop type 2 diabetes at some point during their adult lives. The good news is that most cases of diabetes may be prevented through diet and exercise.

Whether you have diabetes or are trying to prevent it, a healthy high-fiber diet may play an important role in reversing or even avoiding this disease altogether. Swapping whole grains for refined ones seems to be particularly helpful, as a diet high in whole grains is linked with as much as a 30-percent lower risk of developing type 2 diabetes. Likewise, fiber-rich vegetables, legumes, fruits, and nuts offer important protection against diabetes. These foods are all components of the Mediterranean diet, which is perhaps the best dietary pattern for reducing diabetes risk. On the other hand, people who eat a diet low in fiber and high in processed carbs more than double their odds of developing diabetes.

How does fiber fight diabetes? As you know, it slows the absorption of carbohydrates from foods, which leads to a slower rise in blood sugar and less demand for insulin. As a result, the pancreas is less likely to "wear out" prematurely. Viscous fiber in oats, barley, legumes, and psyllium is especially good at stabilizing blood sugar levels. Of course, the weight loss benefits, anti-inflammatory benefits, and abundance of nutrients in a fiber-rich diet all add to this protective effect. For instance many fiber-rich foods are good sources of magnesium and chromium, minerals that protect against diabetes.

Fiber Enhances Heart Health

A high-fiber diet is strong medicine for a healthy heart and cardiovascular system. In fact, a 2013 analysis of twenty-two studies from around the world found that each daily increase of 7 grams of dietary fiber was associated with a 9-percent decrease in risk of cardiovascular disease.

Fiber fights heart disease on many fronts. Viscous fiber, as found in oats, barley, legumes, and psyllium, binds excess cholesterol in the gut and escorts it out of the body. This is why the FDA allows certain products containing psyllium, oats, and barley to feature claims that these items, eaten as part of a diet low in saturated fat and cholesterol, may reduce the risk of heart disease. High-fiber diets also fight heart disease by promoting healthier body weight, stabilizing blood sugar levels, reducing blood triglycerides, and facilitating lower blood pressure. And, of course, fiber-rich plant foods contain a wide variety of nutrients that reduce the risk of blood clots, fight inflammation, and foster a healthy heart and blood vessels.

Fiber Reduces Cancer Risk

The idea that a fiber-rich diet could reduce cancer risk makes scientific sense on many levels. For one thing, fiber sweeps waste quickly through the gut, thereby reducing exposure to toxins. And, as bacteria ferment fibers in the gut, they produce short-chain fatty acids such as butyrate, which may protect against colon cancer. A high-fiber diet may also protect against cancer by promoting a healthy body weight and providing an arsenal of cancer-fighting nutrients. Moreover, when you eat more healthy plant foods, you will likely eat less sugar, meat, trans fat, and processed food products, adding yet another layer of protection against the disease.

High-Fiber Diets and Carbohydrates

If you are watching your carbs, you may know that a high-fiber diet can also be high in carbohydrates. This may be a good thing if you are an athlete or very active, since carbohydrate is needed as fuel for exercise. If you are limiting carbs to treat diabetes, lose weight, or deal with other health problems, however, too much bread, grains, potatoes, or other high-carb foods can be counterproductive.

The good news is that many fiber-containing foods have moderate to low levels of carbohydrates. Salad vegetables and non-starchy vegetables, such as artichokes, asparagus, broccoli, Brussels sprouts, cabbage, and cauliflower, are among foods on the low end of the carbohydrate count. As for fruits, berries are among the high-fiber lower-carb choices. Nuts and avocados are also low-carb foods that supply good amounts of fiber. Keep in mind, too, that fiber-rich foods such as vegetables, fruits, whole grains, and legumes have a gentler effect on blood sugar than refined foods such as white bread or sugar.

The recipes in this book will help you keep both carbs and calories under control by providing lower-carb options for starches and sugars where available. Moreover, grain and pasta recipes feature plenty of non-starchy veggies to add bulk, so you get satisfying portions without an excess of carbohydrates or calories.

Evidence suggests that for every 10 grams of fiber eaten each day, there is a 5-percent reduction in breast cancer risk. One reason for this may be that fiber sequesters excess estrogen in the digestive tract, causing it to be excreted in the stool. The American Institute for Cancer Research and the World Cancer Research Fund have both concluded that there is "convincing" evidence to suggest that foods containing dietary fiber reduce the risk of colorectal cancer. These groups favor a high-fiber plant-based diet as defense against cancer. As an easy way to accomplish this goal, they suggest filling at least two-thirds of your plate with vegetables, fruits, whole grains, and beans, and the remainder with lean meat, poultry, fish, or low-fat dairy items.

Fiber Is Linked to Longevity

Can a high-fiber diet help you live longer? Maybe. Several large studies have linked higher intakes of dietary fiber with a lower risk of death from all causes. For instance, the NIH-AARP Diet and Health Study, which followed 388,122 older adults for an average of nine years, found that men and women with the highest dietary fiber intakes had a 22-percent lower risk of death compared to people who ate the least amount of fiber. A high-fiber diet is thought to increase longevity by virtue of its anti-inflammatory properties and high-nutrient content, both of which protect against many chronic diseases.

HOW MUCH FIBER IS ENOUGH?

According to the Dietary Reference Intakes for Americans, an "Adequate Intake" (AI) of dietary fiber is 14 grams per 1,000 calories. This amounts to about 25 grams for women and 38 grams for men. How did health authorities come up with this ratio? It is based on the intake level shown to protect against heart disease in scientific studies. Most Americans consume only about half this amount—a situation often referred to as the "fiber gap." It should be noted that various experts over the past fifty years have suggested that an optimal fiber intake could be anywhere from 15 to 25 grams per 1,000 calories. These higher intakes may be especially important for the prevention of conditions such as diabetes and colon cancer.

Getting enough fiber can be easy and delicious. Legumes, whole grains, fruits, vegetables, and nuts are all good sources. Some simple ways to fill the fiber gap include making at least half your plate contain vegetables and fruits, enjoying legumes as a main dish or part of a meal or snack, substituting whole grains for refined versions, and substituting snacks such as popcorn or nuts for ones such as chips or pretzels. The following table provides a rough idea of how much fiber is in various groups of foods, but more information on the fiber content of specific foods may be found at the USDA National Nutrient Database (http://ndb.nal.usda.gov).

Approximate Fiber Content of Foods

FOOD	SERVING SIZE	FIBER (G)
Dried beans, peas, lentils	$^1/_2$ cup	5–10
Whole grains (cooked)	$^1/_2$ cup	2–4
Vegetables (cooked)	$^1/_2$ cup	2–5
Fruits	$^1/_2$ cup	2–5
Nuts and seeds	$^1/_4$ cup	3–4

CAN YOU GET TOO MUCH OF A GOOD THING?

As recently discussed, the generally recommended fiber intake is 14 grams per 1,000 calories (or about 25 grams for women and 38 grams for men). This amount can be easily met or even exceeded by consuming a balanced diet that includes whole grains, fruits, vegetables, legumes, nuts, and seeds. The Dietary Reference Intakes did not set an upper limit on dietary fiber, since no level of fiber, when eaten in natural foods, has been shown to have adverse effects. Quite the contrary. A vegetarian diet based on vegetables, fruits, whole grains, nuts, and legumes is known to confer many health benefits. This type of diet can easily provide 50 grams of fiber per day. Our paleolithic ancestors are thought to have consumed over 100 grams of fiber every day.

With that said, adding too much fiber to your diet, or introducing too much fiber too fast, can cause bloating, gas, discomfort, and diarrhea. Due to the bulky nature of fibers, however, overconsumption of natural high-fiber foods tends to be self-limiting. This is a big reason why high-fiber foods help prevent overeating and weight gain. On the other hand, fiber-added foods, such as sweets and snacks, can be problematic because they are easily overeaten, leaving unaware consumers with unpleasant side effects.

If you notice a sudden onset of GI symptoms, inspect the ingredient label on the products you are consuming to see if excess fiber might be the culprit. Also, eating too much fiber along with other "low digestible" carbohydrates such as sugar alcohols (for example sorbitol, mannitol, maltitol) found in some sugar-free foods can make matters worse.

To avoid problems, increase fiber intake gradually, which will give your GI tract time to adapt. And be sure to drink plenty of fluids. As you know, fiber needs water to make its way through the digestive tract efficiently. It is important to note, though, that people with certain GI problems may not be able to tolerate some high-fiber foods and should consult with their healthcare providers before making any dietary changes.

SHOULD YOU SUPPLEMENT?

A diet built around whole foods can provide plenty of fiber in and of itself, while also providing important nutrients. Some people, however, may benefit from specific types of fiber supplements to relieve constipation, reduce blood cholesterol, or address other health issues. A variety of supplements are available, including powders, capsules, chewable tablets, and wafers.

When choosing supplements, be sure the supplement has been well-studied and is known to be effective for the problem you are trying to address. For instance, it is well established that psyllium can promote regularity and help lower blood cholesterol and blood sugar levels. On the other hand, wheat dextrin and methylcellulose may help with regularity, but they have not been shown to affect blood cholesterol or sugar levels.

To work properly, fiber supplements must be taken with adequate amounts of fluid, so read package directions for specific guidelines. Note that fiber supplements may not be safe for people with certain health conditions, including impaired swallowing and GI problems that may lead to obstructions or blockages. Certain fiber supplements may also cause allergic reactions or even anaphylaxis in some people. Finally, fiber supplements may reduce or delay the absorption of some medications. Work with your health-care provider to determine if supplements are right for you.

PUTTING PRINCIPLES INTO PRACTICE

If the ins and outs of fiber seem confusing, don't worry. The good news is you don't have to understand all the particulars to take advantage of a high-fiber lifestyle. Simply eating a diet that is rich in vegetables, fruits, legumes, and whole grains starts you on the road to success. This book will help you create high-fiber meals that are both easy to prepare and highly enjoyable. With just a little practice, you will learn to incorporate healthy and satisfying high-fiber choices into your daily diet.

2

Ingredients for Success

A well-stocked pantry is the first step toward preparing fabulous fiber-rich meals. This chapter features tips for choosing and using the best foods for a healthy high-fiber diet. As you shop for food, keep in mind that only plants naturally contain fiber. Moreover, excessive processing, particularly the refining of grains, strips food of both fiber and nutrients. You may notice that this book favors a diet high in plant foods and low in processed foods. Eating in this way will ensure your meals have the most fiber and best nutritional profiles possible. You will find that fiber-rich meals can be easy to prepare, economical, and absolutely delicious, and that keeping your pantry, refrigerator, and freezer stocked with the right foods can get you on the road to success quickly.

GRAINS AND GRAIN PRODUCTS

Throughout most of history, grains were cooked whole, or coarsely cracked and made into hearty breads or porridges. They retained their fiber and nutrients, and were slowly digested and absorbed, providing a slow-release, long-lasting form of energy. The overly processed grains that people consume today are a world apart. Refining strips away the fibrous bran and nutritious germ. More than half the B vitamins, 90 percent of the vitamin E, most of the minerals, and virtually all of the fiber are lost. Additionally, grinding grains into fluffy white flour causes them to be rapidly digested and absorbed, which spikes blood sugar levels. Switching back to minimally processed whole grains is powerful preventive medicine against obesity, heart disease, type 2 diabetes, and many other health problems. Here are some ways to get the most from grains and grain products.

Bread

From hearty peasant-style loaves and sliced sandwich breads to pitas, flatbreads, tortillas, bagels, and more, bread plays a prominent role in cuisines around the world. But eating too much of the wrong kind of bread adds to a host of health problems. The good news is that there are many excellent options from which to choose. First and foremost, look for 100-percent whole grain bread—foods such as whole wheat, spelt, barley, rye, or oats should appear first in the list of ingredients. Some other ingredients to look for include wheat bran or germ, oat bran, millet, rolled or cracked grains, sprouted grains, flax, nuts, and seeds. These provide a hearty filling texture, extra fiber, and important nutrients. Whole grain bread will have at least 2 grams of fiber per slice. Whole grain bread that contains bran, flax, or added fiber, such as inulin, oat fiber, or cellulose, may have twice as much fiber content.

Watching your carbs? There are reduced-carb versions of just about any kind of bread, from sandwich thins, pitas, wraps, and tortillas to bagels, burger buns, and more. Reduced-carb or "light" breads tend to be especially high in fiber because part of the flour has been replaced with fiber. Since fiber goes largely undigested, many reduced-carb breads have 25 to 50 percent fewer calories and carbs than regular bread. But be sure to read labels, as reduced-carb breads may be higher in sodium, wheat gluten, and other ingredients that you want to avoid. And in some cases, the calories may not be much different if the reduced-carb bread contains extra fat and protein. Chapter 5 provides more tips for choosing bread. (See page 80.)

Cereal

High-fiber ready-to-eat cereals can make a convenient breakfast or snack. As with bread, it's important to check the ingredients to be sure you are getting a truly whole grain product. Look for cereals made with whole wheat, spelt, oats, brown rice, barley, amaranth, wheat bran or germ, flax, or other nutrient-dense ingredients. Most 100-percent whole grain breakfast cereals have at least 4 grams of fiber per 2-ounce serving

Where's the Whole Grain?

Everyone knows that whole grains are healthier than refined versions, but finding authentic 100 percent whole grain products can be tricky. Why? A food needs to contain only 51 percent whole grain in order to be labeled "whole grain." For instance, a bread made with 51 percent whole wheat flour and 49 percent white flour may be labeled whole grain. To make matters more confusing, foods can be labeled "made with whole grain" as long as they contain some whole grain—even a small percentage. And many breads, cereals, and other grain products that are made with mostly white flour boast names such as "honey wheat" or "multigrain," which can be misleading. Here's another tip: Be aware that "wheat flour" and "enriched wheat flour" refer to refined white flour.

What is your best defense? Skip the package claims and go straight to the list of ingredients. Note that ingredients are listed in order of quantity present, so be sure that the first ingredients are whole grains, such as whole wheat, spelt, barley, oats, brown rice, etc. Nutrient-dense grain components such as bran and germ are other wholesome additions. After checking the ingredients, peruse the nutritional information to see the food's calories, fat, fiber, sodium, sugar, and other nutrient levels, as well as any artificial ingredients.

(about 1 cup). Cereals with added bran, psyllium, or isolated or synthetic fibers may have as much as 10 to 14 grams fiber per serving.

Whole grain porridges are excellent choices, as they are made from minimally processed rolled or cracked grains. It's hard to beat a steaming bowl of old-fasioned oatmeal. And there are many other fine choices to be had, such as oat bran, steel-cut oats, and a number of multigrain cereals. For a fresh and creamy hot cereal, make your own from uncooked whole grains such as barley, brown rice, spelt, or whole wheat berries. Simply grind the grain in a blender to a texture similar to grits or cracked grains and cook to a creamy consistency with four parts water, or use part water and part milk. Chapter 4 offers some ideas to get you started.

Cereal can also be used in a myriad of recipes to boost fiber and nutrient levels. For instance, use oat bran or rolled oats as a filler in meatballs or meatloaf. Grind whole grain cereal in a food processor or blender and use instead of graham crackers in pie crusts or as a coating for chicken or fish. Sprinkle some whole grain granola over a bowl of yogurt and fruit, or layer it into parfaits for added crunch and fiber.

Pasta

High-fiber pastas are available in all sizes and shapes. Once again, it's key to look at the ingredients to know what you are getting. High-fiber pastas may contain a myriad of flours, grains, or isolated or synthetic fibers. For the most nutrition, look for whole grains such as whole wheat, whole durum wheat (a high-protein wheat traditionally used to make pasta), kamut, spelt, and quinoa, as well as ingredients such as bran, wheat germ, flax, and legume flours.

While 100-percent whole grain pasta is your best nutritional choice, pastas that are part whole grain are certainly better than white pasta. Some of these boost fiber with isolated or synthetic fibers such as inulin or resistant starch. Whole grain pastas will have 5 to 6 grams fiber per 2-ounce serving (about 1 cup cooked), compared with white pasta, which has about 2 grams of fiber. Pastas made with added fiber or legume flour may contain even more fiber.

Whole Grains and Flours

A wide variety of whole grains are available at your local grocery store, and some cook in a matter of minutes. Whole grains add great texture and flavor to side dishes, soups, salads, and much more. Many are also available as flours or meals for making healthier baked goods.

Whole grains contain anywhere from 4 to 8 grams fiber per 1 cup cooked grain. Compare this with a cup of refined grain such as white rice, which has less than 1 gram fiber. Here are some whole grains, flours, and related products that you may wish to try in your high-fiber recipes.

Amaranth

Amaranth is technically not a grain but rather the tiny golden-colored seed of a South American plant. It smells like fresh corn silk and has an earthy, slightly nutty taste. Unlike most grains, amaranth is a complete protein, supplying all the essential amino acids. It also supplies impressive amounts of iron, magnesium, and zinc. Amaranth cooks into a porridge-like consistency similar to grits in about twenty minutes. It can also be popped like popcorn, although the kernels are much smaller. Amaranth flour may be substituted for up to one-quarter of the wheat flour in breads, muffins, cookies, or other baked goods. Amaranth is naturally gluten-free.

Barley

Barley has a light, nutty flavor and a pleasantly chewy texture. It is delicious in soups, casseroles, pilafs, side dishes, and salads. Like oats, barley is rich in viscous fiber, which helps lower cholesterol, stabilize blood sugar, and fill you up. Several forms of barley are available.

Pearl barley is the type most commonly found in grocery stores. The tough outer hull and bran have been removed. Even though pearl barley is partly refined, it still provides 3 grams of fiber per $1/2$ cup cooked grain. This is because barley contains fiber throughout the entire kernel, unlike many other grains, which concentrate their fiber in their outer bran layers.

Quick-cooking barley is pearl barley that has been steamed and dried to shorten cooking time. It cooks in about twelve minutes and contains the same fiber and nutrients as pearl barley.

Hulled barley is whole grain barley that has only the inedible outer hull removed. It is generally found in natural foods stores. Hull-less barley is also whole grain barley. It comes from a variety of barley that has a very loosely attached outer hull, which reduces the need for mechanical processing. Whole barley has a heartier texture than pearl barley and takes longer to cook.

Barley flour may be ground from either pearl or whole barley. It has a lightly sweet, mild flavor. The viscous fiber in barley flour adds moistness and tenderness to baked goods, reducing the need for fat and sugar. Barley flour can replace up to 50 percent of the wheat flour in many cake, muffin, quick bread, cookie, and pancake recipes.

Buckwheat

Buckwheat is the edible fruit seed of a plant that is closely related to rhubarb. It has a distinctive earthy, nutty flavor. Whole buckwheat kernels (groats) cook in about twelve minutes. Roasted buckwheat groats, also known as kasha, are good in pilafs and hot breakfast cereals. Buckwheat flour is ground from whole buckwheat kernels. It is especially good in pancakes. Asian soba noodles are also made from buckwheat flour. Contrary to what its name implies, buckwheat is not a type of wheat and does not contain gluten.

Chia

Chia is the seed of the *Salvia hispanica* plant, which is native to South America. It was revered as an energizing "super-food" by the ancient Mayans and Aztecs. Chia is about the size of poppyseeds and may be black or white in color. It is rich in the omega-3 fat alpha-linolenic acid (ALA) and supplies impressive amounts of minerals, including calcium, iron, and magnesium. In addition, just 1 tablespoon contains about 4 grams of fiber! To boost fiber and nutrition, sprinkle some chia seeds over yogurt, fruit, cereals, or salads. Add 2 to 3 teaspoons to your breakfast smoothie or add a couple of tablespoons to your batter or dough when making muffins, breads, cookies, or other baked goods.

When mixed with liquids, the viscous fiber in chia causes it to swell, creating a gelatinous tapioca-like texture that can be used to thicken puddings, beverages, and other foods. Chia juice drinks are often sold in natural foods stores, where they come with a hefty price tag. You can easily make these drinks at home for a lot less. (See page 76.) Chia gel can also be used as a substitute for eggs in many baked goods. Stir 1 tablespoon of chia seed into 3 tablespoons water and set aside for about twenty minutes to gel. Use to replace one large egg in baked goods. Note that baked goods made with chia gel will not rise as high as those made with eggs.

People with swallowing problems should consult with their healthcare provider about eating foods like chia seeds, especially in their dry form. Since the seeds absorb many times their weight in water, they may swell and become lodged in the esophagus. This is good advice for any dry or powdered food or supplement that is high in viscous fiber, even for those who do not have swallowing problems.

Coconut Flour

Ground from dried defatted coconut, this flour has a light coconut flavor that complements many baked goods. It also makes a delicious coating for chicken or fish instead of flour or cornmeal. Coconut flour is very high in fiber. With 40 grams fiber per cup, it has more than twice the fiber of most whole grain flours. Coconut flour can replace about 20 percent of the wheat flour in many baked goods. It is very absorbent, though, so substitutions can be tricky. You can either replace a given amount of flour with half as much coconut flour (e.g., replace $\frac{1}{4}$ cup of wheat flour with 2 tablespoons of coconut flour) or replace a given amount of flour with an equal amount of coconut flour and increase the liquid in the recipe by an amount equal to the coconut flour being added (e.g., replace $\frac{1}{4}$ cup of wheat flour with $\frac{1}{4}$ cup coconut flour plus $\frac{1}{4}$ cup liquid).

Be aware that using too much coconut flour in baked goods can cause them to be crumbly, which is why many coconut flour recipes contain a high proportion of eggs or other binders. Too much can also result in a dense, gritty texture. It

may take some experimentation to get your recipe just right. When used as a coating for chicken or fish, a light dusting is usually all that is needed. Use too much, and the coating will be dry and powdery or it will soak up a large amount of oil, adding extra fat and calories to the food.

Corn

Fresh corn is enjoyed as a starchy vegetable, while dried corn is used as a grain. Corn is naturally gluten-free and comes in several colors, including white, yellow, and blue. Much of the cornmeal, corn grits, and polenta found in grocery stores is refined, but whole grain versions can be found in natural foods stores and some grocery stores. To be sure you're getting whole grain corn, look for "whole corn" or "whole grain corn" in the ingredients. Avoid labels that say "bolted" or "degerminated," processing steps that remove bran and germ.

Cornmeal adds a lightly sweet, mellow flavor and distinctive texture to baked goods. Most cornmeal sold in grocery stores is medium grind, but finely ground cornmeal, which adds a softer, more cake-like texture, is also available. Finer still is whole grain corn flour. Coarsely ground cornmeal is sold as both grits (a Southern favorite) and polenta (an Italian porridge).

Popcorn is a special type of whole grain corn that bursts when heated to create a fluffy texture. Moreover, 3 cups of air-popped popcorn has just 80 calories and 3.5 grams fiber.

Couscous

This traditional North African and Middle Eastern dish is actually a tiny pasta that is used like a grain. Couscous cooks in just a couple of minutes and is excellent in pilafs, side dishes, and salads. Be aware that much of the couscous available in grocery stores is made from white flour. Choose whole wheat couscous for the most fiber and nutrition. Israeli, or pearl, couscous is about the size of a pea, and cooks in approximately ten minutes. Again, unless the package specifically states it is whole grain, it is most likely refined.

Flax

This small nutty-tasting seed has long been popular in Canada and Europe. Flax is rich in viscous fibers and the omega-3 fatty acid, alpha-linolenic acid. Whole and ground flaxseeds (flaxmeal) are available in natural foods stores and many grocery stores. Flaxseeds are either reddish-brown or golden-yellow in color. The golden seeds have a milder flavor than the darker seeds but the two are nutritionally similar.

Whole flaxseeds make a fine addition to breads or other baked goods, to which they add color and crunch. But be aware that flax must be ground or thoroughly chewed in order to absorb the ALA and other nutrients. For the freshest flaxmeal possible, grind your own flaxseeds in a coffee grinder or mini blender jar as you need them. Flax can replace 10 to 15 percent of the flour in many baked goods such as muffins, quick breads, and cookies. Flaxmeal can also be sprinkled over yogurt or cereal or added to smoothies. To maintain freshness, refrigerate flaxmeal in an opaque container for up to one month.

Flaxmeal can be used as an egg substitute in some baked goods. To replace one large egg, mix 1 tablespoon flaxmeal with 3 tablespoons water in a small bowl and let sit for about ten minutes, until the mixture forms a thick gel. Add to your recipe as you would an egg. Note that baked goods made with flax will not rise as high as when made with eggs.

Millet

Though it's most often sold as birdseed in the United States, millet is a staple grain in Asia and Africa. Whole grain millet looks like tiny round ivory-colored beads. It has a mild flavor and makes a nice porridge or side dish. Cooked millet can also be mixed with ground meats to make meatloaf or meatballs. Whole grain millet is sometimes added to breads for a hearty and satisfying texture. Whole grain millet flour can replace up to 25 percent of the wheat flour in many baked goods. Millet is gluten-free.

Nut flours

Nut flours such as almond meal and hazelnut meal are simply finely ground nuts. As with the whole nuts, nut flours provide fiber, vitamins, minerals, protein, and healthy fats. Nut flours can replace up to 25 percent of the flour in many baked goods to add tender texture and rich flavor.

Oats

Like barley, oats provide viscous fibers that help lower blood cholesterol and provide many other health benefits. Oats have a mild, lightly sweet flavor that makes them perfect for a wide variety of uses. Here are some delicious ways to add the goodness of oats to your diet.

Rolled oats are whole grain oats that have been rolled into flakes, which allows them to cook more quickly. They're terrific as a breakfast cereal, a filler for meatloaf, and a great addition to cookies and other baked goods. "Old-fashioned" oats, which cook in five to ten minutes (depending on their thickness) are a good choice for breakfast cereal. Being thicker cut than "instant" oats, they take longer to digest and absorb, and keep you feeling fuller longer. "Quick-cooking" (one-minute) oats work well in cookies, muffins, pie crusts, and other baked goods. Steel-cut oats (Irish oats or Scotch oats) are whole grain oats that have been chopped into small pieces. They make a filling and satisfying hot cereal.

Oat bran is made from the outer part of the oat kernel. It cooks into a hearty high-fiber breakfast cereal in a matter of minutes. Add a couple of tablespoons of oat bran to smoothies for a creamy-rich texture. Use it as a filler for meat-loaves and meatballs. And keep some on hand for a versatile baking ingredient. Try replacing 25 percent of the flour in muffins, quick breads, pancakes, pie crusts, and cookies with oat bran for a hearty and satisfying texture. Muffins prepared with all oat bran make an especially filling breakfast on the run. Look for oat bran in the hot cereal section of your grocery store, alongside the rolled oats. For baking, use a quick-cooking (cooks in about two minutes), soft-textured oat bran such as Quaker Oat Bran or, if purchasing in natural foods stores, look for a "fine-textured" oat bran that cooks in a couple minutes.

Oat flour has a lightly sweet, mild flavor that makes it perfect for baking. The viscous fibers in oat flour also add moistness and tenderness to baked goods, reducing the need for fat and sugar. Try replacing 25 to 50 percent of the wheat flour in cakes, muffins, and quick breads with oat flour for a deliciously moist and tender texture.

Quinoa

Quinoa is the seed of a plant related to beets, chard, and spinach. This super-nutritious gluten-free food was a dietary staple of the ancient Incas. Quinoa comes in several colors including ivory, red, and tri-colored. Its light earthy flavor works well in pilafs, salads, and porridges. Perhaps best of all, quinoa cooks in about twelve minutes. Be sure to rinse quinoa well before cooking to remove the bitter coating, which is a natural repellant to birds and insects. Some brands are prewashed, eliminating the need for this step. Read package directions to be sure. Quinoa flour can substitute for up to half of the wheat flour in many baked goods. Its nutty earthy flavor blends well with recipes that feature fruits, nuts, and spices.

Rice

While brown rice is the best known type of whole grain rice, other options include red, black, and even purple. Wild rice, which is technically a seed rather than a grain, is a bit higher in fiber and protein and lower in calories than brown rice. Whole grain rice is naturally gluten-free and has a delightful texture and a light nutty flavor that is delicious in pilafs, salads, soups, side dishes, and desserts. Quick-cooking brown rice is brown rice that has been precooked and dehydrated so that it cooks in about ten minutes.

Brown rice flour has a mild flavor which makes it a good staple for gluten-free baking. Some brands are very finely ground, while others have a texture similar to cornmeal. Try replacing up to 25 percent of the wheat flour in baked goods with brown rice flour.

Teff

This tiny gluten-free grain has been a staple of Ethiopian cuisine for thousands of years. Brown teff has a chocolatey-molasses color and a mild nutty flavor. Ivory teff has a pale yellow color and a milder flavor. Teff is a good source of minerals such as iron, calcium, magnesium, and zinc. Cooked teff has the consistency of farina and is often prepared as a porridge. It can also be made into polenta or added to baked goods, much like cornmeal. Teff flour can be substituted for 25 percent of the wheat flour in many baked goods. It is used to make the fermented Ethiopian flatbread known as injera.

Wheat

Most of the wheat eaten today is in the form of nutrient-poor white flour. However, there are numerous fiber-rich whole grain wheat products to choose from, including some delicious and versatile ancient strains that are making a comeback. It should be noted that some believe these ancient wheats may be better tolerated by people with wheat or gluten sensitivities. All varieties of wheat, however, contain gluten and must be strictly avoided by people with celiac disease. People with wheat allergies must also avoid all types of wheat.

Wheat berries are whole grain wheat kernels. Cooked wheat berries have a deliciously chewy texture and nutty flavor. Use them as you would brown rice in pilafs, casseroles, salads, and other recipes.

Bulgur wheat is cracked wheat berries that have been precooked and dried. Best known as an ingredient in the Middle Eastern salad, Tabbouleh, bulgur wheat is equally tasty in pilafs, stuffings, casseroles, and other dishes. Bulgur

Fiber and Food Labels

In May of 2016, the FDA updated regulations for the Nutrition Facts label that appears on food products. Perhaps the most prominent change is that the label was redesigned to highlight calories and servings, two important elements in making informed food choices. The new Nutrition Facts panel also requires manufacturers to list how much added sugar is in a food and updates the information for a variety of nutrients.

With regard to dietary fiber, two key changes were made. First, a legal definition for dietary fiber was created. Previously, the dietary fiber count on food labels included the fiber that naturally occurs in plants plus a myriad of isolated and synthetic non-digestible carbohydrates that met the chemical definition of fiber. The newly created definition still includes the natural fiber found in foods, of course. However, only those isolated or synthetic fibers that have been determined by FDA to have beneficial health effects will be allowed to count as dietary fiber. These beneficial effects may include such things as lowering blood glucose or cholesterol levels, improving bowel function, lowering blood pressure, or increasing satiety. Seven isolated or synthetic fibers were initially determined to qualify as dietary fiber: Beta-glucan soluble fiber, psyllium husk, cellulose, guar gum, pectin, locust bean gum, and hydroxypropylmethylcellulose. Manufacturers can petition the FDA to request that others be approved.

While some feel that narrowing the definition of dietary fiber is a good thing, it is not without controversy. Perhaps most vexing is that lumping natural and added fibers together as dietary fiber makes it impossible know how much of the fiber in a product comes from food and how much has been added. You can, however, get an idea of where the fiber is coming from by looking at the ingredients list. Ingredients are listed in order of quantity present, so if an isolated or synthesized

wheat is very easy to prepare. All you do is add boiling water and let it sit for thirty minutes.

Einkorn, the most ancient variety of wheat, was harvested as a wild grain around 16,000–15,000 BC and was one of the first grains cultivated for food. Use einkorn as you would wheat berries in salads, pilafs, casseroles, and other dishes.

Kamut is an ancient relative of durum wheat (which is used to make pasta). Kamut berries are about twice the size of wheat berries and have a light buttery taste and a chewy texture. Use kamut as you would brown rice or wheat berries in salads, pilafs, casseroles, and other dishes. Kamut flour is good for making homemade pasta.

Farro is the Italian name for an ancient strain of wheat known as emmer (although some farro may actually be spelt or einkorn). This hearty grain was a dietary mainstay in ancient Rome. Farro has a mild nutty flavor similar to other kinds of wheat, but the texture is fluffier, similar to barley. Farro is available in pearled (perlato) and semi-pearled (semi-perlato) versions. The semi-pearled version retains more of the nutrient-rich bran. Whole (unpearled) farro is also available in some natural foods stores.

Freekeh (also known as farik or frikeh) is a traditional food of the Middle East and Northeastern Africa. It is whole grain wheat that is harvested early (while the kernels are still green) and then roasted. Freekeh has a subtle smoky, nutty

---

fiber is listed first, it is the main ingredient. If the product contains ingredients such as whole wheat, oats, barley, flax, vegetables, fruits, and legumes, you will know that some of the fiber is naturally occurring. Many foods contain a combination of naturally occurring and added fibers.

The other fiber-related change to food labels concerns the Daily Value (DV). Daily values are reference amounts of nutrients that help consumers understand the nutrition information in the context of a total daily diet. The DV for dietary fiber was 25 grams per day, based on a 2,000-calorie diet. That has been updated to 28 grams per day, which reflects the general recommendation to consume 14 grams of fiber per 1,000 calories.

To find out how much fiber is packaged in foods, check the Nutrition Facts panel. The amount of dietary fiber per serving is rounded to the nearest gram. If a serving contains less than 1 gram of fiber, manufacturers do not have to list fiber content. If the serving contains less than 0.5

grams, the fiber content may be expressed as 0.

Some food packages feature terms such as "high, rich in, or excellent source of fiber," "good source of fiber," or "more or added fiber." These terms are regulated by the FDA to mean the following:

- **High, rich in, or excellent source of fiber.** Provides at least 20 percent of the DV for fiber.

- **Good source of fiber.** Provides 10 to 19 percent of the DV for fiber.

- **More or added fiber.** Provides at least 10 percent more fiber per serving than the traditional version of the food.

Changes to the Nutrition Facts panel are slated to take effect over a two- to three-year period. For most manufacturers, these changes must be made by July 26 of 2018. Smaller companies will have an extra year to comply. Keep in mind that these types of deadlines are sometimes extended to give industry more time to adapt.

flavor and pleasant chewy texture that is delicious in salads, pilafs, and other recipes.

Spelt is yet another ancient variety of wheat. It has a light nutty flavor. Spelt berries are delicious in pilafs, casseroles, salads, and other dishes. Whole grain spelt flour works well in quick breads, muffins, cookies, and other baked goods where it lends a more tender texture than regular whole wheat flour.

Whole wheat flour is ground from whole grain wheat. Most of the whole wheat flour sold in grocery stores is made from hard red wheat, which has a bold flavor and high protein (gluten) content that is well-suited for making yeast breads. The high gluten content of hard wheat forms elastic strands that help bread rise. Hard white whole wheat flour is also available in many stores. It has a lighter color and milder flavor than hard red whole wheat flour and also works great in yeast breads. When you want to make recipes such as muffins, quick breads, pie crusts, and cookies, a better choice is whole wheat pastry flour, described below.

Whole wheat pastry flour is ground from soft white wheat berries, which have a milder flavor and less protein (gluten) than the hard red wheat described above. Whole wheat pastry flour produces baked goods with a more tender texture and a lighter, sweeter flavor than hard red wheat. Whole wheat pastry flour is an excellent choice for all baked goods except for yeast breads which need the toughness of hard wheat in order to rise properly. Spelt flour performs much like whole wheat pastry flour in recipes.

Wheat germ is the nutrient-rich inner part of the wheat kernel. It is an excellent source of vitamin E. Wheat germ can replace part of the flour in muffins, quick breads, pancakes, cookies, and other baked goods. It also makes an excellent addition to smoothies, can be sprinkled over cereal or fruit, and makes a good coating for fish or chicken.

Wheat bran is the fiber-rich outer part of the wheat kernel. Wheat bran can be incorporated into breads, muffins, cookies, and many other baked goods. You can also mix it into oatmeal and other hot cereals for a fiber boost.

Storing Whole Grains

Refined grains such as white rice, which have been stripped of the bran and germ, will keep almost indefinitely in the pantry. On the other hand, whole grains, especially if ground into flours or meals, must be stored with care since their natural oils will gradually turn rancid if exposed to light and air.

How do you know if your whole grains are fresh? First, shop at stores where there is a high turnover in product. Next, be sure to check the "sell by" date on packaged grains and flours. Then, store your whole grains and flours in an airtight container in the refrigerator or freezer. This goes for nut flours, coconut flour, and flaxmeal too. Flours and meals should maintain quality for several months if refrigerated and for at least twice as long if stored in the freezer. Intact grains will last longer still. A bitter taste or off-odor indicates that grains have turned rancid.

FRUITS AND VEGETABLES

Low in calories and high in nutrients, vegetables and fruits form the foundation of a healthy high-fiber eating plan. And ongoing research supports that "more matters" when it comes to fighting heart disease, diabetes, cancer, obesity, and many other health problems. The easiest way to be sure you are getting enough vegetables and fruits is to fill at least half your plate with produce.

For the most fiber and nutrients, it's hard to beat fresh produce. And whenever possible, include edible skins and seeds. For instance, try chunky "smashed" potatoes with the skin on instead of mashed peeled potatoes. Eat apples, pears, and peaches unpeeled. And choose whole fruits and vegetables over juices.

One cup of vegetables and fruits provides anywhere from 3 to 8 grams of fiber. Some vegetables, such as lettuce, cucumbers, and mushrooms, have less fiber. But keep in mind that fiber is just one of the good things about vegetables and fruits, so avoid choosing produce based on fiber count alone. A better idea is to aim for a rainbow of colors. This way you get a wide range of disease-fighting vitamins, minerals, phytonutrients, and antioxidants along with the fiber.

When convenience counts, frozen vegetables and fruits are excellent choices. Most frozen produce is picked at the peak of ripeness and flash frozen to preserve nutrients. In fact, if your "fresh" produce is not really all that fresh, frozen may actually be the better choice. Frozen vegetables are great for side dishes, pilafs, soups, and stews. Frozen fruits are perfect for smoothies, fruit sauces, and many desserts. Certain canned and jarred vegetables and fruits are also good convenience foods. For instance, canned tomatoes, marinara sauce, salsa, roasted red peppers, artichoke hearts, and dried beans are all good staples to have on hand for your high-fiber recipes. Organic and lower-sodium versions are available for many of these foods. Last but not least, stock up on an assortment of dried fruits such as raisins, dried cranberries, cherries, apricots, plums, and figs, as well as sun-dried tomatoes to add a burst of flavor to salads, baked goods, and other recipes.

Fiber Content of Selected Fruits

FRUIT	AMOUNT	FIBER
Blackberries, raspberries, guava, pomegranate	1 cup	7–9 g
Avocados	1/2 cup cubes	5 g
Kiwifruit, oranges, bananas, grapefruit, pears, blueberries, fresh figs	1 cup	4–5 g
Apples, cherries, mangoes, apricots, strawberries	1 cup	2.6–3.3 g
Dried figs, plums, dates, blueberries, raisins, apricots	1/4 cup	2.4–3.7 g
Papaya, nectarine, pineapple, plums	1 cup	2.3–2.5 g
Cantaloupe, honeydew melon, seedless grapes	1 cup	1.4–1.6 g
Fruit juice	1 cup	0.2–0.5 g

Fiber Content of Selected Vegetables

VEGETABLE	AMOUNT	FIBER
Dried beans, peas, lentils (cooked or canned)	1 cup	10–20 g
Artichokes, fresh black-eyed peas, fresh lima beans, edamame, green peas, winter squash (hubbard, acorn, butternut)	1 cup	9–10 g
Green peas, corn, collard greens, cooked	1 cup	7–8 g
Brussels sprouts, turnip greens, broccoli, carrots, cooked	1 cup	5–6 g
Spinach, beets, tomatoes, potatoes (with skin), green beans, asparagus, cooked	1 cup	3–4 g
Summer squash, cauliflower, cooked	1 cup	2.6–2.9 g
Cabbage, tomatoes, raw	1 cup	2–2.5 g
Lettuce, spinach, raw	1 cup	1–1.9 g

OILS, SPREADS, DRESSINGS, AND OTHER FAT SOURCES

Making smart fat choices is a high priority in any healthy eating plan. Your best bet is to get most of your fat from whole foods such as nuts, seeds, and avocados, which have their fiber and nutrients intact. These foods can add loads of interest to meals while providing some "good fats." Additionally, including a bit of fat in meals can help you feel fuller longer and boost the absorption of vitamins A, D, E, and K, and many phytonutrients.

Nuts and Seeds

Nuts and seeds are the ultimate "good fats," providing healthy oils in a natural unprocessed package. Nuts and seeds also supply protein, a wide range of phytonutrients, vitamins, minerals, and dietary fiber. For all of these reasons, nuts and seeds rank high on the list of healthful foods. For the most nutrition, purchase nuts with their skins intact, as opposed to blanched nuts, which are processed to remove the papery brown outer seedcoat. Many of the healthful benefits of nuts and seeds are due to fibers and other substances found in the seedcoat. An ounce of most nuts or seeds (about 1/4 cup) contains 3 to 4 grams of fiber. Chia and flaxseeds have more than twice this amount.

There are many ways to perk up meals with nuts and seeds. Sprinkle over yogurt and cereal. Add to smoothies, salads, and baked goods. Toss with steamed green beans. Use in coatings for fish or chicken. Finely ground nuts, such as almond or hazelnut meal, can also replace part of the flour in baked goods. Do keep in mind that nuts and seeds are a concentrated source of calories (about 800 calories per cup!) so use moderately if you are watching your weight.

Avocados

These silky fruits are packed with fiber and nutrients. Avocados are great additons to salads, sandwiches, and many other recipes. Try using mashed avocado as a sandwich spread instead of mayonnaise. One-fourth cup of mashed avocado has just over about 90 calories, about the same as a tablespoon of full-fat mayonnaise. But the avocado also provides 4 grams of fiber along with vitamins E and K, B-vitamins, and much more.

Fats and Oils

Fat plays many important roles in recipes. For instance, fat tenderizes baked goods, enhances flavor, and adds moisture and a rich mouth-feel. But too much fat adds unnecessary calories, so moderation is the best policy. If you like to bake, you may be interested to know that fiber-rich flours can reduce the need for added fats. Oat and barley flours, in particular, are rich in viscous fibers that add tenderness and moistness. For these reasons, some fat substitutes used by the food industry are made with oat and barley fibers. Here are some things to consider when choosing fats and oils.

Butter

Butter has a creamy rich flavor that's hard to beat. Unfortunately, butter is also high in saturated fat. A good compromise is a canola-butter spread, and several brands are available. Blending canola oil with butter reduces saturated fat while adding some omega-3 fat, and preserves buttery flavor. Canola-butter spreads contain varying amounts of fat, ranging from 11 grams per tablespoon for full-fat spreads to 5 grams for light versions. Differences in fat content can make a big difference in the outcome of recipes. For best results, be sure to choose a spread that contains the fat content specified in the recipe you're following.

It's important to note that many environmental contaminants are fat-soluble and especially concentrated in animal fats, since animals are high in the food chain. Therefore, when you use animal fats, such as butter, your best bet is to go with grass-fed organic varieties.

Margarines and Spreads

Margarines and spreads have a bad rap due to their history of being high in hydrogenated oils and trans fats. Some better products are now available. But unfortunately, some spreads are replacing hydrogenated oils with "interesterified" oils. Interesterification is an industrial process that chemically rearranges fats to make them more solid. The best advice is to look for brands with short and simple ingredients lists that include minimally processed oils (such as liquid canola, soybean, and olive oils).

Keep in mind that margarines and spreads contain varying amounts of fat, ranging from 11 grams per tablespoon for a full-fat spread, to 8 grams for intermediate-fat spreads, to 5 grams or less for "light" spreads. Differences in fat content can make a big difference in the outcome of recipes. For best results, be sure to choose a spread that contains the fat content specified in a particular recipe.

Oils

A variety of vegetable oils, including canola, soybean, sunflower, safflower, and peanut oil, will work fine in recipes. For baking, canola oil is a good choice. It has a mild flavor and is a good source of the essential fat ALA, an omega-3 fat

that many people do not get enough of. For salads, extra virgin olive oil is a good choice. It is minimally processed and provides vitamin E and a variety of phytonutrients, while adding delicious flavor to foods. Other good choices are grapeseed oil, as well as walnut, hazelnut, almond, or other nut oils. Whenever possible, choose organic cold-pressed or expeller-pressed oils. Compared with conventionally produced oils, cold-pressed and expeller-pressed oils are subjected to less heat and are not extracted with chemical solvents. In addition, organic foods are GMO-free. To preserve freshness, store oils in the refrigerator. This slows oxidation and helps prevent harmful by-products from forming.

Mayonnaise

Ready-made mayonnaise is a convenient ingredient for salads, sandwiches, and other recipes. If you are watching your weight, choose mayonnaise that is reduced in fat and calories, or use just a small amount of the full-fat product. Be sure to read labels, since some lower-fat brands contain extra sugar and salt. To boost fiber and nutrition, try spreading sandwiches with hummus or mashed avocado instead of mayonnaise. Nut butter is another nutritious alternative to mayonnaise when making sandwiches. Keep in mind that one tablespoon of nut butter has about 90 calories, the same as full-fat mayo, so use just a thin layer.

Salad Dressings

Ready-made salad dressings are convenient for salads, sandwiches, marinades, and more. If you are watching your weight, choose dressings that are reduced in fat and calories, or use just a small amount of the full-fat product. Many people find that they are satisfied with much smaller amounts of light or regular salad dressings than fat-free dressings beause they coat the salad and bring out the flavors better. A good compromise is to look for dressings with about 60 calories and 6 grams of fat per 2-tablespoon serving. Be sure to read labels, since some dressings contain high amounts of added sugar and salt.

PROTEIN SOURCES

Fiber is vitally important for feeling full and satisfied. But also important is protein. Including both protein and fiber in meals is a key to success for people who are watching their weight. While many people are in the habit of eating meat, poultry, and seafood for protein, many plant foods are also good sources of protein. Swapping these for meat can instantly boost your intake of not just fiber, but also a variety of vitamins, minerals, and phytonutrients. As a bonus, you will also consume less saturated fat and cholesterol.

Meat, Poultry, and Seafood

Since only plant foods contain fiber, a meat-based diet is naturally much lower in fiber than a plant-based diet. While totally eschewing meat is not necessary in order to reach your daily fiber goal, making meat a smaller part of the plate makes good sense. Dishes such as soups, stews, casseroles, salads, and sandwiches are a good way to stretch meat portions and increase your intake of fiber-rich vegetables, fruits, and whole grains.

Beef

When buying beef, it is important to choose lean cuts to reduce saturated fat and calories. The leanest cuts have "loin" or "round" in the name.

Examples include eye of round, top round, and sirloin. As for ground beef, look for meat that is at least 93-percent lean. To reduce your intake of pesticides and other environmental contaminants, purchase organic, grass-fed beef as often as possible. The Resource section in the back of this book will guide you to websites that can help you make the best choices.

Chicken and Turkey

When buying poultry, choose skinless cuts or remove the skin and any visible fat before eating. When purchasing ground chicken or turkey, look for meat that is at least 93-percent lean. Fresh chicken and turkey Italian-type sausages are also available. (Again, look for products that are at least 93-percent lean.) These are a much better choice than greasy pork and beef sausages. Choose poultry that is organic and pasture-raised as much as possible.

Pork

Once again, look for leaner cuts. These will have the word "loin" in the name—such as tenderloin and sirloin. Choose pork that is organic and pasture-raised as much as possible.

Seafood

All fish, including fatty fish, are good choices, since the fat in fish provides healthy omega-3 fats. Both fresh and frozen seafood, including fish and shellfish, are good choices. In fact, fish that is fresh-caught and quickly frozen may actually be fresher than some of the "fresh" fish that is offered in supermarkets or seafood stores. Canned seafood, such as tuna, salmon, crab, clams, sardines, and herring, are also convenient foods to keep in your cupboard. When choosing seafood, important issues include safety in regard to both mercury and other environmental contaminants, and sustainability in regard to overfishing. The Resource section of this book (see page 207) will guide you to websites that can help you make the best choices.

Vegetarian Meat Alternatives

Many plant foods are rich in protein and make tasty and budget-friendly alternatives to meat. For instance, one cup of cooked dried beans provides as much protein as 2 to 3 ounces of meat, poultry, or seafood. As a bonus, you get up to 20 grams of fiber, while meat provides none.

Dried Beans, Peas, and Lentils

Also known as legumes, dried beans, peas, and lentils are the seeds of pod-bearing plants that are allowed to fully mature and dry on the vine before being harvested. Legumes are a staple in many delicious cuisines throughout the world. Middle Eastern hummus, Latin American black beans and rice, and Mediterranean white bean cassoulet are just a few examples.

Like meat, legumes provide protein, iron, and zinc. But they also supply nutrients such as fiber, folate, and potassium that concentrate in vegetables. Just one cup of cooked legumes contains 10 to 20 grams of fiber. Some of the fiber found in legumes helps to lower blood cholesterol levels, some improves regularity, and some nourishes good bacteria in the gut. Studies support that legumes can increase feelings of fullness, which may lead to better weight management. Legumes are also a low-glycemic index food, meaning that they have minimal impact on blood sugar levels despite their relatively high carbohydrate content.

It's a good idea to eat legumes daily, or several times a week at a minimum. There are countless ways to feature legumes in meals and snacks. Toss into salads, whip into a savory dip, or cook up a hearty soup, to name a few. You will find a wide variety of legumes in your local grocery store. Choose from black, cannellini, kidney, lima, navy, garbanzo, and pinto beans; black-eyed and split peas; red, green, and brown lentils; and more. Legumes are economical, environmentally conscious, easy to use, and incredibly versatile. Both canned and dried beans are good options. Organic and lower-sodium versions of canned beans are widely available.

Edamame

Edamame is another name for fresh green soybeans. These beans have a light nutty flavor and can be purchased fresh or frozen, either shelled or in the pods. One cup of shelled edamame supplies 8 grams of fiber and 20 grams of protein, along with good amounts of calcium, magnesium, potassium, vitamin K, and other nutrients. Although a type of legume, unlike dried legumes, edamame can be boiled or steamed, and are ready to eat in just a few minutes. Many people enjoy edamame in the pods as a snack, although the pod is not edible. Shelled edamame is delicious in salads, casseroles, soups, pilafs, dips, and many other dishes.

Tofu

Also known as bean curd, tofu is made from soy milk in a process similar to cheese making. It is has a mild taste and absorbs the flavors of the other ingredients in your recipe, making it adaptable to a variety of dishes. Tofu can be used in soups, sauces, dips, smoothies, and more. Try crumbling firm tofu over salads as you would cheese, or substitute it for part or all of the eggs in egg salad. Keep in mind, however, that since tofu is made from soy milk, rather than whole soybeans, it is not a good source of fiber.

Vegetarian Burgers, Sausages, and Crumbles

Foods such as veggie burgers, vegetarian sausage links and patties, and meatless hamburger crumbles are convenient staples to keep in the freezer. Some of these foods provide fiber from ingredients such as legumes, whole grains, vegetables, and isolated or manufactured fibers. Keep in mind that these foods may contain gluten (which lends a chewy, meaty texture), which some people must avoid.

DAIRY

The dairy case has many options to complement your high-fiber lifestyle. Most dairy foods provide protein, minerals such as calcium and potassium, and vitamins A and D. Some dairy foods, such as yogurt and smoothies, may contain added fibers such as inulin or oligofructose.

Cheese

Loaded with calcium and protein, cheese is an excellent way to add flavor and interest to your high-fiber meals. For instance, a sprinkling of Parmesan over whole grain pasta, some feta or goat cheese tossed into a salad, or a slice of cheddar or Swiss melted in a whole grain panini. To minimize saturated fat and calories, look for reduced-fat or 2-percent milk cheeses when possible. If you want or need to avoid dairy, a variety of vegan cheeses made from soy, rice, or nut milks are also available.

Buttermilk

Buttermilk is a great ingredient for adding rich flavor and tender texture to your whole grain breads, muffins, and other baked goods. Choose low-fat or nonfat buttermilk to trim fat and calories. If you do not have buttermilk on hand, a good substitute can be made by mixing half plain yogurt and half milk. Depending on the thickness of the yogurt, you may need to play around with the proportions of yogurt to milk to duplicate the creamy consistency of buttermilk.

Milk

To reduce calories and saturated fat, use reduced-fat (2-percent) milk, low-fat (1-percent) milk, or nonfat (skim) milk. People who cannot tolerate milk sugar (lactose) can choose lactose-free milk products such as Lactaid. Those who wish to avoid dairy foods can use nondairy milks.

Nondairy Milks

If you prefer nondairy milk, many delicious options are available, including almond, coconut, soy, oat, hemp, and rice milks. Some are available in shelf-stable containers and some are in the refrigerator case. All of these milks are lactose-free and work well in smoothies, on cereal, and in baked goods.

Soy milk is nutritionally similar to dairy milk. However, almond, coconut, and rice milks are low in protein compared with dairy milk. Also, be aware that rice milk is higher in carbohydrate than dairy milk. Many nondairy milks are fortified with calcium, vitamin D, and other nutrients in amounts comparable to dairy milk.

Sour Cream

Sour cream is a must-have ingredient for spreads, dressings, sauces, and many other dishes. To trim fat and calories, choose light versions. Flavor and texture can vary greatly among brands, so shop around to find one to your liking. Greek-style yogurt is a nutritious alternative to sour cream in many recipes.

Yogurt

Yogurt adds creamy richness to fruit smoothies, dips, desserts, and many other dishes. Greek-style yogurt has been drained to remove some of the whey, so it is thicker and creamier than regular yogurt. It also contains twice the protein of regular yogurt.

EGGS

From omelets and quiches to casseroles and custards, eggs are an essential ingredient in many recipes. The thinking on eggs has changed a lot in recent years. Whole eggs supply essential nutrients such as choline, lutein, and vitamin D that many people do not consume in adequate amounts. So totally avoiding egg yolks is not necessary. Your healthcare professional can guide you on what is appropriate for your dietary needs. For those who want just the whites, liquid egg whites and egg substitutes are sold in cartons near the dairy case. These products are convenient to use for baking and making omelets. As a rule, one quarter cup of liquid egg whites or egg substitute equals one large egg.

SUGAR AND SWEETENERS

It's no secret that sugar is not the most nutritious food in the pantry. A diet high in sugar can contribute to high blood sugar levels, obesity, and eventually, diabetes. However, when used in moderation, it will not ruin an otherwise healthy diet. How much is too much? The guideline put forth by the American Heart Association (AHA) offers a reasonable upper limit for sweeteners. The AHA recommends no more than six teaspoons of added sugar per day for most women and no more than nine teaspoons for most men. Note that this recommendation refers only to sugar that is added to food, not to sugar that occurs naturally in foods such as fruits, vegetables, and milk products.

To help put these recommendations in perspective, many people consume over three times the recommended intake for added sugars. This is easy to do when you consider that sugar is added to the majority of processed foods. The biggest contributor of sugar to the American diet is sweetened beverages—one 12-ounce soda contains about 10 teaspoons of added sugars.

When a recipe calls for sugar, consider using a less refined version, which may be sold as "natural cane sugar" or "evaporated cane juice." These pale amber to dark brown sugars have a delicious molasses flavor and retain some of the nutrients naturally present in sugar cane. Keep in mind that these less refined sugars provide about the same amount of calories and carbohydrates as regular sugar. Also, choose a finely granulated sugar for baking, as coarse sugars like Demerara and turbinado do not dissolve easily in batters and doughs.

Liquid sweeteners such as honey, maple syrup, sorghum syrup, and molasses also contain an array of nutrients. However, as with the less refined granulated sugars, the nutrients are present in relatively small amounts compared with foods like vegetables and fruits.

The recipes in this book aim to keep added sugars at low to moderate amounts. In some recipes, guidelines are provided for replacing sugar with sugar substitutes to help you meet your nutritional goals. As for sugar substitutes, many kinds are available to choose from, so select one that suits your personal preferences. Just be sure to use a use a heat-stable sugar substitute such as sucralose or stevia for cooking and baking. Also, read the label to determine the amount of sugar substitute needed to replace an equivalent amount of sugar. Some sugar substitutes are very concentrated, while others measure cup-for-cup just like sugar.

SNACK FOOD

Chosen wisely, snacks can boost your intake of fiber and important nutrients. Unfortunately, much of what people have come to think of as snack foods are processed junk foods such as sweets, chips, sugary beverages, and other grab-and-go fare. A healthier mindset is to think of snacks as "mini-meals" and focus on real food. Fresh fruit, yogurt with a sprinkling of nuts, a half-sandwich on whole grain bread, or a cup of vegetable or bean soup are just some examples of smart snacks. Chosen wisely, a few items from the snack aisle can also complement your high-fiber lifestyle.

Cereal bars

Many people find these to be a convenient breakfast or grab-and-go snack. But beware—many "high-fiber" cereal, granola, and breakfast bars are full of refined grains such as crisped (white) rice, sugar, and loads of artificial ingredients, with most of the fiber coming from isolated or manufactured sources. Look for bars with simple ingredient lists, made from whole grains, fruits, nuts, and a minimum of added sugar.

Chips

For those who like their snacks salty and crunchy, chips are a favorite choice. Unfortunately, chips can deliver loads of fat, salt, and calories. That said, a myriad of lighter choices are available. Tortilla chips are often made from whole grain corn, and provide about 2 grams of fiber per one-ounce serving. As a bonus, tortilla chips are good for scooping up fiber-rich salsas and bean dips. To trim calories, look for baked, lower-fat tortilla chips.

Other lower-fat chips include baked potato chips, various "multigrain" chips, and even chips made from vegetables and fruits. The best advice for choosing chips is to look for simple ingredient lists with "real food" as the first ingredients. For instance, in the case of baked tortilla chips, the ingredients may simply be "whole grain corn, vegetable oil, and salt." Also be sure to look at fat grams, calories, carbs, and sodium to see how the food fits into your overall nutrition goals.

Crackers

Paired with cheese or light dips and spreads, whole grain crackers make for a tasty snack or party platter. As with breads, many brands of crackers boast wholesome sounding names such as "multigrain" or "hearty wheat," but contain few actual whole grains and little or no fiber. For the most fiber and nutrition, look for crackers that are high in whole grains and low in added fats. Once again, look for a short and simple ingredients list to reduce your intake of processed fats, sugars, and artificial ingredients.

Popcorn

Many people are unaware that popcorn is a whole grain. A 3-cup serving of air-popped popcorn provides an impressive 3.5 grams of fiber for less than 100 calories. Low-fat microwave popcorn is also a good choice.

STOCKING UP RIGHT

Stocking up on the right ingredients is the first step to a successful high-fiber eating plan. The rest of this book will help you put these ingredients to good use with recipes that can liven up any meal of the day. Get ready to create some new favorites and to experience the pleasures and rewards of cooking the healthy, high-fiber way.

3

Hors d'Oeuvres with a Difference

Delicious food can make any occasion special. Contrary to popular belief, adopting a healthy diet does not mean sacrificing taste. And when it comes to entertaining guests, there are plenty of ways to serve healthful, delicious fiber-rich fare that is sure to please. The easy-to-prepare recipes on the following pages will show you how. You'll find a wide assortment of hot and cold hors d'oeuvres that feature vegetables, fruit, legumes, and whole grains. All are as fiber-filled and nutritious as they are delicious. Best of all, most can be assembled in a flash.

So whether it's a casual get-together or an elegant affair, you can feel confident about serving the dishes in this chapter. Sure to impress, these recipes will prove that festive occasions need not derail your efforts to eat well.

GREAT GUACAMOLE

Yield: 2 ¼ Cups

* * * * * * * *

3 cups diced avocado
(3 to 4 medium)

1 tablespoon lime juice

¼ cup finely chopped red onion
or sweet white onion

2 to 3 tablespoons finely
chopped fresh cilantro

1 tablespoon finely chopped
pickled jalapeño peppers

¼ teaspoon salt

1. In a large bowl, combine the avocado and lime juice. Using a fork, mash the avocado, leaving it slightly chunky. Add the onion, cilantro, jalapeño peppers, and salt. Mix well.

2. Serve immediately, or cover and refrigerate for up to 8 hours before serving. If refrigerating, place a sheet of plastic wrap directly over the surface of the guacamole to prevent it from turning brown.

NUTRITION FACTS (PER ¼-CUP SERVING)

Calories: 82	Carbohydrates: 5 g	Fiber: 3.4 g
Protein: 1.1 g	Fat: 7.3 g	Saturated fat: 1.1 g
Cholesterol: 0 mg	Sodium: 68 mg	Calcium: 6 mg

COWBOY CAVIAR

Yield: 4 Cups

* * * * * * *

15-ounce can reduced-sodium
black beans or black-eyed peas,
drained and rinsed

1 cup frozen whole-kernel
corn, thawed

1 cup seeded and diced plum
tomatoes (about 3 large)

½ cup sliced scallions

¼ cup finely chopped fresh
cilantro

1 tablespoon finely chopped
pickled jalapeño peppers

2 tablespoons pickled jalapeño
pepper juice (from the jar of
jalapeños)

⅛ to ¼ teaspoon salt

1. In a medium-sized bowl, combine the black beans or black-eyed peas, corn, tomatoes, scallions, cilantro, jalapeño peppers, and jalapeño pepper juice. Sprinkle with the salt and toss well.

2. Serve immediately, or cover and refrigerate for up to 3 hours before serving. Serve with baked tortilla chips or small leaves of romaine lettuce.

NUTRITION FACTS (PER ½-CUP SERVING)

Calories: 65	Carbohydrates: 13 g	Fiber: 3.7 g
Protein: 4 g	Fat: 0.3 g	Saturated fat: 0.1 g
Cholesterol: 0 mg	Sodium: 114 mg	Calcium: 17 mg

CLASSIC HUMMUS

1. In a food processor, combine the garbanzo beans, tahini, lemon juice, olive oil, garlic, cumin, salt, cayenne pepper, and 1 tablespoon of the reserved liquid. Process for about 2 minutes, or until smooth and creamy, adding more of the reserved bean liquid if needed.

2. Serve immediately, or cover and refrigerate until ready to serve. Serve with lettuce leaves, fresh-cut celery and carrots, and wedges of whole grain pita bread or whole grain crackers.

NUTRITION FACTS (PER $\frac{1}{4}$-CUP SERVING)

Calories: 125	Carbohydrates: 13 g	Fiber: 3.7 g
Protein: 4.6 g	Fat: 6.6 g	Saturated fat: 0.9 g
Cholesterol: 0 mg	Sodium: 149 mg	Calcium: 45 mg

FOR A CHANGE . . .

To make roasted red pepper hummus, omit the reserved bean liquid and add $\frac{1}{3}$ cup chopped roasted red bell pepper to the food processor along with the beans. Process until smooth, adding some of the reserved bean liquid if needed.

HELPFUL HINT

Whenever a recipe directs you to drain off the liquid from canned or cooked garbanzo beans, consider saving it for another use. Known as *aquafaba*, this liquid can be used as a substitute for eggs in many dishes. Unlike other vegan egg substitutes, aquafaba can be whipped—just like egg whites—and used to make desserts such as meringues and macaroons. (For more information, visit http://aquafaba.com.)

Yield: About 2 Cups

• • • • • • • • • •

19-ounce can reduced-sodium garbanzo beans,
or 2 cups cooked garbanzo beans, drained but not rinsed
(reserve $\frac{1}{4}$ cup of the liquid)

3 tablespoons sesame tahini

3 tablespoons lemon juice

$1\frac{1}{2}$ tablespoons extra virgin olive oil

1 teaspoon crushed garlic

$\frac{3}{4}$ teaspoon ground cumin

$\frac{1}{4}$ teaspoon salt

$\frac{1}{8}$ teaspoon cayenne pepper

HOT & HEARTY BEAN DIP

Yield: 2 Cups

• • • • • • •

15-ounce can reduced-sodium pinto beans, drained but not rinsed

$1/4$ cup chunky-style salsa

1 teaspoon chili powder

$1/2$ teaspoon ground cumin

$3/4$ cup shredded reduced-fat Monterey Jack or Mexican blend cheese

$1/3$ cup thinly sliced scallions

$1/3$ cup chopped black olives

1 tablespoon finely chopped pickled jalapeño peppers

1. Preheat the oven to 400°F.

2. In a food processor, combine the beans, salsa, chili powder, and cumin. Process until smooth.

3. Spread the mixture evenly in a 9-inch glass pie pan. Top with the cheese, scallions, olives, and jalapeño peppers.

4. Cover pie pan with foil and bake for 15 minutes. Remove the foil and bake for about 3 minutes more, or until the cheese is melted. If using a microwave oven, heat uncovered on high for 5 minutes, or until the edges are bubbly and the cheese is melted. Serve hot with baked tortilla chips.

NUTRITION FACTS (PER $1/3$-CUP SERVING)

Calories: 119	Carbohydrates: 14 g	Fiber: 4.4 g
Protein: 8.2 g	Fat: 4.5 g	Saturated fat: 1.8 g
Cholesterol: 10 mg	Sodium: 312 mg	Calcium: 129 mg

The Savvy Hors d'Oeuvres Spread

Make your next get-together as nutritious as it is delicious. Use these tips to create a show-stopping hors d'oeuvres spread and delight guests with guilt-free treats.

- For the most fiber and nutrition, choose dips made with vegetables and legumes, such as spinach and artichoke dips, zesty tomato salsas, or savory hummus.

- Cut fresh vegetables into interesting shapes. Cut carrots, cucumbers, zucchini, yellow squash, or celery stalks on the bias (at a 45° angle) to make fresh "chips," or use a mandolin to create crinkle-cut vegetable slices.

- To perk up your platter, include out-of-the-ordinary vegetables, such as endive leaves, strips of jicama or turnip, or snow peas.

LAYERED BLACK BEAN DIP

1. In a food processor, combine the beans, salsa, chili powder, and cumin. Process until smooth. Spread the mixture evenly in a 9-inch pie pan or shallow dish.

2. Layer on the lettuce, cheese, scallions, tomatoes, jalapeño peppers, and avocado.

3. Serve immediately with baked tortilla chips.

NUTRITION FACTS (PER $1/2$-CUP SERVING)

Calories: 97	Carbohydrate: 11 g	Fiber: 4.5 g
Protein: 5.4 g	Fat: 4.3 g	Saturated Fat: 1.3 g
Cholesterol: 5 mg	Sodium: 166 mg	Calcium: 67 mg

Yield: 4 Cups

• • • • • • • • • •

15-ounce can reduced-sodium black beans, drained but not rinsed

$1/3$ cup chunky-style salsa

$1/2$ teaspoon chili powder

$1/2$ teaspoon ground cumin

TOPPINGS

1 cup shredded romaine lettuce

$1/2$ cup shredded reduced-fat Monterey Jack or Mexican blend cheese

$1/3$ cup sliced scallions

$1/3$ cup seeded and diced plum tomatoes (about 1 large)

1 to 2 tablespoons finely chopped pickled jalapeño peppers

1 medium avocado, finely chopped

- Steam fresh or frozen edamame pods and serve warm or chilled. Add a dish of light ginger or oriental salad dressing for dipping. Or toss with a splash of sesame oil and a sprinkling of sea salt or soy sauce.

- Make colorful skewers of in-season fruits.

- Spread some Greek-style vanilla yogurt in a shallow dish and top with a layer of sliced almonds. Place the dish at the center of a large platter and surround with fresh strawberries or spears of fresh pineapple.

- Spear a combination of fresh mozzarella cubes, cherry tomatoes, and fresh basil leaves with toothpicks and serve with light balsamic dressing or olive oil vinaigrette as a dip.

LENTIL & WALNUT SPREAD

Yield: 2 1/4 Cups

• • • • • • • • • •

1 cup dried brown lentils

2 1/4 cups unsalted vegetable or chicken broth

1 tablespoon extra virgin olive oil

3/4 cup chopped yellow onion

2 teaspoons crushed garlic

1/2 cup chopped walnuts

1 1/2 teaspoons finely chopped fresh lemon or other thyme, or 1/2 teaspoon dried

1/2 teaspoon ground cumin

1/2 teaspoon salt

1/4 teaspoon ground black pepper

1/4 cup finely chopped fresh parsley

1/4 cup thinly sliced scallions

1. In a 2-quart saucepan, combine the lentils and broth. Bring to a boil. Reduce the heat to low, cover, and simmer for about 25 minutes, or until the lentils are soft. Allow the lentils to cool before proceeding with the recipe.

2. In a medium-sized skillet, combine the olive oil and onion. Cover and cook over medium heat, stirring frequently, for about 5 minutes, or until the onion softens. Add a little water if needed to prevent scorching. Add the garlic and cook for about 15 seconds, or until fragrant.

3. Drain the lentils, reserving the liquid. Place the drained lentils, walnuts, onion mixture, thyme, cumin, salt, and black pepper in a food processor, and process until smooth. If needed, add some of the reserved cooking liquid to create a thick but spreadable texture.

4. Spread the lentil mixture evenly in a shallow dish and sprinkle the parsley and scallions over the top. Serve with celery, carrot sticks, and wedges of whole grain pita bread or whole grain crackers.

NUTRITION FACTS (PER 1/4-CUP SERVING)

Calories: 125	Carbohydrates: 13 g	Fiber: 5 g
Protein: 6.4 g	Fat: 6 g	Saturated fat: 0.7 g
Cholesterol: 0 mg	Sodium: 130 mg	Calcium: 24 mg

BAKED ARTICHOKE SPREAD

1. Preheat the oven to 350°F.

2. Place the artichoke hearts in a food processor and process for about 10 seconds, or until coarsely chopped. Add the mayonnaise, $1/4$ cup plus 2 tablespoons of the Parmesan cheese, the mustard, and the black pepper. Process for about 20 seconds, or until well blended but still slightly chunky.

3. Coat a shallow 1-quart casserole dish with cooking spray and spread the artichoke mixture evenly in the dish. Sprinkle the remaining 2 tablespoons of cheese over the top and spray the top lightly with the cooking spray.

4. Cover the dish with aluminum foil and bake for 25 minutes. Remove the foil and bake for 5 minutes, or until the top is lightly browned. Remove from the oven and let sit for 5 minutes.

5. Serve hot with wedges of whole grain pita bread, chunks of whole wheat sourdough bread, or whole grain crackers.

Yield: About $2\,^2/_3$ Cups

• • • • • • •

18 ounces frozen artichoke hearts, thawed,
or two 14-ounce cans artichoke hearts, drained

$3/_4$ cup low-fat or light mayonnaise

$1/_2$ cup grated Parmesan cheese, divided

1 tablespoon plus 1 teaspoon Dijon mustard

$1/_2$ teaspoon ground black pepper

Olive oil cooking spray

NUTRITION FACTS (PER $1/_3$-CUP SERVING)

Calories: 82

Protein: 3.9 g

Cholesterol: 6 mg

Carbohydrates: 9 g

Fat: 3.3 g

Sodium: 318 mg

Fiber: 3.8 g

Saturated fat: 1.1 g

Calcium: 100 mg

CHILI-CHEESE POTATO SKINS

Yield: 12 Potato Skins

6 small baking potatoes, such as Yukon Gold (about 1 1/2 pounds)

3/4 cup Chipotle Black Bean Chili (page 116) or Vegetarian Chili (page 118)

Olive oil cooking spray

1 tablespoon finely chopped pickled jalapeño peppers

1/2 cup shredded reduced-fat cheddar cheese or Mexican blend cheese

1/2 cup light sour cream or Greek-style yogurt

1/4 cup thinly sliced scallions

1. Preheat the oven to 400°F.

2. Wrap the potatoes in aluminum foil. Bake for about 40 minutes, or until easily pierced with a knife. Unwrap the potatoes and let cool for at least 30 minutes. (Bake the potatoes a day in advance if desired).

3. When ready to prepare the potato skins, preheat the oven to 400°F. Cut the potatoes in half lengthwise. Scoop out and discard the pulp, leaving 1/4-inch-thick skins. Place 1 tablespoon of chili in each skin and spray each lightly with the olive oil cooking spray.

4. Arrange the potato skins on a large baking sheet and bake for 8 minutes. Top each potato skin with 1/4 teaspoon of the jalapeño peppers and 2 teaspoons of the cheese. Bake for 4 minutes, or until the filling is hot and the cheese is melted. Serve hot, accompanied by the sour cream and scallions.

NUTRITION FACTS (PER 3-POTATO-SKIN SERVING)

Calories: 162	Carbohydrates: 22 g	Fiber: 3.5 g
Protein: 8 g	Fat: 4.9 g	Saturated fat: 3 g
Cholesterol: 19 mg	Sodium: 168 mg	Calcium: 148 mg

FABULOUS FIBER FACT

Ounce for ounce, potato skins have nearly twice as much fiber as potato flesh. The skins also provide good amounts of potassium, vitamin C, vitamin B$_6$, and other nutrients. Just be sure to avoid potatoes that have sprouts or greenish skins. This indicates the presence of glycoalkaloids, toxins that can cause sickness if eaten in excess.

ROASTED VEGETABLE CROSTINI

1. Preheat the oven to 450°F.

2. Coat an 11-by-14-inch roasting pan or the bottom of a large broiler pan with cooking spray and add the eggplant, tomatoes, zucchini, bell pepper, onion, garlic, basil, thyme, salt, and black pepper. Toss to mix. Spray the top of the vegetable mixture lightly with the cooking spray.

3. Bake uncovered for about 30 minutes, stirring after 10 minutes and then every 5 to 8 minutes until the vegetables are tender and browned in spots. Add the olive oil and set aside.

4. To make the crostini, slice the bread $1/2$-inch thick and cut each slice into halves or quarters, depending on the size of the loaf, to make 30 pieces.

5. Coat a large baking sheet with cooking spray and place the bread slices on the sheet. Spray the tops lightly with the cooking spray. Bake at 350°F for about 12 to 14 minutes, turning after 6 minutes, until toasted.

6. To serve, place the vegetable mixture in a shallow bowl and sprinkle the crushed red pepper and fresh basil over the top. Serve warm or at room temperature accompanied by the crostini. If desired, add small bowls of crumbled reduced-fat feta or goat cheese and chopped black olives as additional toppings.

NUTRITION FACTS
(PER $1/3$-CUP SERVING WITH 5 CROSTINI)

Calories: 148	Carbohydrates: 23 g	Fiber: 5.6 g
Protein: 6 g	Fat: 4.3 g	Saturated fat: 0.9 g
Cholesterol: 0 mg	Sodium: 339 mg	Calcium: 60 mg

Yield: 2 Cups

• • • • • • • • • •

3 cups diced unpeeled eggplant
(about 9 ounces)

$1 1/2$ cups diced plum tomatoes
(about 4 medium)

1 cup diced zucchini
(about 1 medium)

1 cup diced red bell pepper
(about 1 large)

1 cup diced yellow onion
(about 1 medium)

2 teaspoons crushed garlic

1 teaspoon dried basil

$1/2$ teaspoon dried thyme

$1/2$ teaspoon salt

$1/2$ teaspoon ground black pepper

Olive oil cooking spray

1 tablespoon extra virgin olive oil

$1/8$ to $1/4$ teaspoon crushed
red pepper

2 tablespoons thinly sliced
fresh basil

CROSTINI

7 ounces multigrain French
or Italian bread

Olive oil cooking spray

ARTICHOKE & SUN-DRIED TOMATO FLATBREAD

Yield: 24 Pieces

• • • • • • • • •

2 whole grain flatbreads (about 9-x-6 inches each)

1 1/2 tablespoons grated Parmesan cheese

1 cup chopped marinated artichoke hearts, well drained

1/4 cup chopped sun-dried tomatoes

1/4 cup plus 2 tablespoons thinly slivered red onion

1 tablespoon finely chopped fresh basil, or 1 teaspoon dried basil

1/2 cup shredded reduced-fat mozzarella cheese

1. Preheat the oven to 400°F.

2. Coat a large baking sheet with cooking spray and place the flatbreads on the sheet. Bake for 2 minutes. Remove the pan from the oven and turn the flatbreads over.

3. Top each flatbread with half of the Parmesan cheese, artichoke hearts, sun-dried tomatoes, onion, basil, and mozzarella cheese. Bake for 4 to 5 minutes, or until the cheese is melted and the edges of the flatbreads are lightly browned. Cut each flatbread into 12 pieces and serve hot.

NUTRITION FACTS (PER 6-PIECE SERVING)

Calories: 153	Carbohydrates: 15 g	Fiber: 3.5 g
Protein: 10 g	Fat: 6.6 g	Saturated fat: 1.9 g
Cholesterol: 9 mg	Sodium: 348 mg	Calcium: 184 mg

EDAMAME WITH GINGER SAUCE

Yield: 6 Servings

• • • • • • • • •

1 1/2 pounds fresh or frozen edamame pods

GINGER SAUCE

2 tablespoons orange juice

1 tablespoon plus 1 teaspoon finely grated fresh ginger root

1 tablespoon reduced-sodium soy sauce

1 tablespoon sesame or canola oil

1/4 teaspoon salt

1. Combine the ginger sauce ingredients in a small bowl. Mix well and set aside.

2. Fill a 4-quart saucepan halfway with water and bring to a boil. Add the edamame and return to a boil. Cook for about 4 minutes. The cooked edamame should be firm with a slight give.

3. Drain the edamame and return them to the saucepan. Add the prepared sauce and toss to mix. Transfer to a serving dish and serve warm, or refrigerate and serve chilled.

HELPFUL TIP

To eat the edamame, squeeze the edge of the pod with your fingers to extract the beans, or gently pull through clenched teeth, as you would an artichoke leaf. The beans should pop out easily. Discard the empty pods.

NUTRITION FACTS (PER 1-CUP SERVING)

Calories: 130	Carbohydrates: 11 g	Fiber: 5.5 g
Protein: 11.8 g	Fat: 5.4 g	Saturated fat: 0 g
Cholesterol: 0 mg	Sodium: 199 mg	Calcium: 68 mg

ROASTED RED PEPPER FLATBREAD

Yield: 24 Pieces

• • • • • • •

2 whole grain flatbreads (about 9-x-6 inches each)

2 tablespoons grated Parmesan cheese

$\frac{1}{2}$ cup chopped roasted red pepper

$\frac{1}{4}$ cup plus 2 tablespoons thinly slivered yellow onion

$\frac{1}{4}$ cup chopped black olives

1 $\frac{1}{2}$ teaspoons finely chopped fresh oregano or thyme, or $\frac{1}{2}$ teaspoon dried

$\frac{1}{2}$ cup shredded reduced-fat mozzarella cheese

$\frac{1}{4}$ teaspoon crushed red pepper

1. Preheat the oven to 400°F.

2. Coat a large baking sheet with cooking spray and place the flatbreads on the sheet. Bake for 2 minutes. Remove the pan from the oven and turn the flatbreads over.

3. Top each flatbread with half of the Parmesan cheese, roasted red pepper, onion, olives, oregano or thyme, and mozzarella cheese. Bake for 4 to 5 minutes, or until the cheese is melted and the edges of the flatbreads are lightly browned. Sprinkle half of the crushed red pepper over each flatbread. Cut each flatbread into 12 pieces and serve hot.

NUTRITION FACTS (PER 6-PIECE SERVING)

Calories: 133	Carbohydrates: 12 g	Fiber: 3 g
Protein: 8.7 g	Fat: 6.1 g	Saturated fat: 2 g
Cholesterol: 10 mg	Sodium: 314 mg	Calcium: 249 mg

SWISS APPLE TEA SANDWICHES

Yield: 16 Sandwiches
• • • • • • • •

8 slices multigrain, dark rye, or pumpernickel bread

$^1/_2$ cup almond butter

1 medium Granny Smith apple, unpeeled, sliced into very thin wedges

4 ounces thinly sliced reduced-fat Swiss or white cheddar cheese

24 large fresh spinach leaves

1. Place 4 of the bread slices on a work surface and spread each one with 1 tablespoon of the almond butter. Top each bread slice with one-quarter of the apple slices, cheese, and spinach leaves.

2. Spread the remaining bread slices with 1 tablespoon of the remaining almond butter and place on the sandwiches. Trim the crusts if desired and cut each sandwich into four triangles. Arrange on a serving platter and serve immediately.

NUTRITION FACTS (PER 1-TRIANGLE SERVING)

Calories: 118	Carbohydrates: 11 g	Fiber: 2.8 g
Protein: 6.4 g	Fat: 6.1 g	Saturated fat: 1 g
Cholesterol: 5 mg	Sodium: 77 mg	Calcium: 124 mg

HUMMUS ROLL-UPS

Yield: 32 Roll-Ups
• • • • • • • •

4 whole grain flatbreads (about 9-x-6-inches each) or whole wheat flour tortillas (9-inch rounds)

1$^1/_3$ cups Classic Hummus (page 41) or ready-made hummus

$^1/_2$ cup julienne-cut carrot (about 1 medium)

32 thin slices English cucumber

16 thin slices plum tomato

$^1/_3$ cup chopped black olives

24 large fresh spinach leaves

1. Place 1 flatbread on a large cutting board with the long end facing you. Spread $^1/_3$ cup hummus on the flatbread, covering it all the way to the edges. Layer 2 tablespoons carrots, 8 cucumber slices, 4 tomato slices, 1 tablespoon plus 1 teaspoon olives, and 6 spinach leaves over the *bottom half only* of the flatbread.

2. Roll the flatbread up tightly from the bottom and cut into 8 pieces. Place the roll-ups on a serving platter.

3. Repeat Steps 1 and 2 with the remaining flatbreads. Serve immediately, or cover and refrigerate for up to 3 hours before serving.

NUTRITION FACTS (PER 2-ROLL-UP SERVING)

Calories: 78	Carbohydrates: 10 g	Fiber: 2.5 g
Protein: 3.9 g	Fat: 2.3 g	Saturated fat: 0.3 g
Cholesterol: 0 mg	Sodium: 126 mg	Calcium: 58 mg

COLORFUL FRUIT KEBABS

1. To prepare the dip, combine the honey, cinnamon, and 2 tablespoons of the yogurt in a small bowl and stir to mix. Stir in the remaining yogurt. Transfer to a small dish and place in the center of a platter. Set the platter aside.

2. Peel the kiwi fruit and cut each lengthwise into halves. Cut each half into 3 slices to get 6 pieces from each kiwi. Set aside.

3. On a 6-inch wooden skewer, spear 1 strawberry, 1 piece kiwi, 1 strawberry, 1 chunk pineapple, and 1 blackberry.

4. Repeat Step 3 with the remaining skewers. Arrange the kebabs on the prepared platter and serve immediately, or place in a covered container and refrigerate for up to 3 hours before serving.

NUTRITION FACTS
(PER 2-KEBAB SERVING WITH 2 TABLESPOONS DIP)

Calories: 74	Carbohydrates: 16 g	Fiber: 2.5 g
Protein: 3.6 g	Fat: 0.3 g	Saturated fat: 0 g
Cholesterol: 0 mg	Sodium: 12 mg	Calcium: 54 mg

Yield: 24 Kebabs

4 medium-sized kiwi fruit

48 medium-sized strawberries, rinsed, patted dry, and trimmed (about 1 1/4 pounds)

24 (1-inch) chunks fresh pineapple (about 1/2 medium pineapple)

24 large fresh blackberries

24 (6-inch) wooden skewers

CINNAMON-HONEY DIP

1 1/2 tablespoons honey

1 teaspoon ground cinnamon

1 1/2 cups vanilla nonfat or low-fat Greek-style yogurt

STRAWBERRIES & CREAM

1. Place the yogurt in a shallow dish and sprinkle the brown sugar and almonds over the top.

2. Place the dish at the center of a serving platter and surround with the strawberries. Serve immediately.

NUTRITION FACTS
(PER 3/4-CUP SERVING WITH 1/4-CUP DIP)

Calories: 100	Carbohydrates: 14 g	Fiber: 2.6 g
Protein: 6 g	Fat: 3 g	Saturated fat: 0.8 g
Cholesterol: 2 mg	Sodium: 16 mg	Calcium: 72 mg

Yield: 8 Servings

1 1/2 cups plain 2% reduced-fat Greek-style yogurt or light sour cream

3 tablespoons light brown sugar

1/4 cup plus 1 tablespoon sliced almonds

1 1/2 quarts fresh whole strawberries, rinsed

CHOCOLATE-STRAWBERRY SKEWERS

Yield: 8 Skewers
• • • • • • • •

24 medium-large strawberries, rinsed, patted dry, and trimmed (about 1 pound)

$^1/_2$ cup chopped dark chocolate ($2^1/_2$ ounces)

2 tablespoons sliced almonds

8 (6-inch) wooden skewers

1. Thread 3 strawberries onto each skewer. Line the skewers up on a large baking sheet, spacing them about 1 inch apart. Set aside.

2. Fill a 1-quart pot one-third full with water and bring to a boil. Reduce the heat to maintain a simmer. Place the chocolate in a 2-cup heatproof glass measuring cup. Place the cup in the simmering water for about 5 minutes, stirring occasionally, until the chocolate has completely melted. Reduce the heat to low and leave the chocolate in the simmering water so it remains melted while you coat the berries.

3. Dip a spoon into the melted chocolate and drizzle about 1 teaspoon over each of the 3 berries on a skewer. Quickly sprinkle $^1/_4$ teaspoon of almonds over the warm chocolate on each berry. Repeat with the remaining skewers.

4. Place the skewers in the refrigerator for at least 30 minutes to allow the chocolate to harden. Serve immediately or cover and refrigerate for up to 3 hours before serving.

NUTRITION FACTS (PER 1-SKEWER SERVING)

Calories: 75	Carbohydrates: 10 g	Fiber: 1.8 g
Protein: 1.2 g	Fat: 3.7 g	Saturated fat: 0.1 g
Cholesterol: 0 mg	Sodium: 1 mg	Calcium: 15 mg

FABULOUS FIBER FACT

Need another reason to love chocolate? Once ounce of dark chocolate contains 2 to 3 grams of fiber. It also provides some magnesium, potassium, and phytonutrients that may lower blood pressure.

4

Breakfast
& Brunch

There are many reasons to feature fiber at breakfast. Watching your weight? What you eat for breakfast can make all the difference in your success. A morning meal that packs in both fiber and protein revs up your metabolism, keeps you feeling full for hours, and helps prevent overeating later in the day. Looking for an energy boost? A healthy high-fiber breakfast supplies sustained energy—unlike low-fiber processed food, which can trigger a mid-morning energy crash and overeating all day long.

Happily, many breakfast and brunch favorites can feature fiber-rich, nutrient-packed ingredients. This chapter will help you kick-start your day by making the most of your morning meal. As you will see, from fabulous frittatas to sensational smoothies, you can easily start every day the high-fiber way.

How to Build a Better
Breakfast with More Fiber

The morning meal offers plenty of delicious opportunities to fill up on fiber. Aim to get at least one-quarter of your daily fiber needs at breakfast, which amounts to about 7 to 9 grams for most adults. Here are some tips to get you there.

- Make egg sandwiches with whole grain English muffins or bagel thins to instantly add about 4 grams of fiber.

- Cook up a vegetable-packed frittata or omelet. Pair your eggs with a fresh fruit cup to add up to 8 grams of fiber to your meal.

- Make pancakes and waffles with whole grain flour. Prepare French toast with fiber-rich whole grain bread. Top either with fresh fruit or a low-sugar fruit sauce instead of sugary syrup.

- Top a whole grain bagel or waffle with nut butter and fresh fruit instead of cream cheese, butter, jelly, or syrup.

- Add a sprinkling of nuts or seeds to your breakfast. These nutrient-packed morsels are a delicious addition to breakfast parfaits, muffins, hot and cold cereals, or smoothies.

- Stock up on whole grain cereals. Check the label for ingredients such as oats, whole wheat, spelt, barley, bran, or flax. For hot cereals, opt for old-fashioned oats, steel-cut oats, or oat bran, which are more filling than instant oats. Or enjoy a hot multigrain cereal made from a mixture of cracked grains.

- Inspect labels on breakfast bars, choosing those high in whole grain ingredients, fruit, and nuts, and low in sugar and artificial ingredients.

HARVEST
EGG BAKE

1. Preheat the oven to 425°F.

2. Trim off ³⁄₄ inch from each end of the squash and discard. Slice the remaining squash crosswise into 4 rounds, each about ³⁄₄-inch thick. Remove and discard the seeds.

3. Coat a large baking sheet with cooking spray and place the squash slices on the sheet. Sprinkle ¹⁄₄ teaspoon each of salt and black pepper over the squash. Bake at for about 15 minutes, or just until easily pierced with a fork.

4. Remove baking sheet from oven. Crack an egg into the center of each squash slice and sprinkle ¹⁄₈ teaspoon each of salt and black pepper over the eggs. Reduce the oven temperature to 350°F and bake for about 10 minutes, or until eggs are cooked.

5. While the eggs are baking, pour the olive oil into a large skillet and add the spinach and remaining ¹⁄₈ teaspoon salt. Cook over medium heat for 2 to 3 minutes, or until the spinach is wilted.

6. For each serving, place a quarter of the spinach on a plate. Use a spatula to lift one squash ring and egg and place it over the spinach. Sprinkle with a pinch of paprika and a quarter of the bacon. Serve immediately.

Yield: 4 Servings

• • • • • • •

1 large acorn squash (about 1³⁄₄ pounds)

¹⁄₂ teaspoon salt, divided

³⁄₈ teaspoon ground black pepper, divided

4 large eggs

2 teaspoons extra virgin olive oil

6 cups coarsely chopped fresh spinach, moderately packed

¹⁄₄ teaspoon ground paprika

2 slices bacon (vegetarian, turkey, or center-cut pork), cooked and crumbled

NUTRITIONAL FACTS (PER SERVING)

Calories: 188	Carbohydrates: 20 g	Fiber: 3.7 g
Protein: 10 g	Fat: 8.8 g	Saturated fat: 2.2 g
Cholesterol: 208 mg	Sodium: 448 mg	Calcium: 134 mg

FRISÉE WITH PORTOBELLO & POACHED EGG

Yield: 4 Servings

• • • • • • • • • •

4 cups sliced baby portobello mushrooms (about 12 ounces)

$1/4$ teaspoon salt

$1/4$ teaspoon ground black pepper

6 cups coarsely chopped frisée (curly endive) (about 6 ounces)

10 medium red radishes, thinly sliced

4 poached eggs (page 61)

DRESSING

2 tablespoons extra virgin olive oil

1 tablespoon orange juice

1 tablespoon white wine vinegar

1 teaspoon Dijon mustard

$1/4$ teaspoon salt

$1/4$ teaspoon ground black pepper

1. Coat a large nonstick skillet with cooking spray and add the mushrooms, salt, and black pepper. Cook over medium heat for about 5 minutes, or until the mushrooms are tender. Place a lid on the skillet periodically to maintain enough steam to prevent scorching. Remove the skillet from the heat and set aside.

2. In a small bowl, combine the dressing ingredients. Whisk to mix.

3. In a large bowl, combine the frisée and radishes. Drizzle 3 tablespoons of dressing into the bowl. Toss to mix. Add the reserved mushrooms and toss gently.

4. Divide the mixture among 4 serving plates. Top each serving with 1 poached egg. and drizzle with 1 teaspoon dressing. Sprinkle each serving with additional black pepper if desired. Serve immediately.

NUTRITION FACTS (PER SERVING)

Calories: 177	Carbohydrates: 8 g	Fiber: 4 g
Protein: 9.5 g	Fat: 12.4 g	Saturated fat: 2.6 g
Cholesterol: 211 mg	Sodium: 262 mg	Calcium: 76 mg

EGGS WITH SPINACH & ARTICHOKES

1. Coat a large nonstick skillet with cooking spray and add the spinach and artichoke hearts. Cook over medium heat for about 3 minutes, or until the spinach is wilted and the artichokes are heated through.

2. Add the cream cheese, Parmesan cheese, and milk to the skillet and continue to cook for about 3 minutes, or until the cream cheese is melted and the sauce is creamy.

3. For each serving, place about $1/2$ cup of the spinach mixture on each of 4 serving plates. Top with a poached egg and a pinch of paprika. Serve hot.

NUTRITION FACTS (PER SERVING)

Calories: 166	Carbohydrates: 8 g	Fiber: 4.1 g
Protein: 12.2 g	Fat: 9 g	Saturated Fat: 4.3 g
Cholesterol: 200 mg	Sodium: 398 mg	Calcium: 189 mg

Yield: 4 Servings

• • • • • • • • • • •

6 cups moderately packed chopped fresh spinach

$1 1/4$ cups coarsely chopped frozen artichoke hearts, thawed, or coarsely chopped canned artichoke hearts, drained

$1/4$ cup reduced-fat cream cheese

$1 1/2$ tablespoons grated Parmesan cheese

2 tablespoons nonfat or low-fat milk

4 large poached eggs (page 61)

$1/4$ teaspoon ground paprika

FABULOUS FIBER FACT

Looking for an easy way to give recipes a fiber boost? Add artichokes. A half-cup of artichoke hearts provides nearly 5 grams of fiber. Artichokes also supply good amounts of folic acid, vitamins C and K, potassium, magnesium, and antioxidants. Enjoy them in salads, sandwiches, dips, and much more.

SOUTHWESTERN-STYLE BREAKFAST BOWL

Yield: 4 Servings

• • • • • • • • • • •

$1/4$ cup finely chopped yellow onion

I tablespoon water

$1 1/2$ teaspoons extra virgin olive oil

$1/2$ teaspoon ground cumin

$1 1/2$ cups cooked brown rice

I cup canned reduced-sodium black beans, drained (reserve the liquid)

$3/8$ teaspoon salt, divided

4 poached eggs (page 61)

$1/4$ teaspoon ground black pepper

I medium avocado, diced

SALSA

$1/2$ cup chopped seeded tomato

2 tablespoons finely chopped fresh cilantro

2 tablespoons finely chopped red onion

2 teaspoons finely chopped pickled jalapeño pepper

1. In a small bowl, combine the salsa ingredients and stir to mix. Set aside.

2. In a medium-sized skillet, combine the onion, water, olive oil, and cumin. Cover and cook over medium heat for about 3 minutes, or until the onion softens. Add the rice, beans, 2 tablespoons of the reserved bean liquid, and $1/8$ teaspoon salt. Stir to mix. Cook uncovered for about 4 minutes to heat through.

3. For each serving, place a quarter of the rice mixture in a shallow bowl. Top with 1 poached egg. Place a quarter of the salsa on one side of the egg and a quarter of the avocado on the other side. Top each egg with a pinch of salt and black pepper. Serve immediately.

NUTRITIONAL FACTS (PER SERVING)

Calories: 289	Carbohydrates: 32 g	Fiber: 7.9 g
Protein: 13 g	Fat: 12.7 g	Saturated fat: 2.7 g
Cholesterol: 185 mg	Sodium: 354 mg	Calcium: 57 mg

HUEVOS RANCHEROS

1. Preheat the oven to 400°F.

2. Place the beans in a medium-sized bowl and mash with a fork. Stir in 3 tablespoons salsa. Add the chili powder and cumin, stir, and set aside.

3. Coat a large baking sheet with cooking spray and place the tortillas on the sheet. Bake for 3 minutes. Remove from the oven and turn the tortillas over. Spread each one with a quarter of the bean mixture, extending the beans to within $\frac{1}{4}$ inch of the edges. Return to the oven and bake for 3 minutes more to heat the beans.

4. Top each tortilla with 1 egg and 2 tablespoons cheese. Return to the oven for 1 minute to melt the cheese. Place 1 tortilla on each of 4 serving plates, top with 1 tablespoon salsa, 2 tablespoons avocado, $\frac{1}{2}$ tablespoon scallions, and $\frac{1}{2}$ tablespoon cilantro. Serve immediately.

NUTRITION FACTS (PER SERVING)

Calories: 262	Carbohydrates: 23 g	Fiber: 7 g
Protein: 16 g	Fat: 11.9 g	Saturated fat: 4 g
Cholesterol: 218 mg	Sodium: 466 mg	Calcium: 226 mg

Yield: 4 Servings
• • • • • • •

1 cup canned reduced-sodium black or pinto beans, drained but not rinsed

$\frac{1}{4}$ cup plus 3 tablespoons chunky-style salsa, divided

$\frac{1}{2}$ teaspoon chili powder

$\frac{1}{4}$ teaspoon ground cumin

4 corn tortillas

4 large poached or steam-basted eggs (page 61)

$\frac{1}{2}$ cup shredded reduced-fat Mexican blend or Monterey Jack cheese

$\frac{1}{2}$ cup diced avocado

2 tablespoons sliced scallions

2 tablespoons chopped fresh cilantro

FABULOUS FIBER FACT
Viscous fibers (found in foods like oats, barley, legumes, and flaxseed) aid in the regulation of blood sugar levels by slowing digestion and absorption and thus preventing spikes in blood sugar.

EGG & POTATO SKILLET

Yield: 4 Servings
• • • • • • •

1 tablespoon extra virgin olive oil

$^1/_2$ cup finely chopped yellow onion

$^1/_3$ cup finely chopped green bell pepper

$^1/_3$ cup finely chopped red bell pepper

$^1/_3$ cup unsalted vegetable broth or chicken broth, divided

3 cups cooked diced unpeeled potatoes

$^1/_4$ teaspoon salt

$^1/_4$ teaspoon ground black pepper

4 large eggs

$^1/_2$ cup shredded reduced-fat cheddar cheese

1. In a large nonstick skillet, add the olive oil, onion, green bell pepper, red bell pepper, and 1 tablespoon broth. Cover and cook over medium heat for about 4 minutes, or until the vegetables are tender. Add a little more broth if necessary, but only enough to prevent scorching.

2. Add the potatoes, salt, black pepper, and 2 tablespoons broth to the skillet. Stir to mix. Cover and cook over medium heat for about 4 minutes, or until the potatoes are lightly browned.

3. Using a spatula, move the potatoes to one side of the skillet. Spray the bottom of the skillet with cooking spray and redistribute the potatoes to cover the bottom of the skillet.

4. Make 4 wells in the potato mixture. Crack 1 egg and place the contents in 1 well. Repeat with the remaining eggs. Lower the heat to medium-low and drizzle 2 tablespoons vegetable broth over the skillet mixture. Cover and cook for 3 minutes, or until the eggs are almost done.

5. Sprinkle the cheese over the top. Cover and cook for 1 minute, or until the cheese is melted and the eggs are done. Use a spatula to divide the mixture into 4 servings and transfer to serving plates. Serve hot.

NUTRITION FACTS (PER SERVING)

Calories: 245	Carbohydrates: 22 g	Fiber: 3.1 g
Protein: 13.6 g	Fat: 11.9 g	Saturated fat: 4 g
Cholesterol: 218 mg	Sodium: 358 mg	Calcium: 152 mg

Eggs the Way You Like 'Em

If you are looking for a quick meal, eggs are an ideal choice. The protein in an egg-based breakfast can keep you feeling full for hours. By adding some fiber-rich fruit, vegetables, or whole grain to the meal, you will make it all the more satisfying. Here are a few easy ways to cook eggs.

SCRAMBLED

For each serving, whisk together 2 eggs, or use 1 egg plus 2 egg whites. (Whisk briefly for denser scrambled eggs or vigorously for fluffier scrambled eggs.) Coat a large nonstick skillet with cooking spray and preheat over medium heat until a drop of water sizzles when added. Add the eggs, reduce the heat to medium-low, and cook just until they begin to set around the edges. As the eggs begin to set, gently pull a spatula across the bottom and sides of the pan, forming large curds. Cook for about a minute, or just until set.

STEAM-BASTED

Coat a large nonstick skillet with cooking spray and preheat over medium heat until a drop of water sizzles when added. Break 4 eggs and slip them into the pan. Immediately lower the heat to medium-low and add 1 teaspoon water per egg. Place a lid on the pan to hold in the steam. Cook for a couple of minutes, or until the whites are set and the yolks thicken.

POACHED

Fill a pot or deep skillet with 3 inches of water. Add 2 tablespoons white vinegar or lemon juice per quart of water. Bring the liquid to a boil. Lower the heat to keep the water gently simmering. Break an egg into a custard cup. Hold the cup close to the water's surface and slip the egg into the water. Cook until the white is set and the yolk begins to thicken (about 3 to 5 minutes). Use a slotted spoon to lift out the egg.

HARD-BOILED

Place the eggs in a single layer in a pot. Add enough water to cover the eggs by at least 1 inch. Cover, bring the water to a boil, and then turn off the heat. Let the eggs stand covered for 15 minutes (for large size eggs).

Food safety tip: Note that food safety guidelines recommend cooking eggs until both the yolk and the white are firm. Scrambled eggs should not be runny.

EGGS DU PUY

1. In a 1-quart saucepan, combine the lentils and broth. Bring to a boil. Lower the heat to maintain a simmer, cover, and cook for about 30 minutes for French green lentils or 20 minutes for brown lentils, or until the lentils are tender but not mushy. Drain and set aside, uncovered, for 10 minutes to cool slightly.

2. In a small bowl, combine the dressing ingredients and whisk to mix. Set aside.

3. Add the tomatoes, scallions, and 2 tablespoons of the dressing to the lentils. Toss to mix and set aside.

4. Place the salad greens in a medium-sized bowl and drizzle with 1½ tablespoons of the dressing. Toss to mix and divide the mixture among 4 serving plates. Top the greens on each plate with a quarter of the lentil mixture and 1 poached egg. Drizzle 1 teaspoon of the remaining dressing over each serving. Sprinkle each serving with additional black pepper if desired. Serve immediately.

Yield: 4 Servings

• • • • • • • • • •

³/₄ cup dried lentils du Puy (French green lentils) or brown lentils

1½ cups unsalted chicken broth or vegetable broth

½ cup diced plum tomatoes

⅓ cup sliced scallions

4 cups mixed baby salad greens

4 poached eggs (page 61)

DRESSING

2 tablespoons extra virgin olive oil

2 tablespoons white wine vinegar

2 teaspoons Dijon mustard

1 teaspoon crushed garlic

Scant ½ teaspoon salt

¼ teaspoon ground black pepper

NUTRITION FACTS (PER SERVING)

Calories: 273	Carbohydrates: 25 g	Fiber: 11.8 g
Protein: 17 g	Fat: 12 g	Saturated fat: 2.6 g
Cholesterol: 185 mg	Sodium: 471 mg	Calcium: 65 mg

FABULOUS FIBER FACT

A high-fiber diet rich in plant foods helps remove excess estrogen from the body. This may explain why adequate fiber intake has been linked to a reduction in breast cancer risk.

POTATO FRITTATA

1. Coat a large nonstick ovenproof skillet with cooking spray and add the onion, Herbes de Provence or fines herbes, and water. Cover and cook over medium heat for about 3 minutes, or until the onion starts to soften.

2. Add the potatoes, salt, and pepper. Cover and cook for about 4 minutes, turning with a spatula after a couple of minutes, until the potatoes are just beginning to brown. Toss in the kale or spinach and cook uncovered for about 1 minute to wilt.

3. Push the vegetables to one side of the skillet and spread the olive oil over the bottom of the skillet. Add the garlic and cook for 10 seconds. Redistribute the vegetables over the bottom of the skillet. Pour the eggs over the skillet mixture.

4. Cook uncovered without stirring for about 3 minutes, or until set around the edges. Continue to cook for a couple of minutes, lifting the edges with a spatula, allowing the uncooked egg to flow beneath the cooked portion, until the frittata is almost set (the center portion of the top will still be runny).

5. Preheat the oven to broil. Wrap the skillet handle in aluminum foil (to prevent damage from the broiler flame) and place the skillet in the oven, 5 inches from the heat. Cook for about 3 minutes, or until the frittata is almost set. Sprinkle the cheeses over the top and broil for about 30 seconds, or just until the melted. Cut into wedges and serve hot.

NUTRITION FACTS (PER SERVING)

Calories: 223	Carbohydrate: 19 g	Fiber: 3.3 g
Protein: 19 g	Fat: 8 g	Saturated fat: 3.1 g
Cholesterol: 16 mg	Sodium: 457 mg	Calcium: 265 mg

Yield: 4 Servings

• • • • • • •

$1/2$ cup thin wedges yellow onion

1 teaspoon Herbes de Provence or fines herbes

1 tablespoon water

2 cups diced cooked unpeeled new potatoes or Yukon Gold potatoes (about 10 ounces)

$1/4$ teaspoon salt

$1/4$ teaspoon ground black pepper

2 cups chopped kale or spinach, moderately packed

1 tablespoon extra virgin olive oil

$1 1/2$ teaspoons crushed garlic

$1 1/2$ cups liquid egg whites or fat-free egg substitute, or 8 large eggs, beaten

2 tablespoons grated Parmesan cheese

$3/4$ cup shredded reduced-fat mozzarella cheese

ZUCCHINI & CORN FRITTATA

Yield: I Serving
• • • • • • • •

I medium zucchini
(about 6 ounces)

$^1/_2$ cup fresh or frozen
(thawed) whole kernel corn

I tablespoon chopped
sun-dried tomatoes

$^1/_2$ teaspoon dried basil

Pinch salt

Pinch ground black pepper

$^3/_4$ teaspoon extra virgin
olive oil

$^1/_2$ teaspoon crushed garlic

$^1/_2$ cup liquid egg whites or
fat-free egg substitute, or I
egg plus 2 egg whites, beaten

3 tablespoons shredded
reduced-fat mozzarella
cheese

I $^1/_2$ teaspoons grated
Parmesan cheese (optional)

1. Use a julienne vegetable peeler to shred the zucchini into long thin "noodles." Shred only the skin and firm outer portions of the zucchini, stopping when you reach the seeded center portion. (The center can be diced and added to salads or other dishes.)

2. Coat an 8-inch nonstick skillet with cooking spray and preheat over medium-high heat. Add the zucchini and corn and cook for about 4 minutes, or just until the zucchini is tender, tossing frequently. Lower the heat to medium and toss in the sun-dried tomatoes, basil, salt, and black pepper.

3. Push the vegetables to one side of the skillet. Spread the olive oil over the bottom of the skillet. Add the garlic and cook for 10 seconds.

4. Redistribute the vegetables over the bottom of the skillet and pour the eggs over the vegetables. Cook without stirring for about 2 minutes, or until the eggs are set around the edges. Cook for another minute or two, lifting the edges with a spatula, allowing the uncooked egg to flow beneath the cooked portion, until the frittata is almost set.

5. Slide the frittata wet side up onto a large plate. Using potholders, place the skillet upside down over the frittata and invert the frittata back into the skillet. Sprinkle with the cheeses and reduce the heat to low. Cover and cook for 1 minute to melt the cheese. Serve hot.

NUTRITION FACTS (PER SERVING)

Calories: 245	Carbohydrates: 27 g	Fiber: 4.2 g
Protein: 24 g	Fat: 6.2 g	Saturated fat: 2.7 g
Cholesterol: 11 mg	Sodium: 358 mg	Calcium: 207 mg

ITALIAN SAUSAGE FRITTATA

1. Coat a large nonstick ovenproof skillet with cooking spray and add the sausage. Cook over medium heat for about 5 minutes, or until no longer pink, stirring to crumble. Add the leek and garlic. Cover and cook for about 4 minutes, or until the leek softens. Add a little water if the skillet becomes too dry. Stir in the artichoke hearts and peppers. Cook uncovered for a couple of minutes to heat through and evaporate any liquid.

2. Push the sausage mixture to one side of the skillet and respray the skillet. Redistribute the mixture over the bottom of the skillet and pour the eggs over the top. Cook uncovered without stirring for about 3 minutes, or until set around the edges. Continue to cook for a couple of minutes, lifting the edges with a spatula, allowing the uncooked egg to flow beneath the cooked portion, until the frittata is almost set (the center portion will still be runny).

3. Preheat the oven to broil. Wrap the skillet handle in aluminum foil (to prevent damage from the broiler flame) and place the skillet in the oven, 5 inches from the heat. Broil for about 3 minutes, or until the eggs are set. Sprinkle the cheese over the top and broil for about 30 seconds or just until the cheese melts. Cut into wedges and serve hot.

Yield: 4 Servings

• • • • • • •

6 ounces chicken or turkey Italian sausage, casings removed

1 cup sliced leek (white and light green parts only)

1 teaspoon crushed garlic

One 9-ounce package frozen artichoke hearts (thawed), or one 14-ounce can artichoke hearts (drained), and coarsely chopped

$1/4$ teaspoon ground black pepper

$1 1/2$ cups liquid egg whites or fat-free egg substitute, or 8 large eggs, beaten

$3/4$ cup shredded reduced-fat mozzarella or white cheddar cheese

NUTRITION FACTS (PER SERVING)

Calories: 220

Protein: 24 g

Cholesterol: 49 mg

Carbohydrates: 12 g

Fat: 7.8 g

Sodium: 648 mg

Fiber: 4.2 g

Saturated fat: 3.3 g

Calcium: 220 mg

BREAKFAST BAGELWICH

Yield: 1 Serving

• • • • • • • •

1 tablespoon sliced scallions

$1/2$ cup sliced fresh spinach,
moderately packed

2 teaspoons chopped
sun-dried tomatoes

2 egg whites or
1 large egg, beaten

$3/4$ ounce thinly sliced reduced-
fat mozzarella, provolone, or
white cheddar cheese

1 whole grain bagel thin or
whole grain English muffin,
sliced and toasted

1. Coat a 10-inch nonstick skillet with cooking spray and add the scallions. Cover and cook over medium heat for about 2 minutes to soften. Add the spinach and cook for about a minute to wilt. Stir in the sun-dried tomatoes.

2. Pour the egg over the skillet mixture and cook without stirring for about 1 minute, or just until set. Using a spatula, fold the egg in half, and then in half again, so it will fit on the bagel or English muffin.

3. Top the folded egg with the cheese. Turn off the heat and let sit, covered, for about 30 seconds to melt the cheese. Place the eggs and cheese in the bagel or English muffin and serve immediately.

NUTRITION FACTS (PER SERVING)

Calories: 232	Carbohydrates: 31 g	Fiber: 6.5 g
Protein: 19 g	Fat: 5.7 g	Saturated fat: 2.4 g
Cholesterol: 11 mg	Sodium: 429 mg	Calcium: 226 mg

BANANA-DATE-NUT BAGEL

Yield: 1 Serving

• • • • • • • •

3 tablespoons nonfat or low-fat
cottage or ricotta cheese

$1/2$ whole grain bagel thin,
toasted

Pinch ground cinnamon

$1/4$ medium banana, diagonally
sliced

1 date, pitted and thinly sliced

1 tablespoon chopped walnuts

1 teaspoon honey or
maple syrup

1. Spread the cheese over the bagel and sprinkle with the cinnamon. Top with the banana slices and sprinkle with the dates and walnuts.

2. Drizzle the honey over the top. Serve immediately.

NUTRITION FACTS (PER SERVING)

Calories: 200	Carbohydrates: 33 g	Fiber: 4.2 g
Protein: 10.6 g	Fat: 5.1 g	Saturated fat: 0.4 g
Cholesterol: 2 mg	Sodium: 184 mg	Calcium: 78 mg

FOR A CHANGE . . .

Substitute thinly sliced pear for the banana and a dried fig for the date.

EXTRA-FIBER FRENCH TOAST

1. In a shallow bowl, combine the eggs, milk, cinnamon, and vanilla extract. Whisk to mix. Set aside.

2. Coat a large nonstick griddle or skillet with cooking spray and preheat over medium heat until a drop of water sizzles when added. Dip the bread slices in the egg mixture, soaking both sides of each slice to thoroughly saturate the bread.

3. Working in batches as needed, cook the bread slices for about $1\frac{1}{2}$ minutes on each side, or until light golden brown. As the slices are done, transfer to a plate and keep warm in a preheated oven.

4. Serve immediately with Warm Berry Compote (page 68), Spiced Pear Compote (page 68), sliced fresh strawberries and a light sprinkling of powdered sugar, or sliced bananas and a drizzle of honey or maple syrup.

Yield: 8 Slices

• • • • • • •

$\frac{3}{4}$ cup liquid egg whites or fat-free egg substitute, or 4 large eggs, beaten

$\frac{3}{4}$ cup nonfat or low-fat milk

$\frac{1}{2}$ teaspoon ground cinnamon

$\frac{1}{2}$ teaspoon vanilla extract

8 slices whole grain bread (look for 3 to 4 g fiber per slice)

NUTRITION FACTS
(PER 1-SLICE SERVING WITHOUT TOPPINGS)

Calories: 99	Carbohydrates: 17 g	Fiber: 3.1 g
Protein: 7 g	Fat: 1 g	Saturated fat: 0 g
Cholesterol: 1 mg	Sodium: 133 mg	Calcium: 37 mg

FABULOUS FIBER FACT

Fiber-rich foods are slowly digested and absorbed, so they help you feel fuller longer and reduce the urge to graze between meals.

WARM BERRY COMPOTE

Yield: 6 Servings

• • • • • • • •

4 cups fresh or frozen berries such as sliced strawberries, raspberries, blueberries, blackberries, or any combination

$^1/_4$ cup orange or pomegranate juice

3 tablespoons sugar

1. In a 2-quart saucepan, combine the fruit, juice, and sugar. Cover and cook over medium heat for about 5 minutes, or until the berries release their juices and the mixture comes to a boil.

2. Mash the berries with the back of a wooden spoon. Cook uncovered for about 8 minutes, or until the mixture is syrupy and reduced in volume to about $1^1/_2$ cups. Serve warm over pancakes, French toast, or oatmeal, or as a topping for ice cream.

NUTRITION FACTS (PER $^1/_4$-CUP SERVING)

Calories: 73	Carbohydrates: 18 g	Fiber: 3.3 g
Protein: 0.8 g	Fat: 0.4 g	Saturated fat: 0 g
Cholesterol: 0 mg	Sodium: 1 mg	Calcium: 15 mg

SPICED PEAR COMPOTE

Yield: 5 Servings

• • • • • • • •

3 cups sliced peeled pears

2 tablespoons sugar

$^1/_2$ teaspoon ground cinnamon

$^1/_4$ teaspoon ground ginger

$^1/_4$ cup orange juice, divided

1 teaspoon cornstarch

1. In a 2-quart suacepan, combine the pears, sugar, cinnamon, and ginger. Stir to mix. Add $3^1/_2$ tablespoons of the orange juice. Cover and cook over medium heat for about 5 minutes, or until the pears release their juices and the mixture comes to a boil. Lower the heat to simmer and cook for another minute or two, or just until tender.

2. In a small bowl, combine the remaining juice and cornstarch. Stir to mix. Stir into the fruit mixture. Cook, stirring constantly, for about 30 seconds, or until thickened and bubbly. Serve warm over French toast, pancakes, or oatmeal, or as a topping for ice cream.

NUTRITION FACTS (PER $^1/_3$-CUP SERVING)

Calories: 78	Carbohydrates: 20 g	Fiber: 2.7 g
Protein: 0.4 g	Fat: 0.1 g	Saturated fat: 0 g
Cholesterol: 0 mg	Sodium: 2 mg	Calcium: 9 mg

CHIA FRUIT JAM

1. In an 8-inch nonstick skillet, combine the berries and sugar. Cover and cook over medium heat for about 6 to 8 minutes, stirring occationally, until the berries release their juices and the mixture comes to a boil.

2. Mash the berries with a potato masher. Lower the heat to medium-low and stir in the chia seeds. Cook uncovered, stirring frequently, for about 6 to 8 minutes or until the mixture is reduced in volume to 1 cup.

3. Let cool and then transfer to a covered container. Refrigerate for up to 3 days before serving.

NUTRITION FACTS (PER TABLESPOON)

Calories: 31	Carbohydrates: 7 g	Fiber: 1.2 g
Protein: 0.4 g	Fat: 0.7 g	Saturated fat: 0 g
Cholesterol: 0 mg	Sodium: 1 mg	Calcium: 13 mg

Yield: I Cup

2$\frac{1}{2}$ cup fresh or frozen blueberries or pitted and chopped dark sweet cherries

3 tablespoons sugar

2 tablespoons chia seeds

FRUIT & NUT MUESLI

1. In a small bowl, combine all the ingredients except for the yogurt. Stir to mix.

2. Add the yogurt to the bowl. Stir to mix. Let sit for 10 minutes before serving.

NUTRITION FACTS (PER SERVING)

Calories: 300	Carbohydrates: 43 g	Fiber: 6.2 g
Protein: 16 g	Fat: 8.5 g	Saturated Fat: 3.6 g
Cholesterol: 4 mg	Sodium: 143 mg	Calcium: 385 mg

Yield: I Serving

$\frac{1}{3}$ cup old-fashioned oats

I tablespoon wheat bran or wheat germ

I tablespoon dried fruit such as cranberries, blueberries, cherries, raisins, apricots, figs, or dates

I tablespoon sliced almonds, chopped walnuts, raw sunflower seeds, or raw pumpkin seeds

I tablespoon shredded dried coconut

I cup plain or vanilla nonfat or low-fat plain yogurt

CREAMY WHEAT CEREAL

Yield: 4 Servings

• • • • • • •

1 cup whole wheat berries

2 cups water

2 cups nonfat or
low-fat milk

$^1/_2$ cup wheat bran

1. Place the wheat berries in a blender and blend for about 15 seconds, or until the wheat berries have the texture of coarse grits (depending on the power of your blender this could take anywhere from 10 to 30 seconds or more). Set aside.

2. In a 3-quart saucepan, combine the water and milk and bring to a boil. Whisk in the blended wheat berries and wheat bran. Let the mixture return to a boil, and then lower the heat to maintain a simmer. Cover and cook for about 15 minutes, or until the mixture is soft and creamy. Watch the saucepan and stir every few minutes to prevent it from boiling over. Add a little more milk during the last part of cooking if needed.

3. Turn off the heat, cover, and let sit for 10 minutes before serving. Serve hot with toppings such as fresh or dried fruit, walnuts, or ground cinnamon if desired.

NUTRITION FACTS (PER 1 $^1/_8$-CUP SERVING)

Calories: 207	Carbohydrates: 43 g	Fiber: 9.1 g
Protein: 11.3 g	Fat: 0.5 g	Saturated fat: 0.1 g
Cholesterol: 2 mg	Sodium: 52 mg	Calcium: 175 mg

FOR A CHANGE . . .

Substitute other whole grains such as barley or brown rice for the wheat berries.

OVERNIGHT OATS

1. In a medium-sized bowl, combine all the ingredients except for the fruit and stir to mix. Fold in the fruit.

2. Divide the mixture between four 8-ounce containers. Cover and refrigerate overnight or for up to two days.

FOR A CHANGE . . .

Substitute $1/4$ cup plus 2 tablespoons dried blueberries, dried cherries, or chopped dried apricots for the fresh fruit. Increase the milk to $1^1/_2$ cups.

NUTRITION FACTS (PER 1-CUP SERVING)

Calories: 256	Carbohydrates: 38 g	Fiber: 7 g
Protein: 12.7 g	Fat: 7.2 g	Saturated fat: 0.8 g
Cholesterol: 4 mg	Sodium: 98 mg	Calcium: 295 mg

Yield: 4 Servings

• • • • • • •

$1^1/_3$ cups old-fashioned oats

$1^1/_3$ cups plain or vanilla nonfat or low-fat yogurt (not Greek-style)

$1^1/_3$ cups nonfat or low-fat milk

$1/4$ cup sliced almonds or chopped walnuts or pecans

2 tablespoons chia seeds

Low-calorie sweetener to taste (optional)

1 cup fresh fruit such as blueberries, raspberries, diced strawberries, or peaches

Boosting Fiber with Berries

Berries are a great way to boost fiber for relatively few calories. For instance, 1 cup raspberries or blackberries has about 8 grams of fiber and just 60 calories. Pomegranates are also classified as berries. The juicy red seeds of a pomegranate provide 7 grams of fiber per cup. Berries also provide an arsenal of disease-fighting vitamins, minerals, and phytonutrients. Fresh berries are a natural choice for breakfast. Add some to cereal, layer them into a luscious parfait, or use them to create a colorful fruit cup. Frozen berries are perfect to keep on hand for smoothies.

BUTTERMILK BRAN MUFFINS

Yield: 12 Muffins

• • • • • • •

1 cup whole wheat pastry flour (4.25 ounces) (see inset below)

1 1/2 cups wheat bran

3/4 cup oat bran or quick-cooking oats

1/4 cup light brown sugar

1 teaspoon ground cinnamon

3/4 teaspoon baking soda

1 1/2 cups reduced-fat buttermilk

1/4 cup plus 1 tablespoon fat-free egg substitute, or 1 large egg plus 1 egg white, beaten

1/4 cup molasses or honey

2 tablespoons canola oil

1/2 cup chopped walnuts

1/2 cup raisins

1. In a large bowl, combine the flour, wheat bran, oat bran or oats, brown sugar, cinnamon, and baking soda. Stir to mix.

2. In a medium-sized bowl, combine the buttermilk, egg, molasses or honey, and canola oil. Stir to mix. Add the buttermilk mixture to the flour mixture and stir to mix. Stir in the walnuts and raisins.

3. Coat a 12-cup muffin pan with cooking spray. Spoon the batter equally into the muffin cups and bake for about 18 minutes, or until a wooden toothpick inserted into the center of a muffin comes out clean.

4. Remove the muffins from the oven and let sit for 5 minutes. Remove the muffins from the pans and transfer to wire racks to cool completely.

NUTRITION FACTS (PER MUFFIN)

Calories: 195	Carbohydrates: 32 g	Fiber: 5.6 g
Protein: 5.8 g	Fat: 7 g	Saturated fat: 1 g
Cholesterol: 2 mg	Sodium: 120 mg	Calcium: 81 mg

Measuring Flour

The method you use to measure flour can make a big difference in the success of your recipe. When measuring flours for the recipes in this book, for best results, either weigh the flour using a kitchen scale, or use the "spoon and sweep" method described below:

1. Stir the flour with a spoon to break up any lumps.

2. Lightly spoon the flour into a "dry" measuring cup to overflowing. Don't pack the flour down, and don't use a beaker-type liquid measuring cup.

3. Use the flat edge of a knife to scrape off the excess flour.

In contrast, the "dip and sweep" method, in which the measuring cup is dipped directly into a flour canister, scoops up more flour because the flour is compressed. This can cause a significant difference in the outcome of recipes.

ENERGIZER BREAKFAST COOKIES

1. Preheat the oven to 325°F.

2. In a medium-sized bowl, combine the flour, oats, wheat bran, baking soda, and cinnamon. Stir to mix. Add the brown sugar and stir to mix, using the back of a spoon to press out any lumps in the brown sugar.

3. In a small bowl, combine the eggs, canola oil, and vanilla extract. Stir to mix. Add the egg mixture to the flour mixture and stir to mix. Stir in the nuts and dried fruit.

4. Line 2 large baking sheets with aluminum foil and spray lightly with cooking spray. Drop $\frac{1}{4}$ cup measures of dough onto the sheets, spacing them at least 2 inches apart. Using the back of a spoon, flatten each cookie to about $\frac{5}{8}$-inch thickness and $2\frac{1}{4}$ inches in diameter. (The dough may be slightly crumbly and you may have to press it gently for it to hold together.)

5. Bake for 6 minutes, and then switch the position of the baking sheets in the oven. Bake for 5 minutes more, or until the cookies are golden brown. Remove from the oven and let sit for 2 minutes. Transfer the cookies to wire racks to cool completely.

Yield: 16 Cookies

1 cup plus 2 tablespoons whole wheat pastry flour (4.78 ounces) (see inset on page 72)

$\frac{1}{2}$ cup quick-cooking oats

$\frac{1}{2}$ cup wheat bran

$\frac{1}{2}$ teaspoon baking soda

$\frac{1}{2}$ teaspoon ground cinnamon

$\frac{3}{4}$ cup brown sugar

2 egg whites or 1 large egg, beaten

$\frac{1}{4}$ cup canola oil

1 teaspoon vanilla extract

1 cup sliced almonds or chopped walnuts or pecans

$\frac{1}{2}$ cup dried cranberries, cherries, or blueberries

$\frac{1}{2}$ cup chopped dried figs or raisins

NUTRITION FACTS (PER COOKIE)

Calories: 174	Carbohydrates: 27 g	Fiber: 3.7 g
Protein: 3.2 g	Fat: 6.9 g	Saturated fat: 0.6 g
Cholesterol: 0 mg	Sodium: 49 mg	Calcium: 37 mg

HELPFUL TIP

Leftovers can be indivually wrapped and frozen for later use.

Boosting Your Breakfast Fiber
with Bran, Nuts, and Seeds

Starting your day the high-fiber way can be as easy as adding a sprinkling of bran, nuts, or seeds to some of your favorite foods. Here are some great choices:

FOOD	FIBER (PER 2 TBSP)	TIPS
Oat bran	2 g	Swap for a quarter of the flour in pancakes or muffins. Add 1 or 2 tablespoons to smoothies.
Wheat bran	3 g	Swap for a quarter of the flour in muffins or quickbreads. Stir 1 to 2 tablespoons into oatmeal or other hot cereals.
Wheat germ	2 g	Swap for a quarter of the flour in pancakes, muffins, or quickbreads. Add 1 or 2 tablespoons to smoothies. Sprinkle over yogurt and fruit. Stir 1 or 2 tablespoons into oatmeal or other hot cereals.
Nuts and seeds	2 g	Add 1 to 2 tablespoons to smoothies. Sprinkle over cereal or yogurt and fruit.
Coconut flour	5 g	Swap for a fifth of the flour in pancakes, muffins, or quickbreads.
Flaxseed meal	4 g	Swap for a fifth of the flour in muffins or quickbreads. Stir some into oatmeal or add 1 tablespoon to smoothies.
Chia seeds	8 g	Sprinkle over cereals or yogurt, or add 1 tablespoon to smoothies.

In addition to fiber, these options are loaded with vitamins, minerals, and phytonutrients. Flax and chia seeds are also outstanding sources of omega-3 fatty acids.

BERRY BLAST SMOOTHIE

1. Combine all the ingredients in a blender, and blend until smooth.

2. Pour into a 12-ounce glass and serve immediately.

NUTRITION FACTS (PER SERVING)

Calories: 276

Protein: 20 g

Cholesterol: 2 mg

Carbohydrates: 36 g

Fat: 6.7 g

Sodium: 106 mg

Fiber: 9 g

Saturated fat: 0.5 g

Calcium: 370 mg

FOR A CHANGE . . .

Add a handful of fresh spinach or mixed baby salad greens along with the berries. Substitute sliced banana for $1/2$ cup of the berries.

Yield: 1 Serving

$1/2$ cup nonfat or low-fat milk or pomegranate juice

$1/2$ cup plain or vanilla nonfat or low-fat Greek-style yogurt

$1 1/2$ cups mixed frozen or fresh berries, such as strawberries, blueberries, blackberries, and raspberries

$1/2$ cup crushed ice

2 tablespoons sliced almonds or chopped walnuts

1 tablespoon flaxseed meal, chia seeds, oat bran, or wheat germ (optional)

Low-calorie sweetener to taste (optional)

BERRY BREAKFAST PARFAIT

1. Place $1/4$ cup yogurt in a 12-ounce parfait glass or goblet. Top with $1/4$ cup mixed berries and 1 tablespoon plus 1 teaspoon granola.

2. Repeat the layers twice more and serve immediately.

NUTRITION FACTS (PER SERVING)

Calories: 227

Protein: 21 g

Cholesterol: 0 mg

Carbohydrates: 35 g

Fat: 1.5 g

Sodium: 125 mg

Fiber: 6 g

Saturated fat: 0.3 g

Calcium: 224 mg

Yield: 1 Serving

$3/4$ cup plain or vanilla Greek-style yogurt

$3/4$ cup fresh mixed berries, such as strawberries, raspberries, blackberries, blueberries, and pomegranate seeds

$1/4$ cup low-fat granola

ORANGE BREAKFAST BLIZZARD

Yield: I Serving

· · · · · · · · ·

I cup frozen seedless orange segments (mandarin or navel)

$1/2$ cup plain or vanilla nonfat or low-fat Greek-style yogurt

$1/2$ cup nonfat or low-fat milk

2 tablespoons sliced almonds

$1/2$ cup crushed ice

I tablespoon flaxseed meal, oat bran, or wheat germ (optional)

Low-calorie sweetener to taste (optional)

1. Combine all the ingredients in a blender, and blend until smooth.

2. Pour into a 12-ounce glass and serve immediately.

NUTRITION FACTS (PER SERVING)

Calories: 272	Carbohydrates: 39 g	Fiber: 5 g
Protein: 20 g	Fat: 6.4 g	Saturated fat: 0.6 g
Cholesterol: 2 mg	Sodium: 101 mg	Calcium: 403 mg

FOR A CHANGE . . .

Add $1/3$ cup frozen cranberries along with the oranges. Substitute sliced bananas for half of the orange segments.

CHIA JUICE DRINK

Yield: I Serving

· · · · · · · · ·

$1/4$ cup water, room temperature

I tablespoon chia seeds

$1/2$ cup pomegranate or other fruit juice, chilled

1. Place the water in a small container and add the chia seeds. Let sit for 15 minutes, stirring every 3 to 4 minutes, until the mixture forms a thick gel.

2. Stir in the fruit juice. Cover and refrigerate for at least 1 hour, or until ready to serve. You can also make a larger batch and refrigerate for up to 3 days before serving.

NUTRITION FACTS (PER SERVING)

Calories: 141	Carbohydrates: 23 g	Fiber: 5.8 g
Protein: 2.6 g	Fat: 5 g	Saturated fat: 0.6 g
Cholesterol: 0 mg	Sodium: 14 mg	Calcium: 108 mg

WAKE 'EM UP SHAKE

1. Combine all the ingredients in a blender, and blend until smooth.

2. Pour into a 16-ounce glass and serve immediately.

NUTRITION FACTS (PER SERVING)

Calories: 302

Protein: 15 g

Cholesterol: 5 mg

Carbohydrates: 40 g

Fat: 10.8 g

Sodium: 110 mg

Fiber: 6.1 g

Saturated Fat: 3.8 g

Calcium: 342 mg

FOR A CHANGE . . .

Add 1 tablespoon cocoa powder and $\frac{1}{4}$ teaspoon ground cinnamon to the ingredients.

Yield: I Serving
• • • • • • • •

I cup nonfat or low-fat milk

$\frac{1}{2}$ cup sliced frozen banana

$\frac{1}{2}$ cup black coffee, chilled or frozen into cubes

2 tablespoons sliced almonds

2 tablespoons wheat germ or oat bran

I tablespoon shredded unsweetened coconut

I tablespoon chia seeds (optional)

Low-calorie sweetener to taste (optional)

BREAKFAST BANANA SPLIT

1. Lay the bananas split side up in a shallow bowl.

2. Top the bananas with the yogurt, raspberries, blueberries, and nuts or granola. Serve immediately.

NUTRITION FACTS (PER SERVING)

Calories: 235

Protein: 15 g

Cholesterol: 0 mg

Carbohydrates: 34 g

Fat: 6.2 g

Sodium: 46 mg

Fiber: 5.8 g

Saturated fat: 0.5 g

Calcium: 168 mg

Yield: I Serving
• • • • • • • •

$\frac{1}{2}$ banana, split lengthwise

$\frac{1}{2}$ cup vanilla nonfat or low-fat Greek-style yogurt

$\frac{1}{4}$ cup fresh raspberries or sliced strawberries

$\frac{1}{4}$ cup fresh blueberries

2 tablespoons sliced almonds, chopped walnuts, or granola

5

Smart Sandwiches

Versatile, portable, and easy to make, sandwiches are the quintessential quick meal. And when made right, sandwiches can be a smart choice when following a healthy high-fiber eating plan. Replacing white bread with whole grain options is a simple way to boost dietary fiber. Doing this alone adds a good 4 to 6 grams of fiber along with many important nutrients. Pile on plenty of vegetables and you'll end up with even more fiber and nutrients. Substitute mashed avocado or hummus for mayonnaise on your sandwich and you'll truly have a healthy high-fiber meal.

Although many sandwiches are uniquely American, other cuisines feature their own variations on this theme. Pizzas and panini from Italy, tacos and quesadillas from Mexico, and stuffed pitas from the Middle East are just some examples of handheld meals from around the world. Happily, all can easily be made the healthy high-fiber way without sacrificing the tastes you love.

This chapter features a selection of satisfying sandwiches that can be assembled in a snap. Whether you are looking for a portable sandwich to pack for lunch or a hot and hearty creation for a family dinner, you are sure to find something that meets your needs deliciously.

Bread Basics

Bread comes in many different shapes, sizes, and varieties. Whole grain options are ideal, but what about carbohydrate content? Can you have your bread and eat it, too? As long as bread is chosen wisely and eaten in moderation, it can easily fit into a healthy diet. The sandwiches in this chapter are moderate in both calories and carbohydrates. If you want to cut carbs a bit more, you can opt to use light or reduced-carb bread in any of these recipes. Be aware that some reduced-carb breads may be higher in sodium, fat, or other ingredients that you want to avoid. Surprisingly, breads that look quite similar can be very different nutritionally. It pays to compare labels for calories, carbs, sodium, and other ingredients.

SANDWICH BREAD

Look for 100 percent whole grain bread with fiber-rich ingredients such as whole wheat flour, oats, rye meal, sprouted grains, cracked grains, flax, or bran. The "Nutrition Facts" in this chapter are based on using 100 percent whole grain bread with 160 calories, 30 g carbohydrate, and 6 g fiber per 2 slices.

TORTILLAS

This southwestern flatbread, typically 5 to 8 inches in diameter, is used to make tacos, quesadillas, burritos, and other Tex-Mex favorites. Larger tortillas (9 to 10 inches in diameter) are often used to make wrap-style sandwiches. There are many types of whole grain tortillas, including whole wheat, corn, multigrain, and sprouted grain. Tortillas can vary widely in carbohydrate content and calories, so read labels carefully. A 9-inch whole wheat wrap, for instance, can contain anywhere from 140 to 210 calories. The "Nutrition Facts" for wraps in this chapter are based on using a 100 percent whole grain wrap with 140 calories, 24 g carbohydrate, and 3 g fiber per 9-inch wrap.

FLATBREAD

The term "flatbread" encompasses a variety of breads, including tortillas, pitas, naan, and crispy cracker-like breads. A common type of flatbread is a thin, pliable rectangular wrap, also called lavash bread, which is a good option for making sandwich wraps and thin-crust pizzas. As you should when shopping for any type of bread, look for products made with 100 percent whole grain flour and fiber-rich ingredients such as flax, bran, or cracked grains. The "Nutrition Facts" for flatbread sandwiches in this book are based on a 100 percent whole grain flatbread with 100 calories, 15 g carbohydrate, and 3 g fiber per flatbread (about a 9-x-6-inch flatbread).

PITA BREAD

This Middle Eastern bread is also known as pocket bread. Pita is typically split horizontally and stuffed with sandwich filling. It also makes a very good crust for personal-sized pizza. Pita pizza crust is thick and chewy in comparison to tortilla or flatbread pizza crust, which is thinner and crispier. You can also cut pita bread into wedges and use them as an alternative to crackers.

Pita bread varies in size, which directly affects carbohydrate content and calories. The "Nutrition Facts" for the pita in this book are based on a 100 percent whole grain pita with 100 calories, 22 g carbohydrate, and 4 g fiber per 5-inch diameter pita.

NAAN

This Indian-style flatbread looks similar to pita bread but has a softer texture due to the additon of ingredients like yogurt or milk, and sometimes oil or butter. Like pita bread, naan makes a very good crust for personal-sized pizza. Be sure to look for low-fat versions made of whole grain. These will have calorie and carbohydrate content similar to pita bread.

VERY VEGGIE SANDWICHES

1. For each sandwich, place 2 bread slices on a work surface and spread $1^1/_2$ tablespoons hummus on each one.

2. Top 1 bread slice with 3 slices cucumber, 3 slices tomato, 2 tablespoons carrot, 2 rings bell pepper, 1 slice red onion, and 1 sliced mushroom. Drizzle with $1^1/_2$ teaspoons salad dressing. Layer on 1 ounce cheese, 1 lettuce leaf, and $1/_4$ cup cabbage.

3. Top with the remaining bread slice and cut into halves or quarters to serve.

NUTRITION FACTS (PER SANDWICH)

Calories: 353	Carbohydrates: 44 g	Fiber: 10.2 g
Protein: 21 g	Fat: 11 g	Saturated fat: 3.4 g
Cholesterol: 15 mg	Sodium: 538 mg	Calcium: 287 mg

Yield: 4 Sandwiches

• • • • • • • • • • • •

8 slices multigrain, whole wheat, or pumpernickel bread

$3/_4$ cup hummus

12 slices cucumber

12 slices plum tomato

$1/_2$ cup shredded carrot

8 thin rings green bell pepper

4 thin slices red onion

4 medium white button mushrooms, thinly sliced

2 tablespoons light olive oil vinaigrette salad dressing

4 ounces thinly sliced reduced-fat Swiss, mozzarella, or provolone cheese

4 romaine lettuce leaves

1 cup thinly sliced red cabbage

TEMPTING TURKEY SANDWICHES

1. For each sandwich, place 2 bread slices on a work surface and spread 1 tablespoon hummus on each slice.

2. Top 1 bread slice with 2 ounces turkey, 1 ounce cheese, 3 rings bell pepper, 2 tablespoons carrot, 1 slice red onion, $1/_4$ cup artichoke hearts, and 8 leaves spinach. Top with the remaining bread slice and cut into halves or quarters to serve.

NUTRITION FACTS (PER SANDWICH)

Calories: 413	Carbohydrates: 44 g	Fiber: 11.2 g
Protein: 34 g	Fat: 11.1 g	Saturated fat: 3 g
Cholesterol: 35 mg	Sodium: 670 mg	Calcium: 327 mg

Yield: 4 Sandwiches

• • • • • • • • • • • •

8 slices multigrain, pumpernickel, or dark rye bread

$1/_2$ cup hummus

8 ounces thinly sliced cooked turkey breast

4 ounces thinly sliced reduced-fat Swiss, mozzarella, or provolone cheese

12 thin rings red bell pepper

$1/_2$ cup shredded carrot

4 slices red onion

1 cup sliced marinated artichoke hearts, drained

32 large fresh spinach leaves

SUMMER VEGETABLE SANDWICHES

Yield: 4 Sandwiches

• • • • • • • •

8 slices multigrain bread

I cup coarsely mashed avocado (about I medium avocado)

4 ounces thinly sliced reduced-fat mozzarella or Monterey Jack cheese

16 slices cucumber

8 slices tomato

4 romaine lettuce leaves

1. For each sandwich, place 2 bread slices on a work surface. Spread each bread slice with 2 tablespoons mashed avocado. Top 1 bread slice with 1 ounce cheese, and layer on 4 slices cucumber, 2 slices tomato, and 1 leaf lettuce.

2. Place the remaining bread slice on the sandwich. Cut into halves or quarters and serve immediately.

NUTRITION FACTS (PER SANDWICH)

Calories: 289	Carbohydrates: 36 g	Fiber: 8.8 g
Protein: 14 g	Fat: 10.6 g	Saturated fat: 3.2 g
Cholesterol: 14 mg	Sodium: 311 mg	Calcium: 164 mg

GARDEN ARTICHOKE SANDWICHES

Yield: 4 Sandwiches

• • • • • • • •

I $\frac{1}{4}$ cups chopped marinated artichoke hearts, drained

$\frac{1}{4}$ cup reduced-fat cream cheese, softened to room temperature

8 slices multigrain, dark rye, or pumpernickle bread

8 rings red bell pepper

$\frac{1}{4}$ cup grated carrot

4 slices red onion

4 ounces thinly sliced reduced-fat mozzarella, Swiss, or provolone cheese

32 large fresh spinach leaves

4 teaspoons Dijon mustard

1. In a small bowl, combine the artichoke hearts and cream cheese. Stir until well combined.

2. For each sandwich, place 1 bread slice on a work surface and spread with a quarter (about $\frac{1}{3}$ cup) of the artichoke mixture. Layer on 2 rings red bell pepper, 1 tablespoon carrot, 1 red onion slice, 1 ounce cheese, and 8 spinach leaves.

3. Spread 1 bread slice with 1 teaspoon mustard and place on the sandwich. Cut into halves or quarters and serve immediately.

NUTRITION FACTS (PER SANDWICH)

Calories: 355	Carbohydrates: 42 g	Fiber: 9.6 g
Protein: 20 g	Fat: 12.9 g	Saturated fat: 5.4 g
Cholesterol: 31 mg	Sodium: 636 mg	Calcium: 232 mg

COLOSSAL CHICKEN SALAD SANDWICHES

1. In a medium-sized bowl, combine the chicken, celery, scallions, dill, yogurt or sour cream, and $1/4$ cup mayonnaise. Stir to mix.

2. For each sandwich, place 1 bread slice on a work surface and spread with a quarter of the chicken salad (about $1/2$ cup). Top with a quarter of the carrots, avocado, and spinach or lettuce.

3. Spread 1 teaspoon of mayonnaise on 1 bread slice. Place the slice on top of the sandwich, and cut into halves or quarters to serve.

NUTRITION FACTS (PER SANDWICH)

Calories: 355	Carbohydrates: 38 g	Fiber: 9 g
Protein: 30 g	Fat: 9.8 g	Saturated fat: 1.3 g
Cholesterol: 54 mg	Sodium: 398 mg	Calcium: 35 mg

Yield: 4 Sandwiches

• • • • • • • • • • •

2 cups chopped cooked chicken breast

$1/4$ cup plus 2 tablespoons finely chopped celery

$1/4$ cup thinly sliced scallions

1 tablespoon finely chopped fresh dill, or 1 teaspoon dried dill

2 tablespoons nonfat or low-fat Greek-style yogurt or light sour cream

$1/3$ cup low-fat or light mayonnaise, divided

8 slices multigrain, whole wheat, or pumpernickel bread

$1/2$ cup shredded carrots

1 medium avocado, peeled, pitted, and sliced into 16 wedges

32 large fresh spinach leaves, or 4 romaine lettuce leaves

FABULOUS FIBER FACT

Fiber is essentially chains of carbohydrate molecules. However, our digestive enzymes cannot break the bonds between the molecules, so the carbohydrates cannot be digested or absorbed. That's why fiber is often described as "indigestible carbohydrate."

Yield: 4 Pitas

• • • • • • • • • •

4 cups shredded romaine lettuce
or mixed baby salad greens

Two 5-ounce cans tuna in spring
water, drained

$^3/_4$ cup marinated artichoke hearts,
drained (reserve 2 tablespoons
of the marinade)

3 slices red onion,
cut into quarter rings

$^1/_4$ cup plus 2 tablespoons chopped
pitted Kalamata or black olives

$^1/_4$ cup plus 2 tablespoons
crumbled reduced-fat feta cheese

4 whole grain pita pockets
(5-inch rounds), halved

GREEK TUNA PITAS

1. In a large bowl, combine the lettuce or mixed greens, tuna, artichoke hearts, red onion, olives, and feta cheese. Add the reserved marinade and toss to mix.

2. Place about $^3/_4$ cup of the tuna mixture into each pita half and serve immediately.

NUTRITION FACTS (PER PITA)

Calories: 235	Carbohydrates: 28 g	Fiber: 6.5 g
Protein: 20 g	Fat: 6.1 g	Saturated fat: 0.4 g
Cholesterol: 20 mg	Sodium: 603 mg	Calcium: 43 mg

Yield: 4 Wraps

• • • • • • • • • •

2 cups shredded cooked chicken
breast (about 10 ounces)

1 cup julienned Granny Smith apple
(about 1 medium)

$^1/_3$ cup bias-sliced scallions

$^1/_3$ cup julienned celery

$^1/_3$ cup sliced almonds

$^1/_4$ cup low-fat or light mayonnaise

$^1/_4$ cup plain nonfat or low-fat Greek-
style yogurt or light sour cream

$^1/_2$ teaspoon curry powder

4 whole grain tortillas
(9-inch rounds)

4 romaine lettuce leaves

CURRIED CHICKEN WRAPS

1. In a large bowl, combine the chicken, apple, scallions, celery, and almonds. In a small bowl, combine the mayonnaise, yogurt or sour cream, and curry powder. Stir to mix. Add the mayonnaise mixture to the chicken mixture, and toss to mix.

2. For each sandwich, place a tortilla on a work surface. Spread a quarter (about 1 cup) of the chicken mixture over the bottom half of the tortilla, leaving a 1-inch border on each side. Top with a lettuce leaf.

3. Fold the sides in about 1 inch and roll the wrap up snugly from the bottom. Cut into halves and serve immediately.

NUTRITION FACTS (PER WRAP)

Calories: 345	Carbohydrates: 35 g	Fiber: 6 g
Protein: 29 g	Fat: 10.7 g	Saturated fat: 1.5 g
Cholesterol: 54 mg	Sodium: 327 mg	Calcium: 221 mg

COBB-STYLE CHICKEN WRAPS

1. For each sandwich, place a tortilla on a work surface. Spread 1 teaspoon mayonnaise in an even layer over the bottom half of the tortilla, leaving a 1-inch border on each side. Layer on $1/4$ of the chicken, bacon, tomato, blue cheese, avocado, salad dressing, and lettuce.

2. Fold the sides in about 1 inch and roll up snugly from the bottom. Cut into halves and serve immediately.

NUTRITION FACTS (PER WRAP)

Calories: 347	Carbohydrates: 31 g	Fiber: 6.3 g
Protein: 24 g	Fat: 14.8 g	Saturated fat: 3 g
Cholesterol: 48 mg	Sodium: 446 mg	Calcium: 201 mg

Yield: 4 Wraps

• • • • • • • • •

4 whole grain tortillas
(9-inch rounds)

4 teaspoons low-fat or light
mayonnaise

8 ounces thinly sliced cooked
chicken breast

4 slices cooked bacon (vegetarian,
turkey, or center-cut pork)

12 slices plum tomato
(about 2 medium)

$1/4$ cup crumbled reduced-fat
blue cheese

1 medium avocado, cut into 12 slices

2 teaspoons light olive oil
vinaigrette salad dressing

6 large romaine lettuce leaves

HUMMUS-VEGGIE WRAPS

1. For each wrap, place a tortilla on a work surface. Spoon $1/3$ cup hummus in an even layer over the bottom half of the tortilla, leaving a 1-inch border on each side. Layer 2 slices tomato, 1 sliced mushroom, 3 slices cucumber, 1 slice red onion, 1 tablespoon olives, 1 tablespoon feta cheese, and 8 spinach leaves or 1 romaine lettuce leaf over the hummus.

2. Fold in the sides of the tortilla about 1 inch and roll it up snugly from the bottom. Cut into halves and serve immediately.

NUTRITION FACTS (PER SERVING)

Calories: 339	Carbohydrates: 42 g	Fiber: 10.3 g
Protein: 15 g	Fat: 14.6 g	Saturated Fat: 2.8 g
Cholesterol: 8 mg	Sodium: 638 mg	Calcium: 301 mg

Yield: 4 Wraps

• • • • • • • • •

4 whole grain flour tortillas
(9-inch rounds)

$1 1/3$ cups hummus

8 slices plum tomato

4 medium white button
mushrooms, thinly sliced

12 slices English cucumber

4 thin slices red onion, cut into
half-rings

$1/4$ cup chopped black olives

$1/4$ cup crumbled reduced-fat
feta cheese

32 large fresh spinach leaves,
or 4 romaine lettuce leaves

PORTOBELLO MUSHROOM WRAPS

Yield: 4 Wraps
• • • • • • • •

Olive oil cooking spray

4 medium portobello
mushrooms, scrape out the
gills and slice $1/2$-inch thick

4 slices red onion
($3/8$-inch thick)

Olive oil cooking spray

$1/2$ teaspoon ground
black pepper

3 cups mixed baby salad
greens

$1/4$ cup light balsamic
vinaigrette salad dressing

4 whole grain tortillas
(9-inch rounds)

4 ounces soft (log-style)
goat cheese or fresh
mozzarella cheese, sliced

8 slices plum tomato

1. Preheat the oven to 450°F. Line two large baking sheets with aluminum foil and spray with cooking spray. Arrange the mushroom and onion slices on the baking sheets in a single layer. Spray the vegetables lightly with the cooking spray and sprinkle with the pepper.

2. Bake for 10 minutes. Flip the vegetables over and cook for 5 to 8 minutes more, or until nicely browned and tender.

3. While the vegetables are cooking, combine the salad greens and salad dressing in a medium-sized bowl. Toss well and set aside.

4. For each wrap, place 1 tortilla on a work surface. Place a quarter of the salad greens on the bottom half of the tortilla, leaving a $1^1/_2$-inch border on both sides. Layer on a quarter of the mushroom and red onion, 1 ounce goat cheese, and 2 slices tomato.

5. Fold in the sides of the tortilla about 1 inch and roll it up snugly from the bottom. Cut the wrap into halves and serve immediately.

NUTRITION FACTS (PER WRAP)

Calories: 280	Carbohydrates: 35 g	Fiber: 5.3 g
Protein: 13 g	Fat: 9.1 g	Saturated fat: 4.7 g
Cholesterol: 13 mg	Sodium: 559 mg	Calcium: 170 mg

PBJ
PANINI

1. For each sandwich, place 2 bread slices on a work surface and spread each slice with $2^1/_4$ teaspoons peanut butter.

2. Spread $1^1/_2$ tablespoons jam on one of the bread slices. Top with the remaining bread slice, peanut butter side in.

3. Coat a sandwich press or a tabletop grill (such as a George Foreman grill) with cooking spray and place the sandwich inside. Spray the top of the sandwich lightly with cooking spray. (If you don't have a sandwich press or tabletop grill, see the inset below.) Cook for about 5 minutes, or until the bread is toasted and the filling is heated through. Cut into halves or quarters and serve hot.

Yield: 4 Sandwiches

• • • • • • • •

8 slices sprouted grain or multigrain bread

$^1/_4$ cup plus 2 tablespoons peanut butter

$^1/_4$ cup plus 2 tablespoons Chia Fruit Jam (page 69)

Canola oil cooking spray

NUTRITION FACTS (PER SERVING)

Calories: 341

Protein: 14 g

Cholesterol: 0 mg

Carbohydrates: 44 g

Fat: 13.2 g

Sodium: 168 mg

Fiber: 10 g

Saturated fat: 2.2 g

Calcium: 35 mg

Making Panini Without a Press

Don't have a sandwich press or tabletop grill? No problem. You can easily make a hearty panini in a skillet. Coat a nonstick skillet with cooking spray and place the sandwich in the skillet. Spray the top of the sandwich lightly with cooking spray and then top it with a flat object with enough weight to press it down lightly, such as a grill press or a smaller skillet weighted down with a 1-pound can of food. Cook over medium heat for 2 to 3 minutes on each side. (When removing the weighted object, be aware that it may be hot and should be handled with a pot holder.)

PRESSED TUNA MELTS

Yield: 4 Sandwiches
• • • • • • • •

Two 5-ounce cans tuna in spring water, drained

$^1/_2$ cup chopped marinated artichoke hearts, drained

$^1/_4$ cup chopped black olives

$^1/_4$ cup chopped red onion

2 tablespoons chopped sun-dried tomatoes

4 teaspoons low-fat or light mayonnaise

8 slices multigrain bread

4 ounces thinly sliced reduced-fat mozzarella cheese

Olive oil cooking spray

1. In a medium-sized bowl, combine the tuna, artichoke hearts, olives, onion, sun-dried tomatoes, and mayonnaise. Stir to mix. Set aside.

2. For each sandwich, place 1 bread slice on a work surface. Top with a quarter of the tuna mixture (about $^1/_2$ cup) and 1 ounce cheese. Top with 1 bread slice.

3. Coat a sandwich press or a tabletop grill (such as a George Foreman grill) with cooking spray and place the sandwich inside. Spray the top of the sandwich lightly with cooking spray. (If you don't have a sandwich press or tabletop grill, see the inset on page 87.) Cook for about 5 minutes, or until the bread is toasted and the cheese is melted. Cut into halves or quarters and serve hot.

NUTRITION FACTS (PER SANDWICH)

Calories: 352	Carbohydrates: 36 g	Fiber: 7 g
Protein: 28 g	Fat: 11 g	Saturated fat: 3.3 g
Cholesterol: 35 mg	Sodium: 664 mg	Calcium: 219 mg

HARVEST HAM & CHEESE SANDWICHES

1. For each sandwich, place 2 bread slices on a work surface and spread 1 teaspoon mayonnaise and $^1/_2$ teaspoon mustard on each slice.

2. Top 1 bread slice with a quarter of the ham, red onion, apple, spinach, and cheese. Top with the other bread slice.

3. Coat a sandwich press or a tabletop grill (such as a George Foreman grill) with cooking spray and place the sandwich inside. Spray the top of the sandwich lightly with cooking spray. (If you don't have a sandwich press or tabletop grill, see the inset on page 87.) Cook for about 5 minutes, or until the bread is toasted and the cheese is melted. Cut into halves or quarters and serve hot.

NUTRITION FACTS (PER SANDWICH)

Calories: 339	Carbohydrates: 39 g	Fiber: 7.2 g
Protein: 26 g	Fat: 6.5 g	Saturated Fat: 2.6 g
Cholesterol: 40 mg	Sodium: 858 mg	Calcium: 260 mg

Yield: 4 Sandwiches

• • • • • • • •

8 slices multigrain, pumpernickel, or rye bread

2 tablespoons plus 2 teaspoons low-fat or light mayonnaise

4 teaspoons Dijon mustard

8 ounces thinly sliced reduced-sodium lean ham

4 thin slices red onion

1 small Granny Smith apple, cored, unpeeled, and very thinly sliced

24 large fresh spinach leaves

4 ounces thinly sliced reduced-fat Swiss or white cheddar cheese

Olive oil cooking spray

FABULOUS FIBER FACT

A sandwich made with white bread and no vegetables provides only about 1.5 grams of fiber. But if you switch to whole grain bread and pile on plenty of veggies, you can easily increase the fiber by fivefold. This will also add many vital nutrients— not to mention great taste—to your meal.

SPINACH & CHEESE MELTS

Yield: 4 Sandwiches

• • • • • • •

10-ounce package frozen chopped spinach, thawed

2 cups sliced fresh white button mushrooms

2 tablespoons sunflower seeds

2 tablespoons grated Parmesan cheese

4 teaspoons low-fat or light mayonnaise

8 slices multigrain or pumpernickel bread

8 slices plum tomato

4 ounces thinly sliced reduced-fat mozzarella, white cheddar, or Swiss cheese

4 teaspoons Dijon or spicy mustard

1. Squeeze the spinach tightly to remove as much of the liquid as possible. Set aside.

2. Coat a large nonstick skillet with cooking spray and add the mushrooms. Cook over medium heat for about 5 minutes, or until tender and nicely browned. Turn off the heat and stir in the spinach and sunflower seeds. Add the Parmesan cheese and mayonnaise, and stir until well mixed.

3. For each sandwich, place 1 bread slice on a work surface. Top with a quarter of the spinach mixture, 2 slices plum tomato, and 1 ounce cheese. Spread 1 bread slice with 1 teaspoon mustard and place on top.

4. Coat a sandwich press or a tabletop grill (such as a George Foreman grill) with cooking spray and place the sandwich inside. Spray the top of the sandwich lightly with cooking spray. (If you don't have a sandwich press or tabletop grill, see the inset on page 87.) Cook for about 5 minutes, or until the bread is toasted and the cheese is melted. Cut into halves or quarters and serve hot.

NUTRITION FACTS (PER SANDWICH)

Calories: 302	Carbohydrates: 34 g	Fiber: 7 g
Protein: 18 g	Fat: 10.6 g	Saturated fat: 4.2 g
Cholesterol: 22 mg	Sodium: 483 mg	Calcium: 232 mg

FABULOUS FIBER FACT

One reason that fiber-rich foods are so filling is that they often require more chewing and take longer to eat than refined and processed foods. This allows the digestive system to signal a sense of fullness to the brain before too much food can be eaten.

ROASTED VEGETABLE PANINI

1. Preheat the oven to 450°F. Line 2 large baking sheets with aluminum foil and spray with cooking spray. Arrange the vegetables on the baking sheets in a single layer. Spray the vegetables lightly with the cooking spray and sprinkle with the salt and black pepper.

2. Bake for 10 minutes. Flip the vegetables over and cook for 5 to 8 minutes more, or until nicely browned and tender. If necessary, remove the red onion, bell pepper, and mushrooms, set aside, and continue cooking the eggplant until it loses most of its moisture and has a meaty texture.

3. For each sandwich, place 1 bread slice on a work surface and spread with 1 tablespoon pesto. Layer on a quarter of the eggplant, red onion, mushrooms, bell pepper, and cheese. Top with 1 bread slice.

4. Coat a sandwich press or a tabletop grill (such as a George Foreman grill) with cooking spray and place the sandwich inside. Spray the top of the sandwich lightly with cooking spray. (If you don't have a sandwich press or tabletop grill, see the inset on page 87.) Cook for about 5 minutes, or until the bread is toasted and the cheese is melted. Cut into halves or quarters and serve hot.

NUTRITION FACTS (PER SANDWICH)

Calories: 349	Carbohydrates: 38 g	Fiber: 8.4 g
Protein: 19 g	Fat: 14.5 g	Saturated fat: 3.1 g
Cholesterol: 15 mg	Sodium: 629 mg	Calcium: 214 mg

Yield: 4 Sandwiches

• • • • • • • •

8 slices unpeeled eggplant, each $1/4$-inch thick ($1/3$ of a medium eggplant)

4 slices red onion ($1/4$-inch thick)

8 medium white button mushrooms, sliced $3/8$-inch thick

8 rings red bell pepper ($1/4$-inch thick)

Olive oil cooking spray

$1/4$ teaspoon salt

$1/4$ teaspoon ground black pepper

8 slices multigrain Italian-style bread

4 tablespoons basil pesto

4 ounces thinly sliced reduced-fat mozzarella or provolone cheese

FLATBREAD PIZZAS WITH PEPPERONI, ONIONS & OLIVES

Yield: 4 Pizzas

• • • • • • • •

4 whole grain flatbreads
(9-x-6 inches each)

$1/2$ cup marinara sauce

32 slices turkey pepperoni
(about 2 ounces)

$1/2$ cup thinly slivered
yellow onion

$1/2$ cup chopped pitted
black olives

I cup shredded part-skim
mozzarella cheese

$1/2$ teaspoon crushed red
pepper (optional)

1. Preheat the oven to 400°F.

2. Coat 2 large baking sheets with cooking spray. Place 2 flatbreads on each sheet. Bake for 2 minutes. Remove the sheets from the oven and turn the flatbreads over.

3. Spread 2 tablespoons marinara sauce on each flatbread. Top each with 8 slices pepperoni, 2 tablespoons onion, 2 tablespoons olives, and $1/4$ cup cheese. Bake for 4 to 5 minutes, or until the cheese is melted and the edges of the flatbreads are lightly browned. Top each pizza with $1/8$ teaspoon crushed red pepper if desired. Serve hot.

NUTRITION FACTS (PER PIZZA)

Calories: 268	Carbohydrates: 23 g	Fiber: 5 g
Protein: 21 g	Fat: 13.4 g	Saturated fat: 3.8 g
Cholesterol: 28 mg	Sodium: 834 mg	Calcium: 240 mg

FOR A CHANGE . . .

For a thick crust, substitute whole grain pitas or naan (6-inch rounds) for the rectangular flatbreads. Instead of Steps 2 and 3, simply place all the pitas or naan on a large baking sheet, add the toppings, and bake for about 8 minutes.

FLATBREAD PIZZAS WITH SPINACH AND MUSHROOMS

1. Preheat the oven to 400°F.

2. Coat a large nonstick skillet with cooking spray and add the mushrooms. Cook over medium heat for about 5 minutes, or until the mushrooms are nicely browned. Add the garlic and spinach, and cook for a couple of minutes, or until the spinach is wilted. Remove from the heat and set aside.

3. Coat 2 large baking sheets with cooking spray. Place 2 flatbreads on each sheet. Bake for 2 minutes. Remove the sheets from the oven and turn the flatbreads over.

4. Spread 2 tablespoons marinara sauce on each flatbread. Top each with a quarter of the spinach mixture, 2 tablespoons red onion, $3/4$ teaspoon fresh basil (or $1/4$ teaspoon dried), $1/8$ teaspoon fennel, and $1/4$ cup cheese. Bake for 4 to 5 minutes, or until the cheese is melted and the edges of the flatbreads are lightly browned. Serve hot.

Yield: 4 Pizzas

3 cups sliced white button mushrooms (8 ounces)

$1\,1/2$ teaspoons crushed garlic

3 cups moderately packed sliced fresh spinach

4 whole grain flatbreads (9-x-6 inches each)

$1/2$ cup marinara sauce

$1/2$ cup thinly slivered red onion

1 tablespoon finely chopped fresh basil, or 1 teaspoon dried

$1/2$ teaspoon whole fennel seeds

1 cup shredded reduced-fat mozzarella cheese

NUTRITION FACTS (PER PIZZA)

Calories: 222	Carbohydrates: 23 g	Fiber: 5.1 g
Protein: 17 g	Fat: 8.6 g	Saturated fat: 3.1 g
Cholesterol: 15 mg	Sodium: 548 mg	Calcium: 353 mg

FOR A CHANGE . . .

For a thick crust, substitute whole grain pitas or naan (6-inch rounds) for the rectangular flatbreads. Instead of Steps 2 and 3, simply place all the pitas or naan on a large baking sheet, add the toppings, and bake for about 8 minutes.

FLATBEAD WITH LENTILS, LEEKS & MUSHROOMS

Yield: 4 Flatbreads

• • • • • • •

3/4 cup sliced leeks (white and light green parts)

1 tablespoon water

3 cups sliced white button mushrooms (8 ounces)

1 cup cooked brown lentils

1 tablespoon extra virgin olive oil

1 tablespoon finely chopped fresh oregano, or 1 teaspoon dried

4 whole grain flatbreads (9-x-6 inches each)

1/4 cup chopped sun-dried tomatoes (optional)

2 tablespoons grated Parmesan cheese

1 cup shredded reduced-fat mozzarella cheese

1 cup thinly sliced fresh arugula

1. Preheat the oven to 400°F.

2. Coat a large nonstick skillet with cooking spray and add the leeks and water. Cover and cook over medium heat for about 3 minutes, or until the leeks start to soften. Add the mushrooms and cook uncovered for about 4 minutes, or until nicely browned.

3. Add the lentils, olive oil, and oregano to the skillet. Cook for a couple of minutes to heat through and evaporate any liquid in the skillet. Remove from the heat and set aside.

4. Coat two large baking sheets with cooking spray and place the flatbreads on the sheets. Bake for 2 minutes. Remove the pans from the oven and turn the flatbreads over.

5. Top each flatbread with a quarter of the lentil mixture and (if using) 1 tablespoon of sun-dried tomatoes. Sprinkle a quarter of the Parmesan and mozzarella cheeses over each flatbread.

6. Return the flatbreads to the oven and bake for 4 to 5 minutes, or until the cheese is melted and the edges of the flatbreads are lightly browned. Sprinkle a quarter of the arugula over each flatbread and serve immediately.

NUTRITION FACTS (PER FLATBREAD)

Calories: 289	Carbohydrates: 31 g	Fiber: 8 g
Protein: 20 g	Fat: 11.5 g	Saturated fat: 3.5 g
Cholesterol: 17 mg	Sodium: 489 mg	Calcium: 321 mg

BLACK BEAN QUESADILLAS WITH FRESH TOMATO SALSA

1. In a medium-sized bowl, combine all the salsa ingredients. Mix well and set aside.

2. In a medium-sized bowl, coarsely mash the beans. Stir in the chili powder and cumin. Set aside.

3. Place 1 tortilla on a work surface. Spread a quarter of the bean mixture on the bottom half, leaving a $1/2$-inch border. Top with $1/4$ cup cheese. Fold the top half of the tortilla over to enclose the filling. Repeat with the remaining ingredients to make 4 quesadillas.

4. Coat a large nonstick griddle or skillet with cooking spray. Arrange the tortillas on the griddle or in the skillet, working in batches as necessary. Spray the tops of the quesadillas lightly with cooking spray. Cook over medium heat for about $1^1/2$ minutes on each side, or until nicely browned and the cheese is melted. Cut the quesadillas into wedges. Top each serving with a quarter of the salsa and avocado. Serve hot.

NUTRITION FACTS (PER QUESADILLA)

Calories: 374	Carbohydrates: 45 g	Fiber: 11.7 g
Protein: 19 g	Fat: 15.4 g	Saturated Fat: 4.8 g
Cholesterol: 20 mg	Sodium: 494 mg	Calcium: 379 mg

Yield: 4 Quesadillas

• • • • • • • • • • •

15-ounce can reduced-sodium black beans, drained, but not rinsed

1 teaspoon chili powder

$1/2$ teaspoon ground cumin

4 whole wheat flour tortillas (9-inch rounds)

1 cup shredded reduced-fat Monterey Jack or Mexican blend cheese

Olive oil cooking spray

$3/4$ cup mashed avocado (about 1 medium avocado)

SALSA

1 cup chopped fresh tomato

$1/4$ cup finely chopped red onion

$1/4$ cup finely chopped fresh cilantro

1 tablespoon finely chopped pickled jalapeño pepper, or to taste

$1/8$ teaspoon salt

SALSA BURGERS

Yield: 4 Burgers
• • • • • • • •

I pound ground turkey, chicken, or beef (at least 93-percent lean)

I cup finely chopped white button or baby portobello mushrooms

$^1/_3$ cup chunky-style salsa

$^1/_3$ cup finely chopped yellow onion

2 teaspoons low-sodium Southwestern seasoning (such as Mrs. Dash)

4 whole grain burger buns

TOPPINGS

$^1/_3$ cup chunky-style salsa

4 slices red or sweet white onion

4 romaine lettuce leaves

I medium avocado, coarsely mashed

1. Preheat the oven broiler.

2. In a large bowl, combine the ground meat, mushrooms, salsa, onion, and seasoning. Mix well.

3. Shape the mixture into 4 patties of equal size (about $4^1/_2$ inches in diameter). Make the center of each patty a little thinner than the edges to promote even cooking.

4. Coat a broiler pan with cooking spray and place the patties on the pan. Broil for about 5 minutes on each side, or until the centers reach at least 165°F (for poultry) or 160°F (for beef). Avoid pressing down on the patties during cooking, as doing so will cause a loss of moisture. Alternatively, grill over medium coals for about 5 minutes on each side.

5. For each burger, place the bottom of 1 bun on a work surface. Top with 1 burger, 4 teaspoons salsa, 1 slice onion, and 1 lettuce leaf. Spread a quarter of the mashed avocado on the other bun half and place over the sandwich. Serve immediately.

NUTRITION FACTS (PER SERVING)

Calories: 364	Carbohydrates: 31 g	Fiber: 7 g
Protein: 31 g	Fat: 14.9 g	Saturated fat: 4.2 g
Cholesterol: 80 mg	Sodium: 562 mg	Calcium: 121 mg

FRIJOLE TACOS

1. In a medium-sized nonstick skillet, combine the beans, salsa, chili powder, cumin, and salt, stirring to mix. Cook over medium heat, stirring frequently, for about 5 minutes, or until the mixture is reduced to about $1^1/_2$ cups and has the consistency of very thick refried beans.

2. Place the tortillas on a work surface, and spread about 3 tablespoons of the bean mixture over the bottom half of each tortilla to within $1/_4$-inch of the edges. Coat a large nonstick griddle or skillet with cooking spray. Arrange the tortillas on the griddle or in the skillet, working in batches as necessary. Cook over medium heat for about 1 minute, or until the tortillas are soft and pliable enough to fold in half.

3. Fold each tortilla in half to enclose the filling. Spray the tops lightly with cooking spray. Cook for 1 or 2 minutes on each side, or until nicely browned. Open each tortilla slightly and fill with $1/_4$ cup lettuce, 1 tablespoon tomato, 2 avocado slices, and 1 tablespoon cheese. Serve hot.

NUTRITION FACTS (PER 2 TACOS)

Calories: 270	Carbohydrates: 38 g	Fiber: 11.8 g
Protein: 12 g	Fat: 9 g	Saturated fat: 1.8 g
Cholesterol: 10 mg	Sodium: 493 mg	Calcium: 272 mg

Yield: 8 Tacos

• • • • • • • •

15-ounce can reduced-sodium black or pinto beans, drained, but not rinsed, and coarsely mashed

$1/_3$ cup chunky-style salsa

$1/_2$ teaspoon chili powder

$1/_2$ teaspoon ground cumin

Scant $1/_4$ teaspoon salt

8 corn tortillas (5-inch rounds)

Olive oil cooking spray

TOPPINGS

2 cups shredded romaine lettuce

$1/_2$ cup diced fresh tomato

1 medium avocado, cut into 16 slices

$1/_2$ cup crumbled queso fresco or shredded reduced-fat Mexican blend cheese

FABULOUS FIBER FACT

People who eat fiber-rich diets tend to experience healthier body weights, less belly fat, and less weight gain over time than people who eat low-fiber diets.

TEX-MEX TORTILLA PIZZAS

Yield: 4 Pizzas

• • • • • • • • • •

15-ounce can reduced-sodium pinto beans, drained, but not rinsed

1 teaspoon chili powder

$^1/_2$ teaspoon ground cumin

4 whole wheat flour tortillas (9-inch rounds)

$^1/_2$ cup fresh cooked or frozen (thawed) whole kernel corn

$^1/_4$ cup thinly sliced scallions

2 tablespoons finely chopped pickled jalapeño pepper

1 cup shredded reduced-fat Mexican blend or Monterey Jack cheese

TOPPINGS

2 cups shredded romaine lettuce

1 cup chopped fresh tomatoes or salsa

$^1/_3$ cup chopped fresh cilantro

1 medium avocado, diced

1. Preheat the oven to 400°F.

2. In a medium-sized bowl, coarsely mash the pinto beans. Stir in the chili powder and cumin. Set aside.

3. Coat 2 large baking sheets with cooking spray. Place 2 tortillas on each sheet. Bake for 2 minutes. Remove the sheets from the oven and turn the tortillas over.

4. Spread a quarter of the bean mixture on each tortilla, leaving a $^1/_2$-inch border. Top each tortilla with 2 tablespoons corn, 1 tablespoon scallions, $1^1/_2$ teaspoons jalapeño pepper, and $^1/_4$ cup cheese.

5. Bake for 4 minutes, or until the cheese is melted and the pizzas are lightly browned and crispy around the edges. Top each pizza with a quarter of the lettuce, tomato, cilantro, and avocado. Serve hot.

NUTRITION FACTS (PER PIZZA)

Calories: 388	Carbohydrates: 48 g	Fiber: 12.7 g
Protein: 19 g	Fat: 16.1 g	Saturated fat: 4.9 g
Cholesterol: 20 mg	Sodium: 560 mg	Calcium: 292 mg

6

Soups That Satisfy

It's hard to beat a steaming bowl of soup when you are looking for a versatile, economical, and comforting meal. And when made right—with plenty of vegetables, legumes, and whole grains—soups and stews are a perfect fit for a healthy, high-fiber lifestyle. Watching your weight? Soups can be especially helpful, as meals that contain a high proportion of water have been proven to be more filling than drier dishes. The fact is that soup can help you feel fuller for fewer calories when compared with other foods.

Because soups are so versatile, they are as much a boon to the menu planner as they are to the calorie counter. A light soup can be the perfect introduction to a main dish or a lovely side dish with a sandwich. A more substantial soup needs only a crusty whole grain bread and salad to make a hearty and satisfying meal. Whether you are looking for a chicken soup brimming with pasta and vegetables, a hearty chili, or a cool and refreshing gazpacho, here you will find a tasty selection that is sure to satisfy.

ORZO
CHICKEN SOUP

Yield: 6 Cups

• • • • • • •

2 teaspoons extra virgin olive oil

$^1/_2$ cup chopped yellow onion

$4^1/_2$ cups unsalted chicken broth, divided

1 teaspoon crushed garlic

$1^1/_4$ cups diced carrot

$^1/_2$ cup chopped celery

1 teaspoon salt

$^1/_4$ teaspoon ground black pepper

2 boneless skinless chicken breasts (4 ounces each), or 10 ounces skinless bone-in chicken breast

$^1/_2$ cup plus 1 tablespoon whole wheat orzo

$^2/_3$ cup frozen green peas

2 cups moderately packed chopped fresh spinach

2 tablespoons finely chopped fresh parsley, or 2 teaspoons dried

1. In a 4-quart saucepan, combine the olive oil, onion, and 2 table-spoons broth. Cover and cook over medium heat for about 4 minutes, or until the onion softens. Add the garlic and cook for 30 seconds, or until the garlic begins to turn color and smells fragrant.

2. Add the carrot, celery, salt, black pepper, and remaining broth to the saucepan. Bring to a boil and then add the chicken. Lower the heat to a simmer, cover, and cook for 30 minutes, or until the vegetables are tender and the chicken is cooked through.

3. Transfer the chicken to a cutting board and set aside. Use a slotted spoon to transfer about half of the vegetables to a blender. Add about $1^1/_2$ cups of the broth and blend at low speed until smooth. (Remove the center piece of the blender lid to allow steam to escape, placing a clean towel over the opening to prevent splatters while blending.) Pour the mixture back into the saucepan.

4. Bring the soup to a boil and add the orzo. Lower the heat to a simmer, cover, and cook for 8 minutes, stirring occasionally. Dice or pull the chicken into small pieces and add it to the soup along with the peas. Cover and simmer for 3 minutes. Add the spinach and cook for 2 minutes, or until the orzo is tender, the peas are cooked, and the spinach is wilted. Stir in the parsley and turn off the heat. Allow the soup to sit covered for 3 minutes before serving.

NUTRITION FACTS (PER CUP)

Calories: 154	Carbohydrates: 19 g	Fiber: 4.6 g
Protein: 13 g	Fat: 3 g	Saturated fat: 0.5 g
Cholesterol: 24 mg	Sodium: 427 mg	Calcium: 47 mg

CHICKEN, BARLEY & CORN CHOWDER

1. In a 3-quart saucepan, combine the chicken broth, sweet potato, onion, celery, thyme, garlic, salt, and white pepper. Bring to a boil and then lower the heat to simmer. Cover and cook for 15 minutes, or until the vegetables are tender.

2. Using an immersion blender, purée the soup until smooth. Alternatively, use a slotted spoon to transfer the vegetables to a blender, add 2 cups of the broth, and blend at low speed until smooth. (Remove the center piece of the blender lid to allow steam to escape, placing a clean towel over the opening to prevent splatters while blending.) Return the mixture to the saucepan.

3. Add the chicken and barley to the saucepan. Cover and simmer for 40 minutes. Transfer the chicken to a cutting board and continue to simmer the soup for another 10 minutes, or until the barley is tender. Remove the chicken from the bone, dice the meat, and return the meat to the saucepan.

4. Add the corn to the saucepan. Cover and simmer for 5 minutes. Stir in the parsley and turn off the heat. Allow the soup to sit covered for 5 minutes before serving.

NUTRITION FACTS (PER CUP)

Calories: 161	Carbohydrates: 24 g	Fiber: 3.8 g
Protein: 14 g	Fat: 1.6 g	Saturated fat: 0.3 g
Cholesterol: 30 mg	Sodium: 413 mg	Calcium: 25 mg

Yield: 8 Cups

· · · · · · ·

5 cups unsalted chicken broth

2 cups diced peeled sweet potato (about 2 medium)

$1/2$ cup plus 2 tablespoons chopped yellow onion

$1/2$ cup finely chopped celery

1 teaspoon dried thyme

$1 1/2$ teaspoons crushed garlic

1 teaspoon salt

$1/8$ teaspoon ground white pepper

1 pound skinless bone-in chicken breast

$1/2$ cup pearl barley

$1 1/2$ cups fresh or frozen corn

1 tablespoon finely chopped fresh parsley

ITALIAN WEDDING SOUP

Yield: 6 Cups

• • • • • • • • • • •

4 cups unsalted chicken broth

$^1/_4$ cup finely chopped yellow onion

1 $^1/_2$ teaspoons crushed garlic

$^3/_4$ cup diced carrot, divided

$^3/_4$ teaspoon salt

$^1/_2$ teaspoon ground black pepper

$^1/_2$ cup whole wheat orzo

3 cups thinly sliced fresh escarole or spinach

Grated Parmesan cheese (optional)

MEATBALLS

8 ounces ground beef or turkey (at least 93-percent lean)

$^1/_4$ cup finely chopped yellow onion

2 tablespoons oat bran or quick-cooking oats

1 egg white, beaten

1 tablespoon grated Parmesan cheese

$^1/_4$ teaspoon dried Italian seasoning

1. Prepare the meatballs first by combining the meat, onion, oat bran or oats, egg white, Parmesan cheese, and Italian seasoning in a medium-sized bowl. Mix well. Shape into 18 meatballs (about 1 inch in diameter). Set aside.

2. To prepare the soup, combine the chicken broth, onion, garlic, and $^1/_4$ cup plus 2 tablespoons of the carrots in a blender. Blend until smooth.

3. Pour the blended broth mixture into a 3-quart saucepan over medium-high heat. Add the salt, black pepper, and remaining carrots. Bring to a boil, lower the heat to medium, and add the meatballs one at a time. Lower the heat to a simmer. Cover and cook for 12 minutes.

4. Add the orzo to the saucepan. Cover and simmer for about 10 minutes, or until tender. Add the escarole or spinach and cook for 3 minutes longer, or until wilted. Serve hot, topping each serving with a sprinkling of grated Parmesan cheese if desired.

NUTRITION FACTS (PER CUP)

Calories: 139	Carbohydrates: 15 g	Fiber: 4 g
Protein: 13 g	Fat: 3.4 g	Saturated fat: 1.3 g
Cholesterol: 25 mg	Sodium: 401 mg	Calcium: 46 mg

BEEF & BARLEY SOUP

1. Coat a 4-quart saucepan with cooking spray and add the ground beef. Cook over medium heat for about 6 minutes, or until lightly browned, stirring to crumble. Add the mushrooms, onion, and garlic. Cover and cook for 5 minutes, or until tender.

2. Add the broth, vegetable juice, carrot, barley, thyme, bay leaf, black pepper, and salt, and bring to a boil. Lower the heat to a simmer. Cover and cook for about 50 minutes, or until the barley is tender.

3. Remove the bay leaf and stir in the parsley. Cover and turn off the heat. Allow the soup to sit for 5 minutes before serving.

NUTRITION FACTS (PER CUP)

Calories: 165	Carbohydrates: 16 g	Fiber: 3.3 g
Protein: 15 g	Fat: 4.2 g	Saturated fat: 1.7 g
Cholesterol: 36 mg	Sodium: 420 mg	Calcium: 32 mg

Yield: 8 Cups

1 pound ground beef (at least 93-percent lean)

3 cups sliced white button mushrooms

$3/4$ cup finely chopped yellow onion

2 teaspoons crushed garlic

4 cups unsalted beef broth

$1\frac{1}{2}$ cups low-sodium vegetable juice cocktail, such as V8

1 cup grated carrot

$1/2$ cup pearl barley

1 teaspoon dried thyme

1 bay leaf

$1/2$ teaspoon ground black pepper

$3/4$ teaspoon salt

2 tablespoons finely chopped fresh parsley, or 2 teaspoons dried

FABULOUS FIBER FACT

In addition to providing fiber, whole grains are often good sources of many important nutrients, including B vitamins, magnesium, manganese, selenium, copper, iron, and zinc.

Yield: 4 Cups

3 cups chopped fresh tomatoes

$1^{1}/_{2}$ cups peeled and diced cucumber

$1^{1}/_{4}$ cups chopped red or yellow bell pepper

$^{3}/_{4}$ cup chopped red onion

$^{1}/_{2}$ cup low-sodium vegetable juice or tomato juice

2 tablespoons extra virgin olive oil

$1^{1}/_{2}$ tablespoons sherry vinegar

1 teaspoon smoked paprika

1 teaspoon crushed garlic

$^{1}/_{2}$ teaspoon salt

$^{1}/_{4}$ teaspoon ground black pepper

Pinch cayenne pepper

$^{1}/_{4}$ cup thinly sliced scallions

GARDEN FRESH GAZPACHO

1. In a blender, combine all the ingredients except for the scallions. Blend until smooth.

2. Divide the mixture between 4 serving bowls and top each serving with 1 tablespoon scallions, or cover and chill until ready to serve.

NUTRITION FACTS (PER CUP)

Calories: 128	Carbohydrates: 14 g	Fiber: 4 g
Protein: 2.8 g	Fat: 7.4 g	Saturated fat: 1 g
Cholesterol: 0 mg	Sodium: 325 mg	Calcium: 35 mg

Yield: 9 Cups

2 cups dried split peas

7 cups unsalted chicken or vegetable broth

1 cup chopped yellow onion

1 cup thinly sliced celery

1 cup chopped carrot

1 teaspoon dried sage

2 bay leaves

$^{1}/_{2}$ teaspoon ground black pepper

1 large meaty ham bone, or 2 cups diced lean ham

$^{1}/_{2}$ teaspoon salt

SPLIT PEA SOUP WITH HAM

1. In a 4-quart saucepan, combine all the ingredients except for the salt. Bring to a boil and then lower the heat to a simmer. Cover and cook for $1^{1}/_{2}$ hours, or until the split peas are soft.

2. Remove the ham bone and let it cool slightly. Remove 2 cups of the soup and purée it in a blender. (Remove the center piece of the blender lid to allow steam to escape, placing a clean towel over the opening to prevent splatters while blending.) Return the puréed soup to the saucepan.

3. Remove the meat from the ham bone, chop it, and return it to the saucepan. Stir in the salt. If needed, simmer uncovered for a few minutes to thicken the soup. Serve hot.

NUTRITION FACTS (PER CUP)

Calories: 217	Carbohydrates: 31 g	Fiber: 12 g
Protein: 19 g	Fat: 2.3 g	Saturated fat: 0.7 g
Cholesterol: 14 mg	Sodium: 440 mg	Calcium: 40 mg

HELPFUL HINT

To prepare this soup in a slow cooker, place all the ingredients in a 4-quart slow cooker and cook for about 4 hours on high power, or for 8 hours on low power.

ESCAROLE, SAUSAGE & WHITE BEAN SOUP

1. Coat a 2-quart saucepan with cooking spray and add the sausage. Cook over medium heat for about 6 minutes, or until the meat is lightly browned, stirring to crumble. Add the onion, cover, and cook for 4 minutes, or until the onion is tender. Add the garlic and cook for 30 seconds more.

2. Add the broth and beans to the saucepan. Bring to a boil and then lower the heat to a simmer. Cover and cook for 10 minutes. Add the escarole and bring to a boil. Lower the heat to a simmer, cover, and cook for 3 minutes, or until the escarole is wilted and tender.

3. Serve hot, topping each serving with a sprinkling of the Parmesan cheese if desired.

Yield: 5 Cups

• • • • • • • • • •

8 ounces chicken or turkey hot Italian sausage, casings removed

$3/4$ cup chopped yellow onion

$1^{1}/_{2}$ teaspoons crushed garlic

2 cups unsalted chicken broth

15-ounce can reduced-sodium cannellini or white beans, undrained

4 cups chopped escarole

Grated Parmesan cheese (optional)

NUTRITION FACTS (PER CUP)

Calories: 176	Carbohydrates: 17 g	Fiber: 4 g
Protein: 15 g	Fat: 5.9 g	Saturated fat: 1.5 g
Cholesterol: 42 mg	Sodium: 462 mg	Calcium: 82 mg

SLOW-COOKED BRUNSWICK STEW

Yield: 8 Cups
. . . .

3 cups chopped fresh tomatoes, or 14.5-ounce can unsalted tomatoes, undrained

$^2/_3$ cup chopped carrot

$^1/_3$ cup chopped celery

1 cup barbecue sauce

3 cups chopped or pulled cooked chicken, turkey, pork, or beef, or any combination

1 $^1/_2$ cups fresh or frozen (thawed) whole kernel corn

1 $^1/_2$ cups fresh or frozen (thawed) baby lima beans

1 cup chopped yellow onion

2 bay leaves

$^1/_2$ teaspoon ground black pepper

1 $^1/_2$ cups unsalted chicken broth

1. In a blender, combine the tomatoes, carrots, and celery. Blend until smooth. Pour the mixture into a 3-quart slow cooker. Add the remaining ingredients and stir to mix.

2. Cook for 3 hours on high power, or 6 hours on low power. Remove the bay leaves and serve hot.

NUTRITION FACTS (PER CUP)

Calories: 237	Carbohydrates: 33 g	Fiber: 4.2 g
Protein: 21 g	Fat: 2.7 g	Saturated fat: 0.6 g
Cholesterol: 45 mg	Sodium: 432 mg	Calcium: 50 mg

FABULOUS FIBER FACT

The best evidence to date indicates that the fiber in real foods—rather than isolated or synthetic fiber—is protective against disease. This is likely due to the interaction of fiber, vitamins, minerals, antioxidants, and other components that make up whole plant foods.

SAVORY BLACK-EYED PEA SOUP

1. Soak the peas according to package directions and drain.

2. In a 4-quart saucepan, combine all the ingredients except for the salt over medium-high heat. Bring to a boil and then lower the heat to a simmer. Cover and cook for about $1^{1}/_{2}$ hours, or until the peas are soft and the liquid is thick, stirring occasionally. Add a little water during cooking if needed.

3. Remove the ham bone and let it cool slightly. Remove the meat from bone, chop it, and return it to the saucepan. Remove and discard the bay leaves. Stir in the salt, and serve hot.

NUTRITION FACTS (PER CUP)

Calories: 179

Protein: 16 g

Cholesterol: 14 mg

Carbohydrates: 26 g

Fat: 1.4 g

Sodium: 448 mg

Fiber: 5 g

Saturated fat: 0.4 g

Calcium: 14 mg

FOR A CHANGE . . .

Add $2^{1}/_{2}$ cups chopped fresh collard greens to the soup during the last 20 minutes of cooking. Trim and discard any tough stems from the collard leaves before adding them to the soup.

Yield: 9 Cups

• • • • • • • • • •

2 cups dried black-eyed peas

1 large meaty ham bone, or 2 cups diced lean ham

1 cup chopped yellow onion

2 bay leaves

2 teaspoons crushed garlic

$1^{1}/_{2}$ teaspoons dried sage

$^{1}/_{2}$ teaspoon ground black pepper

4 cups unsalted chicken or vegetable broth

$1^{1}/_{4}$ cups low-sodium vegetable juice cocktail, such as V8

$^{1}/_{2}$ teaspoon salt

SOUTHWESTERN BLACK BEAN SOUP

Yield: 4 Cups

2 teaspoons extra virgin olive oil

$^1/_2$ cup chopped yellow onion

$^1/_3$ cup chopped green bell pepper

$^3/_4$ cup unsalted chicken or vegetable broth, divided

1 teaspoon crushed garlic

$^1/_2$ cup plus 2 tablespoons chunky-style salsa

Two 15-ounce cans reduced-sodium black beans, undrained

1 teaspoon chili powder

$^1/_2$ teaspoon ground cumin

TOPPINGS

$^1/_4$ cup plus 2 tablespoons shredded reduced-fat Mexican blend or Monterey Jack cheese

$^1/_4$ cup thinly sliced scallions

6 teaspoons finely chopped fresh cilantro

1. In a 2-quart saucepan, combine the olive oil, onion, bell pepper, and 2 tablespoons broth. Cover and cook over medium heat for 5 minutes, or until the vegetables soften, stirring occasionally. Add the garlic and cook for 15 seconds more.

2. Add the remaining broth and the salsa, black beans, chili powder, and cumin to the saucepan. Cover and bring to a boil. Lower the heat to a simmer and cook for 15 minutes.

3. Using an immersion blender, purée the soup until smooth. Alternatively, using a regular blender, purée the soup 2 cups at a time on low speed. (Remove the center piece of the blender lid to allow steam to escape, placing a clean towel over the opening to prevent splatters while blending.)

4. Serve hot, topping each serving with $1^1/_2$ tablespoons cheese, 1 tablespoon scallions, and $1^1/_2$ teaspoons cilantro.

NUTRITION FACTS (PER CUP)

Calories: 250	Carbohydrates: 38 g	Fiber: 12.2 g
Protein: 16 g	Fat: 6.9 g	Saturated fat: 1.8 g
Cholesterol: 7 mg	Sodium: 509 mg	Calcium: 183 mg

FABULOUS FIBER FACT

A good way to raise your dietary fiber intake is to eat more vegetarian meals. Some tasty options include beans and brown rice; whole grain pasta with vegetables; split pea, lentil, and black bean soups; vegetable stir fries; and hummus with whole grain pita bread.

VEGETARIAN TORTILLA SOUP

1. To prepare the tortilla strips, preheat the oven to 350°F. Coat a large baking sheet with cooking spray and arrange the strips in a single layer on the sheet. Spray the strips lightly with the cooking spray and sprinkle with the salt. Bake for about 8 minutes, or just until crisp. Remove from the oven and set aside.

2. In a $2\frac{1}{2}$-quart saucepan, combine the onion, carrots, and $\frac{1}{2}$ cup broth. Cover and cook over medium heat for 5 minutes, or until the vegetables soften.

3. Add the tomatoes, cumin, oregano, salt, black pepper, and remaining 2 cups broth to the saucepan and bring to a boil. Lower the heat to a simmer. Cover and cook for 10 minutes.

4. Add the beans and corn to the saucepan and return to a boil. Lower the heat to a simmer. Cover and cook for 10 minutes with the lid slightly ajar to allow steam to escape. Stir in the olive oil.

5. For each serving, ladle 1 cup soup into a bowl and top with one fifth of the tortilla strips (about $\frac{1}{4}$ cup), 3 tablespoons avocado, and 1 tablespoon cilantro. Serve hot.

NUTRITION FACTS (PER CUP PLUS TOPPINGS)

Calories: 250	Carbohydrates: 39 g	Fiber: 10.4 g
Protein: 9 g	Fat: 8.1 g	Saturated fat: 1.1 g
Cholesterol: 0 mg	Sodium: 429 mg	Calcium: 126 mg

Yield: 5 Cups

• • • • • • • • • •

$\frac{3}{4}$ cup chopped yellow onion

$\frac{1}{2}$ cup diced carrot

$2\frac{1}{2}$ cups no-salt-added chicken broth, divided

14.5-ounce can Mexican-style tomatoes, undrained and puréed in a blender

$\frac{3}{4}$ teaspoon ground cumin

$\frac{3}{4}$ teaspoon dried oregano

$\frac{1}{2}$ teaspoon salt

$\frac{1}{4}$ teaspoon ground black pepper

15-ounce can reduced-sodium black beans, drained and rinsed

$1\frac{1}{4}$ cups fresh or frozen whole kernel corn

1 tablespoon extra virgin olive oil

1 cup diced avocado (about 1 large)

$\frac{1}{4}$ cup plus 1 tablespoon chopped fresh cilantro

TORTILLA STRIPS

5 thin corn tortillas (5-inch rounds), cut into $1\frac{1}{2}$-x-$\frac{1}{2}$-inch strips

Olive oil cooking spray

$\frac{1}{8}$ teaspoon salt

POROTOS GRANADOS (CHILEAN BEAN STEW)

Yield: 7 Cups

• • • • • • • • • • •

1 ½ tablespoons extra virgin olive oil

1 cup chopped yellow onion

¾ cup thinly sliced celery

2 tablespoons water

1 ½ teaspoons crushed garlic

2 cups cubed butternut squash or diced carrot

3 cups unsalted chicken or vegetable broth

¾ teaspoon salt

¼ teaspoon ground white pepper

1 cup fresh or frozen baby lima beans

15-ounce can reduced-sodium white beans, drained

2 cups fresh or frozen corn

2 tablespoons finely chopped fresh basil, or 2 teaspoons dried

1. In a 3-quart saucepan, combine the olive oil, onion, celery, and water. Cover and cook over medium heat for 5 minutes, or until the vegetables soften. Add the garlic and cook for 30 seconds.

2. Stir in the squash or carrots, broth, salt, and white pepper. Bring to a boil, and then lower the heat to a simmer. Cover and cook for 15 minutes.

3. Use an immersion blender to blend the soup until smooth. Alternatively, use a regular blender to purée the soup 2 cups at a time on low speed. (Remove the center piece of the blender lid to allow steam to escape, placing a clean towel over the opening to prevent splatters while blending.)

4. Add the lima beans to the soup. Cover and cook for 15 minutes. Add the white beans, corn, and basil. Cover and cook for 10 minutes. Serve hot.

NUTRITION FACTS (PER CUP)

Calories: 180	Carbohydrates: 31 g	Fiber: 7.7 g
Protein: 8 g	Fat: 3.9 g	Saturated fat: 0.7 g
Cholesterol: 0 mg	Sodium: 373 mg	Calcium: 71 mg

LENTIL SOUP WITH ITALIAN SAUSAGE

1. Coat a 3-quart saucepan with cooking spray and add the Italian sausage. Cook over medium heat for about 5 minutes, or until the sausage is no longer pink, stirring to crumble. Add the onion, carrot, and celery. Cover and cook for 4 minutes, until the vegetables soften. Add the garlic and cook for 15 seconds more.

2. Add the lentils, sage, basil, black pepper, water, and vegetable juice to the saucepan. Bring to a boil, and then lower the heat to a simmer. Cover and cook for 1 hour, or until the lentils are soft and the liquid is thick. Add a little more water during cooking if needed. Stir in the salt and serve hot.

NUTRITION FACTS (PER CUP)

Calories: 215	Carbohydrates: 28 g	Fiber: 12.6 g
Protein: 17.5 g	Fat: 3.5 g	Saturated fat: 1.1 g
Cholesterol: 35 mg	Sodium: 370 mg	Calcium: 60 mg

Yield: 8 Cups

$3/4$ pound chicken or turkey Italian sausage, casings removed

$3/4$ cup chopped onion

$3/4$ cup diced carrot

$1/2$ cup finely chopped celery

$1 1/2$ teaspoons crushed garlic

$1 1/2$ cups dried brown lentils

$3/4$ teaspoon dried sage

$3/4$ teaspoon dried basil

$1/4$ teaspoon ground black pepper

5 cups water or unsalted chicken broth

$1 1/2$ cups low-sodium vegetable juice cocktail, such as V8

$1/4$ teaspoon salt

FABULOUS FIBER FACT

While dried beans, peas, and lentils are best known for their cholesterol-lowering soluble fiber, they also contain good amounts of insoluble fiber, which speeds the passage of food through the intestines, reducing our exposure to carcinogens and other harmful substances.

ITALIAN SAUSAGE & VEGETABLE SOUP

Yield: 8 Cups
• • • • • • • • • • • •

3 cups unsalted chicken broth

3 cups chopped fresh tomatoes, or 14.5-ounce can unsalted tomatoes, undrained

$^3/_4$ pound chicken or turkey Italian sausage, casings removed

$^1/_2$ cup chopped yellow onion

$1^1/_2$ teaspoons crushed garlic

$^3/_4$ cup diced carrot

$1^1/_2$ teaspoons dried basil

1 teaspoon dried parsley

$^3/_4$ teaspoon dried oregano

3 ounces whole wheat rotini or penne pasta

1 medium zucchini, quartered lengthwise and sliced $^1/_4$-inch thick (about 1 cup)

$^3/_4$ cup frozen green peas

Grated Parmesan cheese (optional)

1. In a blender, combine the broth and tomatoes. Purée until smooth. Set aside.

2. Coat a 3-quart saucepan with cooking spray and add the sausage. Cook over medium heat for 5 minutes, or until the meat is no longer pink, stirring to crumble. Add the onion, cover, and cook for 5 minutes to soften. Add the garlic and cook for 30 seconds more.

3. Add the blended tomato mixture, carrot, basil, parsley, and oregano to the saucepan. Bring to a boil, and then lower the heat to a simmer. Cover and cook for 12 minutes, or until the carrot is tender.

4. Add the pasta to the saucepan and bring to a boil. Lower the heat to a simmer, cover, and cook for 3 minutes. Add the zucchini and peas. Cover and simmer for 5 to 8 minutes, or until the pasta is al dente and the zucchini is tender. Serve hot, topping each serving with a sprinkling of the Parmesan cheese if desired.

NUTRITION FACTS (PER CUP)

Calories: 137	Carbohydrates: 16 g	Fiber: 3.5 g
Protein: 12 g	Fat: 4.1 g	Saturated fat: 1 g
Cholesterol: 38 mg	Sodium: 434 mg	Calcium: 43 mg

SAVORY BUTTERNUT SQUASH SOUP

1. In a $2\frac{1}{2}$-quart saucepan, combine the olive oil, onion, celery, and 2 tablespoons broth. Cover and cook over medium heat for 5 minutes, until the vegetables start to soften, shaking the pan occasionally.

2. Add the remaining broth and the butternut squash, thyme, salt, and black pepper. Bring to a boil, and then lower the heat to a simmer. Cover and cook for 20 minutes, or until the butternut squash is soft.

3. Use an immersion blender to purée the soup until smooth. Alternatively, using a regular blender, purée the soup 2 cups at a time on low speed. (Remove the center piece of the blender lid to allow steam to escape, placing a clean towel over the opening to prevent splatters while blending.) Serve hot.

Yield: 5 Cups

2 tablespoons extra virgin olive oil

$\frac{3}{4}$ cup chopped yellow onion

$\frac{1}{2}$ cup thinly sliced celery

$2\frac{1}{2}$ cups unsalted chicken broth, divided

5 cups cubed butternut squash ($\frac{3}{4}$-inch pieces)

$\frac{1}{4}$ teaspoon dried thyme

$\frac{1}{2}$ teaspoon salt

$\frac{1}{2}$ teaspoon ground black pepper

NUTRITION FACTS (PER CUP)

Calories: 128	Carbohydrates: 20 g	Fiber: 3.5 g
Protein: 2.8 g	Fat: 5.6 g	Saturated fat: 0.8 g
Cholesterol: 0 mg	Sodium: 282 mg	Calcium: 79 mg

FOR A CHANGE . . .

Add 1 cup chopped peeled apple such as Granny Smith, Jonathan, or winesap, along with the butternut squash. Garnish each serving with 1 tablespoon julienned apple, 1 teaspoon sliced almonds, and $\frac{3}{4}$ teaspoon crumbled blue cheese or goat cheese.

MAMA'S MINESTRONE

Yield: 9 Cups

• • • • • • • • • •

2 tablespoons extra virgin olive oil, divided

1 cup chopped yellow onion

$^1/_2$ cup finely chopped celery

1 tablespoon water

2 teaspoons crushed garlic

4 cups unsalted vegetable, chicken, or beef broth

14.5-ounce can unsalted tomatoes, undrained, or 3 cups chopped fresh tomatoes, puréed

$^1/_2$ cup low-sodium vegetable juice cocktail, such as V8

1$^1/_2$ cups coarsely shredded cabbage

1 cup julienned carrot

2 teaspoons dried Italian seasoning

1 teaspoon salt

$^1/_2$ teaspoon ground black pepper

5 ounces uncooked whole grain penne pasta

15-ounce can reduced-sodium red kidney beans, drained but not rinsed

1$^1/_2$ cups 1-inch pieces fresh or frozen green beans

3 tablespoons finely chopped fresh basil

Grated Parmesan cheese (optional)

1. Add 1 tablespoon of the olive oil to a 4-quart saucepan. Add the onion, celery, and water. Cover and cook over medium heat for 5 minutes, or until the vegetables soften. Add the garlic and cook for 30 seconds.

2. Add the broth, tomatoes, vegetable juice, cabbage, carrot, Italian seasoning, salt, and black pepper. Bring to a boil, and then lower the heat to a simmer. Cover and cook for 15 minutes.

3. Add the pasta, kidney beans, and green beans. Bring to a boil, and then lower the heat to a simmer. Cover and cook for 10 minutes, or until the pasta and green beans are tender. Stir in the remaining olive oil. Serve hot, topping each serving with 1 teaspoon of the fresh basil and, if desired, a sprinkling of Parmesan cheese.

NUTRITION FACTS (PER CUP)

Calories: 162	Carbohydrates: 26 g	Fiber: 6 g
Protein: 7 g	Fat: 3.6 g	Saturated fat: 0.5 g
Cholesterol: 0 mg	Sodium: 393 mg	Calcium: 35 mg

HELPFUL HINT

For best results when slicing julienned carrots, use a julienne slicer. This inexpensive kitchen tool quickly shreds carrots into thin strips with a uniform, restaurant-quality appearance. Julienne slicers are also perfect for making zucchini noodles.

FARRO SOUP WITH WHITE BEANS & SPINACH

1. Add 1 tablespoon of the olive oil to a 4-quart saucepan. Add the onion, celery, carrot, and water. Cover and cook over medium heat for 5 minutes, or until the vegetables soften. Add a little water if needed to prevent scorching. Add the garlic and cook for 30 seconds.

2. Add the farro, broth, basil, fennel, salt, and black pepper. Bring to a boil, and then lower the heat to a simmer. Cover and cook for 30 minutes, or until the farro is almost tender.

3. Add the tomatoes and white beans. Bring to a boil, and then lower the heat to a simmer. Cover and cook for 15 minutes, or until the farro is tender. Add the spinach and remaining olive oil. Simmer for 2 minutes, or until the spinach is wilted. Serve hot, topping each serving with a sprinkling of Parmesan cheese if desired.

NUTRITION FACTS (PER CUP)

Calories: 187	Carbohydrates: 29 g	Fiber: 6.7 g
Protein: 8 g	Fat: 4 g	Saturated fat: 0.6 g
Cholesterol: 0 mg	Sodium: 362 mg	Calcium: 63 mg

Yield: 8 Cups

2 tablespoons extra virgin olive oil, divided

1 cup chopped yellow onion

$3/4$ cup thinly sliced celery

$3/4$ cup diced carrot

2 tablespoons water

2 teaspoons crushed garlic

$3/4$ cup uncooked farro

4 cups unsalted chicken or vegetable broth

2 teaspoons dried basil

$1/2$ teaspoon whole fennel seed

$3/4$ teaspoon salt

$1/2$ teaspoon ground black pepper

14.5-ounce can unsalted diced tomatoes, undrained

15-ounce can white beans, drained

2 cups chopped fresh spinach

Grated Parmesan cheese (optional)

CHIPOTLE
BLACK BEAN CHILI

Yield: 8 Cups

• • • • • • • • • • •

8-ounce can chipotle chiles in adobo sauce

1 pound ground beef or turkey (at least 93-percent lean)

1 cup chopped yellow onion

14.5-ounce can unsalted diced tomatoes, undrained, or 3 cups chopped fresh tomatoes

Two 15-ounce cans reduced-sodium black beans, undrained

8-ounce can unsalted tomato sauce

2 tablespoons chili powder

1 teaspoon ground cumin

$^3/_4$ teaspoon dried oregano

$^1/_2$ teaspoon salt

TOPPINGS (optional)

$^3/_4$ cup shredded reduced-fat Monterey Jack cheese

$^1/_2$ cup sliced scallions

1. Drain the sauce from the chipotle chiles into a blender. Wearing protective gloves, cut open the chiles and scrape out and discard the seeds and the inner membranes (this tones down the heat). Add the chiles to the blender and purée until smooth. Pour into a small bowl and set aside.

2. Coat a 3-quart saucepan with cooking spray and add the ground meat. Cook over medium heat for about 6 minutes, stirring to crumble, until the meat is lighlty browned. Add the onion, cover, and cook for about 5 minutes, or until the onion softens.

3. Add the tomatoes, black beans, tomato sauce, chili powder, cumin, oregano, salt, and 2 tablespoons of the puréed chili peppers (the remaining purée can be frozen for later use). Bring to a boil, and then lower the heat to a simmer. Cover and cook for 30 minutes, stirring occasionally. If necessary, simmer uncovered for the last 5 minutes to thicken.

4. Serve hot, topping each serving with some of the cheese and scallions if desired.

NUTRITION FACTS (PER CUP)

Calories: 234	Carbohydrates: 28 g	Fiber: 9.2 g
Protein: 20 g	Fat: 4.8 g	Saturated fat: 1.8 g
Cholesterol: 36 mg	Sodium: 406 mg	Calcium: 44 mg

SPICY SWEET POTATO SOUP

1. Drain the sauce from the chipotle chiles into a blender. Wearing protective gloves, cut open the chiles and scrape out and discard the seeds and inner membranes (this tones down the heat). Add the chiles to the blender and purée until smooth. Pour into a small bowl and set aside.

2. In a 2-quart saucepan, combine the olive oil, onion, celery, and water. Cover and cook over medium heat for about 6 minutes, stirring occasionally, or until the vegetables soften. Add the garlic and cook for 30 seconds.

3. Add the broth, sweet potato, and salt. Bring to a boil, and then lower the heat to a simmer. Cover and cook for 12 minutes, or until the potatoes are soft.

4. Add 2 teaspoons of the puréed chipotle chiles to the saucepan (the remaining purée can be frozen for later use). Use an immersion blender to blend the soup until smooth. Alternatively, carefully purée the soup 2 cups at a time in a blender. (Remove the center piece of the blender lid to allow steam to escape and place a clean towel over the lid to prevent splatters while blending.) Add a little more broth if the soup seems too thick.

5. Serve hot, topping each serving with a quarter of the bacon and scallions.

Yield: 5 Cups

- - - - - - - - - - -

8-ounce can chipotle chiles in adobo sauce

1 tablespoon extra virgin olive oil

$1/_2$ cup chopped yellow onion

$1/_2$ cup chopped celery

2 tablespoons water

2 teaspoons crushed garlic

$2^{1}/_4$ cups unsalted chicken or vegetable broth

$3^{1}/_2$ cups diced peeled sweet potato (about 2 medium, or $1^{1}/_4$ pounds total)

$1/_2$ teaspoon salt

2 slices crisp-cooked bacon (turkey, center-cut pork, or vegetarian), crumbled

3 tablespoons thinly sliced scallions

NUTRITION FACTS (PER CUP)

Calories: 165	Carbohydrates: 27 g	Fiber: 4.3 g
Protein: 4.5 g	Fat: 4.8 g	Saturated fat: 0.8 g
Cholesterol: 5 mg	Sodium: 399 mg	Calcium: 62 mg

VEGETARIAN CHILI

Yield: 8 Cups

• • • • • • •

1 tablespoon plus
1 teaspoon extra virgin
olive oil

1 cup chopped yellow onion

1 cup water, divided

14.5-ounce can diced
tomatoes with green chilies,
undrained

$1/_2$ cup diced carrot

1 $1/_4$ cups low-sodium
vegetable juice

$1/_2$ cup uncooked bulgur
wheat

2 tablespoons chili powder

1 teaspoon ground cumin

$3/_4$ teaspoon dried oregano

Scant $1/_2$ teaspoon salt

1 cup fresh or frozen corn

Two 15-ounce cans
reduced-sodium dark red
kidney beans, drained
(reserve $1/_2$ cup of
the liquid)

TOPPINGS (optional)

1 cup shredded reduced-fat
Mexican blend or
Monterey Jack cheese

$1/_2$ cup thinly sliced scallions

1. In a 4-quart saucepan, combine the olive oil, onion, and 2 tablespoons of the water. Cover and cook over medium heat for 5 minutes, or until the onion softens.

2. In a blender, combine the tomatoes and carrots. Purée until smooth. Add the mixture to the saucepan along with the vegetable juice, bulgur wheat, chili powder, cumin, oregano, salt, and remaining water. Bring to a boil, and then lower the heat to a simmer. Cover and cook for 15 minutes, stirring occasionally.

3. Add the corn, beans, and reserved bean liquid, and return the pot to a simmer. Cover and cook for 10 minutes. If necessary, simmer uncovered for a few minutes to thicken. Serve hot, topping each serving with some of the cheese and scallions if desired.

NUTRITION FACTS (PER CUP)

Calories: 190	Carbohydrates: 34 g	Fiber: 9 g
Protein: 9 g	Fat: 3.3 g	Saturated fat: 0.5 g
Cholesterol: 0 mg	Sodium: 413 mg	Calcium: 56 mg

HELPFUL HINT

You can substitute 3 cups chopped fresh tomatoes plus 1 tablespoon pickled jalapeño peppers and $1/_2$ teaspoon salt for the canned tomatoes with green chilies.

7

Main Dish Salads

Main dish salads are the superstars of any healthy eating plan. Unfortunately, many people are leery of salad as a meal and think of it mainly as diet food. This may be because all too often, salads are bland, boring, and underwhelming. The goal of this chapter is to change that mindset.

A myriad of glorious greens can form the foundation of a great salad, from colorful European blends to zesty arugula, or from crisp cabbage to super-nutritious spinach or kale. Add pizzazz to the plate by using fresh colorful vegetables and fruits, hearty whole grains, or crunchy nuts and seeds. You can even kick it up a notch with gourmet garnishes such as capers, olives, or fresh herbs. A handful of garbanzo beans, edamame, lentils, or any other legume will boost both protein and fiber amounts in a salad, making your meal even more satisfying.

It's hard to beat the ease and versatility of main dish salads. Whether you are looking for a dish with a spicy southwestern slant, something marvelous and Mediterranean, or a colorful chopped variety, many exciting salads can be created in a matter of minutes. Get ready to experience a world of sensational and ultimately satisfying salads. It's time to banish the boredom forever.

TEX-MEX TACO SALAD

Yield: 4 Servings

• • • • • • • • • • •

12 ounces ground beef, turkey, or chicken (at least 93-percent lean)

$3/4$ cup chopped yellow onion

15-ounce can reduced-sodium black or pinto beans, undrained

1 cup chunky-style salsa

1 teaspoon ground cumin

1 teaspoon chili powder

12 cups shredded romaine lettuce

1 cup chopped fresh tomatoes

$1/3$ cup chopped fresh cilantro

$1 1/3$ cups coarsely mashed avocado (about $1 1/2$ medium avocados)

$3/4$ cup shredded reduced-fat Mexican blend cheese

1. Coat a large nonstick skillet with cooking spray and add the ground meat. Cook over medium heat for about 6 minutes, or until the meat is no longer pink, stirring to crumble. Add the onion, cover, and cook for 4 minutes, or until tender, stirring occasionally.

2. Add the undrained beans, salsa, cumin, and chili powder. Lower the heat to a simmer, cover, and cook for 5 minutes. Remove the lid and simmer uncovered for 3 to 5 minutes to thicken the sauce. Remove from the heat and set aside.

3. In a large bowl, combine the lettuce, tomatoes, and cilantro. Toss to mix.

4. Divide the lettuce mixture equally among 4 serving plates or bowls. Top each serving with a quarter of the meat mixture (about $7/8$ cup) and garnish with a quarter of the mashed avocado and cheese. Serve immediately.

NUTRITION FACTS (PER SERVING)

Calories: 433	Carbohydrates: 33 g	Fiber: 13.5 g
Protein: 33 g	Fat: 19.2 g	Saturated fat: 3.7 g
Cholesterol: 54 mg	Sodium: 632 mg	Calcium: 137 mg

BALSAMIC & BERRY CHICKEN SALAD

1. In a small bowl, combine all the dressing ingredients and whisk to mix. Set aside. In another small bowl, combine the garlic powder, black pepper, and salt. Set aside.

2. If necessary, cut the chicken breasts in half horizontally or butterfly them so they are no more than $3/4$-inch thick. Sprinkle both sides of the chicken breasts with the spice mixture.

3. Coat a large nonstick skillet with cooking spray and preheat over medium heat. Add the chicken and cook for 1 minute on each side to lightly brown. Lower the heat to medium-low. Cover and cook for 12 minutes, turning after 6 minutes, or until the chicken is cooked through. If necessary, remove the lid and cook uncovered for a couple of minutes to evaporate any liquid in the skillet. Remove the skillet from the heat, cover, and set aside.

4. In a large bowl, combine the spinach or mixed greens and scallions. Add $1/4$ cup plus 2 tablespoons of the dressing and toss to mix. Divide the mixture equally among 4 serving plates.

5. Thinly slice or dice 1 cooked chicken breast and place on each salad. Arrange a quarter of the berries around the chicken on each salad. Drizzle each salad with a quarter of the remaining dressing (about $1^1/_2$ teaspoons) and sprinkle with a quarter of the nuts and cheese. Serve immediately.

NUTRITION FACTS (PER SERVING)

Calories: 438	Carbohydrates: 20 g	Fiber: 9.2 g
Protein: 35 g	Fat: 25.4 g	Saturated fat: 4.4 g
Cholesterol: 71 mg	Sodium: 733 mg	Calcium: 215 mg

FOR A CHANGE . . .

Substitute diced pears and halved red grapes for the berries.

Yield: 4 Servings

$1/2$ teaspoon garlic powder

$1/2$ teaspoon ground black pepper

$1/4$ teaspoon salt

1 pound boneless skinless chicken breast, cut into 4 equal pieces

12 cups fresh spinach or mixed baby salad greens

$3/4$ cup thinly sliced scallions

$1^1/_2$ cups fresh raspberries or sliced strawberries

$1^1/_2$ cups fresh blackberries or blueberries

$1/4$ cup plus 2 tablespoons chopped walnuts or pecans

$1/4$ cup plus 2 tablespoons crumbled reduced-fat blue cheese or feta cheese

DRESSING

$1/4$ cup extra virgin olive oil

$1^1/_2$ tablespoons balsamic vinegar

$1^1/_2$ tablespoons orange juice

2 teaspoons Dijon mustard

$1/2$ teaspoon salt

Arugula Salad with Lemon Pepper Shrimp

Yield: 4 Servings

• • • • • • • •

2 teaspoons low-sodium lemon pepper seasoning

$^1/_2$ teaspoon garlic powder

$^1/_4$ teaspoon salt

1 pound medium shrimp, peeled and deveined

8 cups baby arugula

4 slices red onion, cut into quarter-rings

15-ounce can reduced-sodium white beans or cannellini beans, rinsed and drained

2 tablespoons grated Parmesan cheese

DRESSING

2 tablespoons lemon juice

2 tablespoons extra virgin olive oil

1 teaspoon crushed garlic

$^1/_4$ teaspoon salt

$^1/_4$ teaspoon ground black pepper

1. In a small bowl, combine the lemon pepper, garlic powder, and salt. Place the shrimp in a large bowl. Sprinkle the lemon pepper mixture over the shrimp and toss to mix. Set aside.

2. Combine the arugula, onion, and beans in a large bowl. Toss and set aside.

3. In a small bowl, combine all the dressing ingredients. Stir to mix. Set aside.

4. Coat a large nonstick skillet with cooking spray and preheat over medium heat. Add the shrimp to the skillet in a single layer. Cook for a couple of minutes on each side, or until the shrimp turn opaque and are cooked through.

5. Pour the dressing over the salad and toss to mix. Divide the salad equally among 4 serving plates. Sprinkle each serving with $1^1/_2$ teaspoons Parmesan cheese and top with a quarter of the shrimp. Serve immediately.

Nutrition Facts (Per Serving)

Calories: 261	Carbohydrates: 22 g	Fiber: 7 g
Protein: 26 g	Fat: 8.5 g	Saturated fat: 1.6 g
Cholesterol: 139 mg	Sodium: 560 mg	Calcium: 246 mg

Helpful Hint

If using regular lemon pepper seasoning, omit the salt in the shrimp coating.

SOUTHWESTERN CHICKEN CHOPPED SALAD

1. Divide the first 9 ingredients (lettuce through jalapeño peppers) equally between 4 serving bowls.

2. Drizzle each salad with 2 tablespoons dressing and toss to mix. Add a little more dressing if needed. Add a quarter of the avocado to each salad and toss gently to mix. Serve immediately.

NUTRITION FACTS (PER SERVING)

Calories: 409   Carbohydrates: 32 g   Fiber: 11 g

Protein: 34 g   Fat: 19 g   Saturated fat: 5.1 g

Cholesterol: 69 mg Sodium: 494 mg   Calcium: 246 mg

HELPFUL HINT

In this recipe, the individual salads are mixed in 4 separate dishes because most people don't have a bowl large enough to accommodate all the ingredients. If you do own a 6-quart bowl or pot, you can mix all of the ingredients together in that dish, toss in the dressing, and then divide the salad among the individual serving dishes.

Yield: 4 Servings

12 cups shredded romaine lettuce

2 cups diced cooked chicken breast

1 cup diced fresh tomatoes

1 cup frozen (thawed) or fresh-cooked whole kernel corn

1 cup canned reduced-sodium black beans, rinsed and drained

1 cup sliced scallions or chopped red onion

$3/4$ cup shredded reduced-fat Monterey Jack or Mexican blend cheese

$1/2$ cup chopped fresh cilantro

2 tablespoons finely chopped pickled jalapeño peppers, or to taste

$1/2$ cup light olive oil vinaigrette or sun-dried tomato salad dressing

1 medium avocado, diced

GREEK CHICKEN CHOPPED SALAD

Yield: 4 Servings

• • • • • • • • • • •

12 cups chopped or shredded romaine lettuce

1 1/3 cups chopped cucumber

1 1/3 cups quartered grape tomatoes

1/2 cup chopped red onion

2 cups chopped cooked chicken breast

1 1/3 cups garbanzo beans (reduced-sodium if canned)

1 1/3 cups chopped marinated artichoke hearts, drained

1/2 cup coarsely chopped pitted Kalamata olives

4 pickled pepperoncini peppers, sliced into thin rings

1/4 cup plus 2 tablespoons crumbled reduced-fat feta cheese

1/2 cup light olive oil vinaigrette salad dressing

1. Divide the first 10 ingredients (lettuce through feta cheese) equally among 4 serving bowls.

2. Drizzle each salad with 2 tablespoons dressing, and toss to mix. Add a little more dressing if needed. Serve immediately.

NUTRITION FACTS (PER SERVING)

Calories: 362

Carbohydrates: 31 g

Fiber: 9.5 g

Protein: 31 g

Fat: 13.9 g

Saturated fat: 2.6 g

Cholesterol: 58 mg

Sodium: 718 mg

Calcium: 113 mg

HELPFUL HINT

In this recipe, the individual salads are mixed in 4 separate dishes because most people don't have a bowl large enough to accommodate all the ingredients. If you do own a 6-quart bowl or pot, you can mix all of the ingredients together in that dish, toss in the dressing, and then divide the salad among the individual serving dishes.

SUMMERTIME COBB SALAD

1. In a large bowl, combine the lettuce and dressing. Toss to mix. Divide the lettuce equally among 4 serving plates.

2. Top each serving with a quarter of the corn, blue cheese, tomato, chicken, bacon, avocado, and egg. Serve immediately.

NUTRITION FACTS (PER SERVING)

Calories: 352	Carbohydrates: 22 g	Fiber: 7 g
Protein: 26 g	Fat: 20 g	Saturated fat: 5 g
Cholesterol: 146 mg	Sodium: 545 mg	Calcium: 126 mg

FOR A CHANGE . . .

Substitute cooked shrimp or crabmeat for the chicken.

Yield: 4 Servings

• • • • • • • • • •

10 cups shredded romaine lettuce

$\frac{1}{2}$ cup light olive oil vinaigrette salad dressing

1 $\frac{1}{3}$ cups frozen (thawed) or fresh-cooked whole kernel corn

$\frac{1}{4}$ cup plus 2 tablespoons crumbled reduced-fat blue cheese

1 $\frac{1}{3}$ cups chopped tomato

1 $\frac{1}{3}$ cups diced or pulled cooked chicken

4 slices cooked bacon (turkey, center-cut pork, or vegetarian), crumbled

1 medium avocado, diced

2 hard-boiled eggs, chopped

FABULOUS FIBER FACT

When snacking, don't forget fiber. Grab some fresh fruit, raw vegetables, low-fat popcorn, or a small handful of nuts or seeds. Leftovers, such as a cup of vegetable soup or salad, also make a good snack.

WEST COAST CHOPPED SALAD

Yield: 4 Servings
• • • • • • • • • • •

12 cups chopped romaine lettuce

2 cups diced cooked chicken or turkey breast

$1\frac{1}{3}$ cups chopped broccoli florets

$1\frac{1}{3}$ cups grape tomatoes, quartered

$\frac{1}{2}$ cup grated carrot

$\frac{1}{2}$ cup chopped red onion

$\frac{1}{3}$ cup sunflower seeds

$\frac{1}{3}$ cup raisins or dried cranberries

1 medium avocado, diced

$\frac{1}{4}$ cup plus 2 tablespoons crumbled reduced-fat blue cheese

$\frac{1}{2}$ cup plus 2 tablespoons light balsamic or olive oil vinaigrette salad dressing

1. Divide all the ingredients except for the salad dressing equally among 4 serving bowls.

2. Drizzle each salad with $2\frac{1}{2}$ tablespoons dressing and toss to mix. Add a little more dressing if needed. Serve immediately.

NUTRITION FACTS (PER SERVING)

Calories: 415	Carbohydrates: 29 g	Fiber: 8.5 g
Protein: 29 g	Fat: 22.8 g	Saturated fat: 4.5 g
Cholesterol: 59 mg	Sodium: 515 mg	Calcium: 149 mg

HELPFUL HINT

In this recipe, the individual salads are mixed in 4 separate dishes because most people don't have a bowl large enough to accommodate all the ingredients. If you do own a 6-quart bowl or pot, you can mix all of the ingredients together in that dish, toss in the dressing, and then divide the salad among the individual serving dishes.

CAESAR SALAD WITH CHICKEN & PENNE PASTA

1. Cook the pasta according to package directions. Drain the pasta, rinse with cool water, and drain again. In a small bowl, combine all the dressing ingredients. Stir to mix. Set aside.

2. In a large bowl, combine the lettuce, tomatoes, and onion. Add the dressing and toss to mix. Add the pasta and Parmesan cheese and toss again.

3. Divide the salad equally among 4 serving plates. Top each serving with a quarter of the chicken. Serve immediately.

NUTRITION FACTS (PER SERVING)

Calories: 358	Carbohydrates: 32 g	Fiber: 7 g
Protein: 32 g	Fat: 12.9 g	Saturated fat: 2.2 g
Cholesterol: 70 mg	Sodium: 422 mg	Calcium: 94 mg

Yield: 4 Servings

4 ounces uncooked whole grain penne pasta

12 cups shredded romaine lettuce

1 cup halved grape tomatoes

4 slices red onion, cut into quarter-rings

2 to 3 tablespoons grated Parmesan cheese

$2^1/_2$ cups diced cooked chicken breast

DRESSING

$^1/_4$ cup plus 2 tablespoons light mayonnaise

2 tablespoons extra virgin olive oil

1 tablespoon plus 1 teaspoon lemon juice

1 tablespoon plus 1 teaspoon Dijon mustard

1 teaspoon crushed garlic

$^1/_4$ teaspoon ground black pepper

FABULOUS FIBER FACT

High-fiber pastas are available in all sizes and shapes. It's key to look at the ingredients to know what you are getting. For the most nutrition, look for whole grains such as whole wheat, whole durum wheat (a high-protein wheat traditionally used to make pasta), kamut, spelt, brown rice, and quinoa, as well as ingredients such as bran, wheat germ, flax, and legume flours.

CHICKEN & BROCCOLI PASTA SALAD

Yield: 4 Servings

• • • • • • • • • • •

6 ounces uncooked whole grain penne pasta

2$^1/_2$ cups small fresh broccoli florets

2 cups diced cooked chicken breast

$^1/_2$ cup thinly sliced scallions

$^1/_3$ cup chopped black olives

DRESSING

$^1/_2$ cup light mayonnaise

$^1/_3$ cup Greek-style yogurt (2-percent or 4-percent fat) or light sour cream

1 tablespoon Dijon mustard

1 tablespoon plus 1 teaspoon finely chopped fresh dill, or 1$^1/_4$ teaspoons dried

$^1/_4$ teaspoon ground white pepper

1. Cook the pasta al dente according to package directions. Drain the pasta, rinse with cool water, and drain again.

2. In a large bowl, combine the pasta, broccoli, chicken, scallions, and olives. Toss to mix.

3. In a small bowl, combine all the dressing ingredients. Stir to mix. Add the dressing to the salad. Toss to mix. Add a little more mayonnaise if the salad seems too dry. Serve immediately, or cover the salad and chill until ready to serve.

NUTRITION FACTS (PER 1$^3/_4$-CUP SERVING)

Calories: 385	Carbohydrates: 38 g	Fiber: 7 g
Protein: 32 g	Fat: 12 g	Saturated fat: 2.4 g
Cholesterol: 56 mg	Sodium: 498 mg	Calcium: 92 mg

FABULOUS FIBER FACT

The amount of resistant starch in a food increases after it has been cooked and cooled. Therefore, chilled pasta or potato salad has more resistant starch—a source of nourishment for "good" bacteria—than hot cooked pasta or potatoes.

SPICY SHRIMP SALAD

1. Place the shrimp in a medium-sized bowl. Add the Cajun seasoning, and toss to mix.

2. Coat a large nonstick skillet with cooking spray and preheat over medium heat. Add the shrimp to the skillet in a single layer. Cook for a couple of minutes on each side, or until the shrimp turn opaque and are cooked through.

3. In a large bowl, combine the lettuce, tomatoes, and onion. Drizzle with the dressing and toss to mix. Divide the salad equally among 4 serving plates. Top each serving with a quarter of the shrimp, corn, avocado, bacon, and blue cheese. Serve immediately.

NUTRITION FACTS (PER SERVING)

Calories: 347 Carbohydrates: 28 g Fiber: 8.5 g

Protein: 26 g Fat: 18 g Saturated fat: 3.4 g

Cholesterol: 154 mg Sodium: 641 mg Calcium: 150 mg

HELPFUL HINT

If you don't have any low-sodium Cajun seasoning on hand, substitute 1 teaspoon ground paprika, $\frac{1}{2}$ teaspoon garlic powder, $\frac{1}{4}$ teaspoon dried thyme, $\frac{1}{4}$ teaspoon dried oregano, $\frac{1}{4}$ teaspoon ground black pepper, and $\frac{1}{8}$ teaspoon cayenne pepper.

Yield: 4 Servings

1 pound medium shrimp, peeled and deveined

2 to 3 teaspoons low-sodium Cajun seasoning

12 cups shredded romaine lettuce

1 cup diced tomatoes

4 slices red onion, cut into quarter-rings

$\frac{1}{2}$ cup plus 2 tablespoons light olive oil vinaigrette or sun-dried tomato salad dressing

1 cup frozen (thawed) or fresh-cooked whole kernel corn

1 medium avocado, diced

4 slices cooked bacon (turkey, center-cut pork, or vegetarian), crumbled

$\frac{1}{4}$ cup crumbled reduced-fat blue cheese

TUSCAN TUNA SALAD

Yield: 4 Servings

. . . .

$3/4$ cup uncooked farro

10 cups shredded romaine lettuce

1 cup diced cucumber

1 cup grape tomatoes, quartered

$3/4$ cup chopped fresh parsley

4 slices red onion, cut into quarter-rings

Two 5-ounce cans tuna in spring water, drained and separated into chunks

$1/4$ cup chopped pitted Kalamata olives

$1/4$ cup crumbled reduced-fat feta cheese.

DRESSING

$1/4$ cup extra virgin olive oil

$1/4$ cup lemon juice

1 teaspoon crushed garlic

$1/2$ teaspoon salt

$1/2$ teaspoon ground black pepper

1. Cook the farro according to package directions. Chill the farro before proceeding with the recipe.

2. In a large bowl, combine the cooked farro, lettuce, cucumber, grape tomatoes, parsley, and onion. Toss to mix. In a small bowl, combine all the dressing ingredients. Stir to mix. Pour all except for 2 tablespoons of the dressing over the salad and toss to mix.

3. Divide the salad equally among 4 serving plates. Top each serving with a quarter of the tuna and drizzle $1\frac{1}{2}$ teaspoons dressing over the tuna on each plate. Top each salad with a quarter of the olives and feta cheese. Serve immediately.

NUTRITION FACTS (PER SERVING)

Calories: 359	Carbohydrates: 33 g	Fiber: 7 g
Protein: 20 g	Fat: 18 g	Saturated fat: 2.6 g
Cholesterol: 23 mg	Sodium: 696 mg	Calcium: 80 mg

FOR A CHANGE . . .

Wheat berries, spelt, or einkorn can be substituted for the farro in this recipe. Or substitute 2 cups cooked chilled whole grain penne pasta for the farro.

ANTIPASTO SALAD

1. Cook the pasta according to package directions. Drain, rinse with cool water, and drain again. Set aside.

2. Divide the pasta, lettuce, garbanzo beans, artichoke hearts, tomatoes, olives, pepperoni, onion, and cheese equally among 4 serving bowls.

3. Drizzle each salad with 2 tablespoons dressing and toss to mix. Serve immediately.

NUTRITION FACTS (PER SERVING)

Calories: 411	Carbohydrates: 46 g	Fiber: 10.5 g
Protein: 20.5 g	Fat: 19 g	Saturated fat: 4.4 g
Cholesterol: 22 mg	Sodium: 743 mg	Calcium: 244 mg

HELPFUL HINT

In this recipe, the individual salads are mixed in 4 separate dishes because most people don't have a bowl large enough to accommodate all the ingredients. If you do own a 6-quart bowl or pot, you can mix all of the ingredients together in that dish, toss in the dressing, and then divide the salad among the individual serving dishes.

Yield: 4 Servings

. . . .

4 ounces uncooked whole grain penne pasta

10 cups shredded romaine lettuce

1 cup cooked garbanzo beans (reduced-sodium if canned)

1 cup chopped marinated artichoke hearts, drained

1 cup quartered grape tomatoes

$1/2$ cup chopped black olives

$1 1/2$ ounces turkey pepperoni, cut into thin strips (about 20 slices)

4 slices red onion, cut into quarter-rings

$3/4$ cup coarsely shredded or diced reduced-fat mozzarella or provolone cheese

$1/2$ cup light olive oil vinaigrette or Italian salad dressing

TUNA SALAD WITH PASTA & ROASTED RED PEPPERS

Yield: 4 Servings

• • • • • • • • • • •

4 ounces uncooked whole grain penne pasta

$1/3$ cup thinly sliced (on the bias) scallions

$1/4$ cup quartered pitted Kalamata or black olives

Two 5-ounce cans tuna in spring water, drained and separated into chunks

6 cups shredded romaine lettuce or mixed baby salad greens

I cup quartered marinated artichoke hearts, drained (reserve 3 tablespoons of the marinade)

I tablespoon plus I teaspoon capers, drained

DRESSING

$1/4$ cup diced roasted red bell peppers

$1/2$ cup light mayonnaise

$1/2$ teaspoon crushed garlic

I teaspoon dried basil, or I tablespoon fresh

$1/4$ teaspoon ground black pepper

1. Cook the pasta according to package directions. Drain, rinse with cool water, and drain again. In a large bowl, combine the cooked pasta, scallions, and olives. Set aside.

2. In a mini food processor, combine all the dressing ingredients and process until smooth. Add the dressing to the pasta mixture and toss to mix. Add the tuna and toss gently to mix.

3. Place the lettuce in a large bowl and pour the reserved artichoke marinade on top. Toss to mix. Divide the lettuce equally among 4 serving plates. Top each serving with a quarter of the pasta mixture (about $1^1/4$ cups). Arrange $1/4$ cup artichoke hearts around the pasta, and sprinkle 1 teaspoon capers over each salad. Serve immediately.

NUTRITION FACTS (PER SERVING)

Calories: 242

Carbohydrates: 33 g

Fiber: 7 g

Protein: 18 g

Fat: 5.5 g

Saturated fat: 0.2 g

Cholesterol: 23 mg

Sodium: 634 mg

Calcium: 54 mg

QUINOA SALAD WITH SPINACH & EDAMAME

1. Cook the quinoa according to package directions. Chill the quinoa before proceeding with the recipe.

2. In a large bowl, combine the quinoa, edamame, spinach, cranberries, pumpkin seeds, and scallions. In a small bowl, combine all the dressing ingredients and stir to mix. Pour the dressing over the salad and toss to mix. Let sit for 10 minutes before serving, or cover and refrigerate until ready to serve.

NUTRITION FACTS (PER 1 $\frac{1}{3}$-CUP SERVING)

Calories: 321	Carbohydrates: 36 g	Fiber: 7 g
Protein: 14 g	Fat: 14.8 g	Saturated fat: 1.9 g
Cholesterol: 0 mg	Sodium: 310 mg	Calcium: 73 mg

Yield: 4 Servings

$\frac{3}{4}$ cup tricolor or white quinoa

1 $\frac{3}{4}$ cups shelled cooked edamame

2 cups moderately packed sliced fresh spinach

$\frac{1}{3}$ cup dried cranberries

$\frac{1}{3}$ cup pumpkin seeds

$\frac{1}{3}$ cup thinly sliced scallions

DRESSING

1 $\frac{1}{2}$ tablespoons extra virgin olive oil

1 $\frac{1}{2}$ tablespoons white wine vinegar

1 $\frac{1}{2}$ tablespoons orange juice

$\frac{1}{2}$ teaspoon salt

$\frac{1}{2}$ teaspoon ground black pepper

FABULOUS FIBER FACT

The recommended daily intake for fiber is 14 grams for every 1,000 calories eaten. This amounts to about 28 grams per day for most women and 36 grams for most men. Many experts believe that a fiber intake closer to 50 grams per day is even better. Unfortunately, most adults in the United States consume only 16 grams per day.

LENTIL SALAD WITH SPINACH, CORN & TOMATOES

Yield: 4 Servings

• • • • • • • • • • •

1 cup dried lentils du Puy (French green lentils) or brown lentils

2¼ cups unsalted vegetable or chicken broth

8 cups moderately packed sliced fresh spinach

1¼ cups frozen (thawed) or fresh-cooked whole kernel corn

¾ cup diced grape tomatoes

¾ cup sliced scallions

½ cup crumbled queso fresco cheese

3 tablespoons pumpkin seeds

DRESSING

2½ tablespoons extra virgin olive oil

1½ tablespoons lime juice

1 tablespoon orange juice

2 teaspoons finely chopped pickled jalapeño peppers

1 teaspoon crushed garlic

¾ teaspoon salt

½ teaspoon ground black pepper

1. In a 2-quart saucepan, combine the lentils and broth over medium-high heat. Bring to a boil, and then lower the heat to a simmer. Cover and cook for about 25 to 30 minutes for French green lentils, 20 minutes for brown lentils, or until tender. Drain the excess liquid. Cool the lentils before assembling the salad.

2. In a small bowl, combine all the dressing ingredients and whisk to mix. Set aside.

3. In a large bowl, combine the lentils, spinach, corn, tomatoes, and scallions. Drizzle with the dressing and toss to mix.

4. Divide the mixture equally among 4 serving plates or bowls (about 2 cups each). Top each serving with a quarter of the cheese and pumpkin seeds. Serve immediately.

NUTRITION FACTS (PER SERVING)

Calories: 382	Carbohydrates: 45 g	Fiber: 18.2 g
Protein: 21 g	Fat: 15 g	Saturated fat: 3 g
Cholesterol: 10 mg	Sodium: 588 mg	Calcium: 210 mg

CHOPPED SALAD WITH CHICKPEAS, FARRO & FETA

1. Cook the farro according to package directions. Chill before proceeding with the recipe.

2. In a small bowl, combine all the dressing ingredients and stir to mix. Set aside.

3. Divide the cooked farro, lettuce, garbanzo beans, cucumber, tomatoes, onion, bell pepper, olives, feta cheese, and dill equally between 4 serving bowls. Drizzle each salad with $1^1/_2$ tablespoons dressing. Toss to mix. Serve immediately.

NUTRITION FACTS (PER SERVING)

Calories: 387	Carbohydrates: 46 g	Fiber: 12.1 g
Protein: 14.5 g	Fat: 17.4 g	Saturated fat: 2.7 g
Cholesterol: 5 mg	Sodium: 702 mg	Calcium: 124 mg

FOR A CHANGE . . .

Substitute wheat berries, spelt, or einkorn for the farro.

HELPFUL HINT

In this recipe, the individual salads are mixed in 4 separate dishes because most people don't have a bowl large enough to accommodate all the ingredients. If you do own a 6-quart bowl or pot, you can mix all of the ingredients together in that dish, toss in the dressing, and then divide the salad among the individual serving dishes.

Yield: 4 Servings

$^1/_4$ cup plus 2 tablespoons uncooked farro

8 cups chopped romaine lettuce

2 cups cooked garbanzo beans (chickpeas), rinsed and drained (reduced-sodium if canned)

1 cup diced English cucumber

1 cup diced grape tomatoes

$^3/_4$ cup chopped red onion

$^3/_4$ cup chopped yellow or orange bell pepper

$^1/_2$ cup chopped black olives

$^1/_2$ cup crumbled reduced-fat feta cheese

$^1/_4$ cup finely chopped fresh dill

DRESSING

3 tablespoons extra virgin olive oil

3 tablespoons lemon juice

1 teaspoon crushed garlic

$^1/_2$ teaspoon salt

$^1/_2$ teaspoon ground black pepper

FRIJOLE & GUACAMOLE SALAD

Yield: 4 Servings

• • • • • • • • • • •

2$^{1}/_{2}$ cups cooked pinto or black beans, undrained and coarsely mashed (reduced-sodium if canned)

$^{2}/_{3}$ cup chunky-style salsa

1 teaspoon chili powder

$^{1}/_{2}$ teaspoon ground cumin

12 cups shredded romaine lettuce

1$^{1}/_{3}$ cups frozen (thawed) or fresh-cooked whole kernel corn

1$^{1}/_{3}$ cups diced tomato

$^{3}/_{4}$ cup chopped red onion

2 tablespoons finely chopped pickled jalapeño peppers

1$^{1}/_{3}$ cups coarsely mashed avocado (about 1$^{1}/_{2}$ medium avocados)

1 cup shredded reduced-fat Monterey Jack or Mexican blend cheese or crumbled queso fresco

1. In a large nonstick skillet, combine the beans, salsa, chili powder, and cumin over medium heat, stirring to mix. Bring to a boil. Cook uncovered for about 5 minutes, or until the consistency of refried beans, stirring frequently. Turn off the heat, cover, and set aside to keep warm.

2. For each salad, spread a quarter of the warm bean mixture (about $^{1}/_{2}$ cup) over the bottom of a serving plate or shallow bowl. Cover the beans with 3 cups lettuce. Top the lettuce with $^{1}/_{3}$ cup corn, $^{1}/_{3}$ cup tomatoes, 3 tablespoons onion, and 1$^{1}/_{2}$ teaspoons jalapeño peppers. Dollop $^{1}/_{3}$ cup avocado over the salad in 3 mounds and top with $^{1}/_{4}$ cup cheese. Serve immediately.

NUTRITION FACTS (PER SERVING)

Calories: 393	Carbohydrates: 47 g	Fiber: 17 g
Protein: 20 g	Fat: 16 g	Saturated fat: 4.7 g
Cholesterol: 20 mg	Sodium: 608 mg	Calcium: 335 mg

BEAN FUSION SALAD

1. In a large bowl, combine the edamame, black beans, garbanzo beans, kale, and cabbage.

2. In a small bowl, combine all the dressing ingredients and whisk to mix. Pour the dressing over the salad and toss to mix. Let sit for at least 20 minutes before serving, or cover and refrigerate until ready to serve.

NUTRITION FACTS (PER 1-CUP SERVING)

Calories: 267	Carbohydrates: 31 g	Fiber: 9.9 g
Protein: 14 g	Fat: 11.1 g	Saturated fat: 1.5 g
Cholesterol: 0 mg	Sodium: 352 mg	Calcium: 130 mg

Yield: 4 Servings

• • • • • • • • • •

1 cup shelled cooked edamame

1 cup canned reduced-sodium black beans, rinsed and drained

1 cup canned reduced-sodium garbanzo beans, rinsed and drained

1 cup thinly sliced kale (remove any tough stems)

1 cup thinly sliced red cabbage

DRESSING

2 tablespoons extra virgin olive oil

$1\frac{1}{2}$ tablespoons white wine vinegar

1 tablespoon Dijon mustard

1 tablespoon orange juice

$\frac{1}{4}$ teaspoon salt

$\frac{1}{4}$ teaspoon ground black pepper

FABULOUS FIBER FACT

Animal products do not contain any fiber at all. On the other hand, plant foods, such as vegetables, fruits, whole grains, legumes, nuts, and seeds, are naturally rich in fiber. Simply eat more plant foods and you will be sure to increase your fiber intake.

FARRO & ARTICHOKE SALAD

Yield: 4 Servings

• • • • • • • • •

$3/_4$ cup uncooked farro

10 cups shredded romaine lettuce or mixed baby salad greens

2 cups coarsely chopped marinated artichoke hearts, drained (reserve $1/_2$ cup of the marinade)

2 cups julienned or coarsely shredded carrot

1 cup thinly slivered red onion

$1^1/_2$ cups diced fresh mozzarella cheese (6 ounces)

$1/_4$ teaspoon ground black pepper

1. Cook the farro according to package directions. Chill before proceeding with the recipe.

2. Divide the cooked farro, lettuce, artichoke hearts, carrot, onion, and mozzarella cheese equally among 4 serving bowls.

3. Sprinkle each serving with a pinch of black pepper and drizzle with 2 tablespoons of the reserved marinade. Toss to mix. Serve immediately.

NUTRITION FACTS (PER SERVING)

Calories: 401	Carbohydrates: 46 g	Fiber: 12 g
Protein: 17 g	Fat: 15.5 g	Saturated fat: 5.1 g
Cholesterol: 30 mg	Sodium: 568 mg	Calcium: 298 mg

HELPFUL HINT

In this recipe, the individual salads are mixed in 4 separate dishes because most people don't have a bowl large enough to accommodate all the ingredients. If you do own a 6-quart bowl or pot, you can mix all of the ingredients together in that dish, toss in the dressing, and then divide the salad among the individual serving dishes.

Spinach, Orzo & White Bean Salad

1. Cook the orzo according to package directions. Drain, rinse with cool water, and drain again.

2. In a large bowl, combine the orzo, spinach, tomatoes, beans, mozzarella cheese, olives, scallions, and basil. In a small bowl, combine the dressing ingredients and stir to mix. Pour the dressing over the salad and toss to mix.

3. Divide the salad equally among 4 serving bowls. Serve immediately.

NUTRITION FACTS (PER SERVING)

Calories: 373	Carbohydrates: 49g	Fiber: 12 g
Protein: 15 g	Fat: 13.4 g	Saturated fat: 2.5 g
Cholesterol: 8 mg	Sodium: 606 mg	Calcium: 220 mg

Yield: 4 Servings

1 cup whole wheat orzo (6 ounces)

4 cups moderately packed thinly sliced fresh spinach

2 cups grape tomatoes, quartered lengthwise

15-ounce can cannellini or white beans, drained and rinsed

$1/2$ cup shredded part-skim mozzarella cheese

$1/3$ cup chopped black olives

$1/4$ cup thinly sliced scallions

$1/4$ cup chopped fresh basil

DRESSING

2 tablespoons extra virgin olive oil

2 tablespoons lemon juice

$1/2$ teaspoon crushed garlic

$1/2$ teaspoon salt

$1/2$ teaspoon ground black pepper

FABULOUS FIBER FACT

A diet high in fiber-rich foods is thought to increase longevity by virtue of its anti-inflammatory properties and high nutrient content, both of which protect against many chronic diseases.

8

Fiber-Rich
Main Dishes

The main course, or entrée, often includes a piece of beef, poultry, or fish. While these foods provide important nutrients, they do not provide any fiber. One way to enhance your meal with fiber is to add wholesome side dishes like those in Chapter 9. Another option is to combine beef, poultry, or seafood with whole grains, pastas, vegetables, or beans to create entrées with both fiber and flair. Of course, you can also go meatless and feature legumes, vegetables, and whole grains in an infinite number of enticing main dishes.

This chapter offers a tasty array of recipes that are simple to make and sure to satisfy. As you will see, a wide variety of family favorites, including pasta, skillet dinners, meatballs, and more, can easily be made the healthy, high-fiber way.

CHICKEN WITH ARTICHOKES & SUN-DRIED TOMATOES

1. If necessary, cut the the chicken breasts in half horizontally or butterfly them so that they are no more than $^3/_4$-inch thick. In a small bowl, combine the garlic powder, black pepper, and salt. Stir to mix. Rub some of the spice mixture on both sides of the chicken breasts.

2. Coat a large nonstick skillet with cooking spray and preheat over medium heat. Add the chicken and cook for 1 to 2 minutes on each side, or until lightly browned.

3. Pour the wine or broth into the skillet and bring to a boil. Lower the heat to a simmer. Cover and cook for 5 minutes. Turn the chicken over and scatter the mushrooms around the chicken. Cover and cook for 8 minutes.

4. Add the artichokes and sun-dried tomatoes to the skillet. Cover and simmer for 5 minutes, or until the chicken and vegetables are cooked through and the flavors are blended.

5. Using a slotted spoon, place 1 chicken breast on each of 4 serving plates. Top each piece of chicken with a quarter of the vegetable mixture. Stir the olive oil into the pan juices. Cook for a couple of minutes over medium-high heat to reduce to 3 tablespoons. Drizzle about 2 teaspoons of the pan juices over each serving and top with 1 tablespoon cheese and 1$^1/_2$ teaspoons fresh basil. Serve immediately.

NUTRITION FACTS (PER SERVING)

Calories: 231	Carbohydrates: 11 g	Fiber: 5 g
Protein: 28 g	Fat: 7.2 g	Saturated fat: 1.7 g
Cholesterol: 62 mg	Sodium: 551 mg	Calcium: 58 mg

SPICY RED BEANS & RICE

Yield: 5 Servings
• • • • • • •

1. Coat a large nonstick skillet with cooking spray and add the sausage. Cook over medium heat for about 4 minutes to lightly brown, stirring frequently. Add the onion, bell pepper, and celery. Cover and cook for 5 minutes, or until tender. Add the garlic and cook for 30 seconds.

2. Add the kidney beans, tomatoes, Cajun seasoning, paprika, and thyme to the skillet. Bring to a boil and then lower the heat to a simmer. Cover and cook for 25 minutes, stirring occasionally. Uncover and simmer for about 10 minutes more to thicken the sauce.

3. For each serving, spread $1/2$ cup brown rice in a shallow bowl. Top with $1/4$ of the kidney bean mixture (about $1^1/_8$ cups). Sprinkle with a quarter of the scallions, and serve hot.

12 ounces chicken andouille sausage or smoked turkey sausage, sliced $1/_4$-inch thick

$3/_4$ cup chopped onion

$3/_4$ cup chopped green bell pepper

$3/_4$ cup chopped celery

1 teaspoon crushed garlic

Two 15-ounce cans reduced-sodium red kidney beans, undrained

14.5-ounce can no-salt-added diced tomatoes, undrained

2 teaspoons Cajun seasoning

1 teaspoon smoked paprika

$1/_2$ teaspoon dried thyme

$2^1/_2$ cups cooked brown rice

$1/_3$ cup thinly sliced scallions

NUTRITION FACTS (PER SERVING)

Calories: 308	Carbohydrates: 43 g	Fiber: 11 g
Protein: 20 g	Fat: 7.7 g	Saturated fat: 1.8 g
Cholesterol: 52 mg	Sodium: 848 mg	Calcium: 93 mg

FABULOUS FIBER FACT

The fiber and protein in legumes increase feelings of fullness. Legumes are also a low-glycemic index food, meaning they have minimal impact on blood sugar levels despite being relatively high in carbohydrates.

MEATBALLS FLORENTINE

Yield: 4 Servings

• • • • • • • • • • •

10-ounce package frozen chopped spinach, thawed

1 pound ground turkey (at least 93-percent lean)

$1/2$ cup finely chopped yellow onion

$1/4$ cup uncooked whole wheat couscous

$1/4$ cup grated Parmesan cheese

2 egg whites, or 1 large egg

$1 1/2$ teaspoons crushed garlic

1 teaspoon dried basil

$1/2$ teaspoon ground black pepper

$2 1/2$ cups ready-made marinara sauce

$3/4$ cup unsalted beef or vegetable broth

1. Squeeze the spinach tightly to remove as much of the liquid as possible.

2. Place the spinach in a large bowl and add the ground turkey, onion, couscous, Parmesan cheese, egg, garlic, basil, and black pepper. Mix well. Shape into 12 meatballs and set aside.

3. Pour the marinara sauce and broth into a large deep nonstick skillet and stir to mix. Bring to a boil, and then lower the heat to a simmer. Add the meatballs to the simmering sauce one at a time. Cover and cook for 40 minutes, or until cooked through and the flavors are well blended (the meatballs should reach at least 165°F), turning every 10 minutes. If necessary, remove the cover and simmer for a few minutes to thicken the sauce. Serve hot. If desired, serve over Zucchini Noodles (page 187) or spaghetti squash.

NUTRITION FACTS (PER 3-MEATBALL SERVING)

Calories: 328	Carbohydrate: 26 g	Fiber: 6.8 g
Protein: 34 g	Fat: 12.4 g	Saturated fat: 4.6 g
Cholesterol: 85 mg	Sodium: 640 mg	Calcium: 250 mg

Main Dish Makeovers

There are plenty of simple ways to boost both the fiber content and nutritional value of a main dish, giving it a healthy makeover. You could substitute whole grain pasta for the refined variety in lasagna or any other pasta dish. You could make pizza with whole grain crust. You could replace part of the meat in casseroles, stews, tacos, or other dishes with legumes. Try black beans and pintos in Tex-Mex dishes, red kidney beans in Cajun dishes, white beans and lentils in Mediterranean fare, or garbanzo beans in Middle Eastern favorites. When making meatloaf, burgers, or meatballs, why not add finely chopped mushrooms, onions, or other vegetables, and use whole grain bread, rolled oats, or oat bran as a filler instead of white bread? If you are making risotto, use brown rice, barley, or farro instead of white rice. There is no shortage of delicious options at your disposal when you are trying to enhance your favorite meal with more fiber.

SAUSAGE STUFFED CABBAGE ROLLS

1. Preheat the oven to 350°F.

2. Coat a large nonstick skillet with cooking spray and add the onion and bell pepper. Cover and cook over medium heat for about 8 minutes, or until the vegetables soften. If the skillet becomes too dry, lower the heat slightly or add a little water, but only enough to prevent scorching. Remove the skillet from the heat and stir in the orzo. Set aside.

3. In a blender, combine the tomatoes and broth. Purée until smooth. Stir $1/2$ cup of the purée into the skillet. Add the sausage to the skillet and mix well. Set aside.

4. Cut the cabbage leaves in half along the tough center veins, trimming away the veins and discarding them. Place $1/4$ cup packed sausage mixture along the bottom of 1 cabbage leaf and roll the leaf up to enclose the filling. (Don't worry if the leaves do not fit snugly around the filling. The filling will expand a bit during cooking and the leaves will shrink as they cook.) Repeat this process to make 15 rolls.

5. Coat a 10-x-13-inch baking pan with cooking spray and arrange the rolls in a single layer in the pan. Set aside.

6. Add the flour to the remaining puréed tomatoes in the blender. Blend until smooth and then pour into a 2-quart saucepan and bring to a boil, stirring frequently. Pour the mixture evenly over the cabbage rolls.

7. Cover the baking pan with aluminum foil and bake for 45 minutes, or until the filling is firm and the orzo is cooked. The filling should reach at least 165°F. Let sit for 10 minutes before serving.

Yield: 5 Servings

• • • • • • •

$1^1/_2$ cups chopped yellow onion

1 cup chopped red bell pepper

$3/_4$ cup uncooked whole wheat orzo

14.5-ounce can tomatoes with Italian seasoning, undrained

1 cup unsalted chicken or vegetable broth

1 pound turkey or chicken Italian sausage, casings removed

8 large cabbage or collard leaves

1 tablespoon whole wheat pastry flour

NUTRITION FACTS (PER 3-ROLL SERVING)

Calories: 296	Carbohydrates: 35 g	Fiber: 8 g
Protein: 22 g	Fat: 8.3 g	Saturated fat: 2.2 g
Cholesterol: 76 mg	Sodium: 919 mg	Calcium: 116 mg

SHEPHERD'S PIE

Yield: 5 Servings

• • • • • • •

1 pound ground beef (at least 93-percent lean)

³/₄ cup chopped yellow onion

³/₄ cup diced carrot

1 ¹/₂ teaspoons crushed garlic

2¹/₄ cups unsalted beef broth, divided

3 tablespoons whole wheat pastry flour

2 tablespoons tomato paste

¹/₂ teaspoon dried rosemary

³/₄ teaspoon dried thyme

³/₄ teaspoon salt

¹/₂ teaspoon ground black pepper

1 cup fresh or frozen corn

1 cup fresh or frozen green peas

TOPPING

1 pound 1-inch chunks unpeeled Yukon Gold potatoes (about 3¹/₂ cups)

¹/₃ cup light sour cream or Greek-style yogurt

1 tablespoon margarine or butter

¹/₄ teaspoon salt

¹/₄ teaspoon ground paprika

1. Preheat the oven to 350°F.

2. To prepare the topping, place the potatoes in a 4-quart saucepan and barely cover them with water over medium-high heat. Bring to a boil. Lower the heat to medium and boil for about 10 minutes, or until soft.

3. Drain the potatoes, reserving ¹/₂ cup of the liquid. Return the potatoes to the saucepan and add the sour cream, margarine or butter, ¹/₄ teaspoon salt, and ¹/₄ cup of the reserved potato water. Use a potato masher to mash until smooth. Add a little more of the potato water, if needed, to bring the potatoes to a creamy consistency. Cover and set aside.

4. To prepare the filling, coat a large nonstick skillet with cooking spray and add the ground beef. Cook over medium heat for about 8 minutes, or until the meat is lightly browned, stirring to crumble.

5. Add the onion, carrot, garlic, and ¹/₄ cup of the broth to the skillet. Cover and cook for 5 minutes, or until the vegetables are tender. If necessary, cook uncovered for a minute or two to evaporate any excess liquid.

6. Sprinkle the flour over the skillet mixture and stir to distribute evenly. Cook and stir for 30 seconds. Add the remaining broth, tomato paste, rosemary, thyme, salt, and black pepper and bring to a boil. Lower the heat to simmer. Cover and cook for 10 minutes, stirring occasionally.

7. Add the corn and peas to the skillet. Cover and simmer for 5 minutes, or until the vegetables are cooked through.

8. Place a fifth of the filling (about 1 cup) in each of five 16-ounce ramekins. Spread a fifth of the potatoes (about ¹/₂ cup) evenly over the filling in each ramekin. Sprinkle with a pinch of paprika. Bake for about 15 minutes, or until bubbly around the edges. Let sit for 5 minutes before serving.

NUTRITION FACTS (PER SERVING)

Calories: 353	Carbohydrates: 39 g	Fiber: 6.3 g
Protein: 27 g	Fat: 10.6 g	Saturated fat: 4.6 g
Cholesterol: 62 mg	Sodium: 622 mg	Calcium: 69 mg

HELPFUL HINT

To make one large Shepherd's Pie, spread the filling evenly in a 2-quart casserole dish. Spread the topping over the filling, and sprinkle with paprika. Bake for about 30 minutes.

STUFFED ACORN SQUASH

1. Cook the bulgur wheat according to package directions. Set aside.

2. Preheat the oven to 375°F.

3. Cut each squash in half and scoop out and discard the seeds. Trim a small piece of rind from each squash half so that the halves can sit steadily on their rinds once cooked. Coat a 9-x-13-inch baking pan with cooking spray. Place the squash halves flesh side down on the pan. Bake for about 30 minutes, or until tender. Remove from the oven and flip the squash over. Set aside.

4. While the squash is cooking, coat a large nonstick skillet with cooking spray and add the sausage. Cook over medium heat for about 6 minutes, or until no longer pink. Add the onion and garlic. Cover and cook for 5 minutes, or until the onion is tender. Add the spinach and cook for 2 minutes, or until the spinach wilts, tossing frequently. Add the bulgur wheat or couscous and 1 tablespoon Parmesan cheese. Toss to mix.

5. Stuff each squash half with a quarter of the sausage mixture. Sprinkle $^3/_4$ teaspoon of the remaining cheese over the filling of each squash half. Spray the tops lightly with cooking spray. Return the squash to the oven and bake for 10 minutes, or until the topping is lightly browned. Serve hot.

Yield: 4 Servings

• • • • • • •

$^1/_3$ cup uncooked bulgur wheat or whole wheat couscous

2 medium acorn squash (about 1 $^1/_4$ pounds each)

8 ounces chicken or turkey Italian sausage, casings removed

$^3/_4$ cup finely chopped yellow onion

1 teaspoon crushed garlic

3 cups (packed) coarsely chopped fresh spinach or baby kale

2 tablespoons grated Parmesan cheese, divided

Olive oil cooking spray

NUTRITION FACTS (PER SERVING)

Calories: 245	Carbohydrate: 37 g	Fiber: 6.3 g
Protein: 16 g	Fat: 5.3 g	Saturated fat: 1.9 g
Cholesterol: 49 mg	Sodium: 403 mg	Calcium: 167 mg

CHICKEN & BARLEY RISOTTO

Yield: 5 Servings

• • • • • • • • • •

12 ounces boneless skinless chicken breast, cut into 1-inch pieces

3 cups sliced white button mushrooms

$^3/_4$ cup chopped yellow onion

2 teaspoons crushed garlic

1 cup uncooked pearl barley

$2^1/_2$ cups unsalted chicken broth

$^1/_2$ cup dry white wine

$^1/_2$ cup low-sodium vegetable juice cocktail, such as V8

1 teaspoon dried thyme

$^1/_2$ teaspoon salt

$^1/_2$ teaspoon ground black pepper

$^3/_4$ cup fresh or frozen green peas

1. Coat a large, deep nonstick skillet with cooking spray and preheat over medium heat. Add the chicken and cook for about 3 minutes to lightly brown.

2. Add the mushrooms, onion, and garlic to the skillet. Cover and cook for 5 minutes, or until the vegetables are tender. Add the barley, chicken broth, white wine, vegetable juice, thyme, salt, and black pepper. Bring to a boil, and then lower the heat to a simmer. Cover and cook for 45 minutes, or until the barley is tender and most of the liquid has been absorbed, stirring occasionally. Add a little more broth during cooking if needed.

3. Add the peas to the skillet. Cover and cook for 5 minutes. Serve hot.

NUTRITION FACTS (PER 1 $^1/_3$-CUP SERVING)

Calories: 284	Carbohydrates: 40 g	Fiber: 8.2 g
Protein: 22 g	Fat: 2.6 g	Saturated fat: 0.6 g
Cholesterol: 43 mg	Sodium: 390 mg	Calcium: 38 mg

FABULOUS FIBER FACT

Barley is rich in the soluble fiber beta glucan, which helps to lower cholesterol and blood sugar levels and may increase feelings of fullness. Unlike most grains, the fiber in barley is distributed throughout the entire barley kernel rather than being concentrated in the outer bran layer.

CHICKEN & BROCCOLI CASSEROLE

1. Preheat the oven to 350°F.

2. Coat a large deep nonstick skillet with cooking spray and add the mushrooms and onion. Cover and cook over medium heat for 6 minutes, or until tender. Add the broccoli and water, cover, and cook for 2 minutes, or until crisp-tender. Add a little more water if the skillet becomes too dry, but only enough to prevent scorching. Remove from the heat. Add the barley or rice and the chicken to the skillet and toss to mix. Set aside.

3. To prepare the sauce, combine the milk and flour in a pint-sized jar with a tight-fitting lid and shake until smooth. Pour the milk mixture into a 1-quart saucepan over medium heat. Bring to a boil, stirring frequently. Whisk in the cheddar cheese, white pepper, and 2 tablespoons Parmesan cheese. Cook for about 1 minute to melt the cheese, stirring regularly. Remove from the heat and whisk in the sour cream.

4. Pour the sauce over the skillet mixture and toss to mix. Coat an 8-inch square baking dish with cooking spray and spread the mixture evenly in the dish. Bake for 20 minutes. Sprinkle the remaining 2 tablespoons Parmesan cheese over the top and bake for an additional 5 to 10 minutes, or until heated through.

NUTRITION FACTS (PER 1½-CUP SERVING)

Calories: 360	Carbohydrates: 38 g	Fiber: 7 g
Protein: 29 g	Fat: 10.3 g	Saturated fat: 5.8 g
Cholesterol: 62 mg	Sodium: 359 mg	Calcium: 354 mg

Yield: 5 Servings

• • • • • • • • • •

3 cups sliced white button mushrooms

$^3/_4$ cup chopped yellow onion

3 cups chopped fresh broccoli florets ($^3/_4$-inch pieces)

2 tablespoons water

$2^1/_2$ cups cooked barley or brown rice

1$^1/_2$ cups diced cooked chicken breast

SAUCE

1 cup nonfat or low-fat milk

1 tablespoon whole wheat pastry flour or unbleached all-purpose flour

1 cup shredded reduced-fat sharp cheddar cheese

$^1/_8$ teaspoon ground white pepper

$^1/_4$ cup grated Parmesan cheese, divided

$^1/_2$ cup light sour cream

Yield: 5 Servings

- 1 pound ground beef or turkey (at least 93-percent lean)
- 1 medium yellow onion, chopped
- 14.5-ounce can Mexican-style diced tomatoes, undrained and crushed
- 15-ounce can reduced-sodium dark red kidney beans, drained but not rinsed
- 1 cup unsalted beef broth
- 1 cup low-sodium vegetable juice cocktail, such as V8
- 1 tablespoon chili powder
- 1 teaspoon ground cumin
- $^1/_2$ teaspoon dried oregano
- 5 ounces uncooked whole grain elbow macaroni or penne pasta

CHILI-MACARONI

1. Coat a large deep nonstick skillet with cooking spray and add the ground meat. Cook over medium heat for about 8 minutes, or until the meat is lightly browned, stirring to crumble. Add the onion, cover, and cook for 5 minutes, or until softened.

2. Add the tomatoes, beans, broth, vegetable juice, chili powder, cumin, and oregano to the skillet. Bring to a boil.

3. Add the pasta to the skillet and stir to mix. Lower the heat to medium-low, cover, and cook for about 12 minutes, or until most of the liquid has been absorbed and the pasta is tender, stirring occasionally. Add a little more broth if needed. Serve hot.

NUTRITION FACTS (PER 1 $^1/_2$-CUP SERVING)

Calories: 348	Carbohydrates: 41 g	Fiber: 8.4 g
Protein: 29 g	Fat: 7.7 g	Saturated fat: 2.9 g
Cholesterol: 57 mg	Sodium: 410 mg	Calcium: 64 mg

Yield: 2 Servings

- 2 large zucchini (about 9 ounces each)
- 2 ounces thinly sliced lean ham, cut into thin strips
- 6 cloves garlic, thinly sliced
- $^2/_3$ cup frozen green peas, thawed
- 3 tablespoons chopped walnuts
- 2 teaspoons extra virgin olive oil
- $^1/_4$ teaspoon ground black pepper
- 2 tablespoons grated Parmesan cheese, divided

ZUCCHINI NOODLES WITH HAM & PEAS

1. Using a vegetable peeler, julienne the zucchini into long noodles, slicing only the skin and firm outer portions of the zucchini, and stopping when you reach the seeded portion. Set aside.

2. Coat a large, deep nonstick skillet with cooking spray and add the ham and garlic. Cook over medium heat for about 5 minutes, or until the ham is lightly browned and the garlic is fragrant, stirring frequently. Add the zucchini, green peas, and walnuts. Raise the heat to medium-high and cook for 5 minutes, or just until the zucchini is crisp-tender, tossing frequently.

3. Toss the olive oil and black pepper into the skillet mixture. Divide the mixture equally between 2 plates and top each serving with 1 tablespoon Parmesan cheese. Serve immediately.

NUTRITION FACTS (PER SERVING)

Calories: 237

Protein: 14 g

Cholesterol: 17 mg

Carbohydrates: 18 g

Fat: 13.6 g

Sodium: 444 mg

Fiber: 5 g

Saturated fat: 2.5 g

Calcium: 127 mg

ORZO PAELLA WITH CHICKEN & SAUSAGE

1. Coat a large deep nonstick skillet with cooking spray and add the chicken and sausage. Cook over medium-high heat for about 8 minutes, or until the sausage is no longer pink and the chicken is lightly browned, stirring to crumble the sausage. Lower the heat to medium and add the onion and garlic. Cover and cook for 4 minutes, or until soft. Add a little water if needed to prevent scorching.

2. Stir in the broth, wine, tomato, saffron, oregano, salt, and orzo. Bring to a boil, and then lower the heat to a simmer. Cover and cook for 10 minutes, or until most of the liquid has been absorbed and the orzo is almost tender.

3. Stir in the peas and cook for 3 minutes, or until the orzo is done and the peas are cooked through. Turn off the heat, cover, and let sit for 5 minutes. Serve hot.

Yield: 5 Servings

8 ounces boneless skinless chicken breast, cut into $3/4$-inch chunks

8 ounces hot turkey or chicken Italian sausage, casings removed

1 cup chopped yellow onion

2 teaspoons crushed garlic

2 cups unsalted chicken broth

$1/2$ cup dry white wine

1 cup diced plum tomato (about 2 large)

$1/4$ to $3/8$ teaspoon loosely packed saffron threads

$1/2$ teaspoon dried oregano

$1/4$ teaspoon salt

$1 1/2$ cups uncooked whole wheat orzo (9 ounces)

$3/4$ cup fresh or frozen green peas

NUTRITION FACTS (PER 1 $1/3$-CUP SERVING)

Calories: 349

Protein: 26 g

Cholesterol: 69 mg

Carbohydrates: 45 g

Fat: 6.2 g

Sodium: 598 mg

Fiber: 8.7 g

Saturated fat: 1.4 g

Calcium: 80 mg

SKILLET LASAGNA

Yield: 5 Servings
• • • • • • • • • •

12 ounces ground beef, turkey, or chicken (at least 93-percent lean), or 12 ounces turkey Italian sausage, casings removed

2 cups sliced white button mushrooms

$3/4$ cup chopped yellow onion

$2^1/_2$ cups ready-made marinara sauce

$1^1/_4$ cups water

6 ounces uncooked whole grain penne or rotini pasta

$3/4$ cup nonfat or reduced-fat ricotta cheese

$1^1/_2$ tablespoons grated Parmesan cheese

$3/4$ cup shredded reduced-fat mozzarella cheese

1. Coat a large deep nonstick skillet with cooking spray and add the ground meat. Cook over medium heat for about 6 minutes, or until lightly browned, stirring to crumble. Add the mushrooms and onion, cover, and cook for about 5 minutes, or until the vegetables are tender.

2. Add the marinara sauce and water and bring to a boil. Stir in the pasta and let the mixture return to a boil. Lower the heat to a simmer. Cover and cook for about 12 minutes, or until the pasta is al dente and most of the liquid has been absorbed.

3. Drop rounded tablespoonful of the ricotta over the pasta to make 5 mounds. Sprinkle the Parmesan and then the mozzarella over the top. Cover and cook for 1 minute. Turn off the heat and let sit for 3 minutes to melt the mozzarella cheese. Lift out each serving with a spatula, taking care not to break up the ricotta cheese. Serve hot.

NUTRITION FACTS (PER $1^1/_2$-CUP SERVING)

Calories: 372	Carbohydrates: 42 g	Fiber: 7.3 g
Protein: 32 g	Fat: 10.1 g	Saturated fat: 4.1 g
Cholesterol: 54 mg	Sodium: 638 mg	Calcium: 314 mg

FABULOUS FIBER FACT
A fiber-rich diet plays an important role in both treating and preventing diabetes. Fiber slows the absorption of carbohydrates from foods, which leads to a slower rise in blood sugar and less demand for insulin.

SAUSAGE & WHITE BEAN CASSOULET

1. Preheat the oven to 350°F.

2. Coat a large nonstick skillet with cooking spray and add the sausage. Cook over medium heat for about 6 minutes, or until lightlty browned, stirring to crumble. Add the next 7 ingredients (mushrooms through sage). Cover and cook for about 10 minutes, stirring occasionally, or until the vegetables are tender. Lower the heat or add a little water if needed to prevent scorching.

3. Add the puréed tomatoes and vegetable juice to the skillet and bring to a boil. Lower the heat to simmer. Cover and cook for 10 minutes. Stir in the beans, cover, and simmer for 5 minutes. If needed, simmer uncovered for a few minutes to thicken the sauce. Set aside.

4. To prepare the topping, place the bread in a food processor and process into crumbs. Add the garlic, olive oil, and Parmesan cheese. Process for a few seconds to mix.

5. Coat five 16-ounce ramekins with cooking spray. Divide the bean mixture evenly among the ramekins. Top the bean mixture in each ramekin with some of the crumbs.

6. Bake uncovered for about 12 minutes, or until the crumbs are lightly toasted. Let sit for 5 minutes before serving. (Alternatively, bake in a 2-quart casserole dish for about 20 minutes.)

NUTRITION FACTS (PER 1½-CUP SERVING)

Calories: 346	Carbohydrates: 44 g	Fiber: 11.2 g
Protein: 24 g	Fat: 9.5 g	Saturated fat: 2 g
Cholesterol: 60 mg	Sodium: 753 mg	Calcium: 132 mg

Yield: 5 Servings

12 ounces chicken or turkey Italian sausage, casings removed

3 cups sliced white button mushrooms

1½ cups chopped yellow onion (about 2 medium)

2 carrots, halved lengthwise and thinly sliced

¾ cup thinly sliced celery

2 teaspoons crushed garlic

1 teaspoon dried thyme

1 teaspoon dried sage

3 cups chopped fresh plum tomatoes (about 6 to 8 medium), puréed in a blender

¾ cup low-sodium vegetable juice cocktail, such as V8

Two 15-ounce cans reduced-sodium cannellini or white beans, drained but not rinsed

TOPPING

2 slices whole grain bread, torn into pieces

2 teaspoons crushed garlic

2 teaspoons extra virgin olive oil

1 tablespoon grated Parmesan cheese

PENNE PASTA BAKE

Yield: 5 Servings

• • • • • • •

8 ounces uncooked whole grain penne pasta

12 ounces ground beef or chicken, or turkey Italian sausage, casings removed

3 cups sliced white button mushrooms

$^{3}/_{4}$ cup chopped yellow onion

$2^{1}/_{2}$ cups ready-made marinara sauce

2 cups moderately packed chopped fresh spinach

$2^{1}/_{2}$ tablespoons grated Parmesan cheese

$^{3}/_{4}$ cup shredded reduced-fat mozzarella cheese

1. Cook the pasta al dente according to package directions. Drain and set aside. Preheat the oven to 350°F.

2. Coat a large, deep skillet with cooking spray and add the ground meat. Cook over medium heat for about 6 minutes, or until lightly browned, stirring to crumble. Add the mushrooms and onion. Cover and cook for 5 minutes, or until the vegetables soften.

3. Add the marinara sauce to the skillet. Bring to a boil, and then lower the heat to a simmer. Add the spinach, cover, and cook for 2 minutes, or until wilted. Turn off the heat, add the pasta, and toss to mix.

4. Coat a $2^{1}/_{2}$-quart casserole dish with cooking spray and spread the pasta mixture evenly in the dish. Sprinkle the Parmesan and mozzarella cheeses over the top. Cover the dish with aluminum foil (spray the underside of the foil with cooking spray to prevent sticking) and bake for 20 minutes. Remove the foil and bake for about 7 minutes more, or until the edges are bubbly and the cheese is melted. Remove the dish from the oven and let sit for 5 minutes before serving.

NUTRITION FACTS (PER $1^{3}/_{4}$-CUP SERVING)

Calories: 376	Carbohydrates: 43 g	Fiber: 8 g
Protein: 29 g	Fat: 11.5 g	Saturated fat: 4.3 g
Cholesterol: 54 mg	Sodium: 556 mg	Calcium: 237 mg

FOR A CHANGE . . .

To make individual casseroles, divide the pasta mixture equally among five 16-ounce ramekins. Cover and bake for 15 minutes. Bake uncovered for an additional 5 minutes. In addition, feel free to omit the spinach and add $^{3}/_{4}$ cup diced red bell pepper along with the mushrooms and onion.

SPAGHETTI WITH BRUSSELS SPROUTS, PINE NUTS & PARMESAN

1. Cook the pasta according to package directions. Drain, reserving $\frac{1}{2}$ cup of the liquid, and set aside to keep warm.

2. Rinse the Brussels sprouts and trim away any tough or discolored outer leaves. Slice the Brussels sprouts very thinly, discarding the tough stem ends. Separate the slices into shreds. There should be about $4\frac{1}{2}$ cups of loosely packed shreds.

3. Pour the olive oil and water into a large, deep nonstick skillet, and add the Brussels sprouts, black pepper, and salt. Cook over medium heat for about 4 minutes, or until crisp-tender, tossing frequently. Add the pine nuts and garlic and cook for another minute.

4. Add the spaghetti and $\frac{1}{3}$ cup of the reserved pasta liquid to the Brussels sprouts and toss to mix. Add a little more of the reserved liquid if needed. Remove from the heat and toss in the Parmesan cheese. Serve immediately.

Yield: 4 Servings

8 ounces uncooked thin whole wheat spaghetti

12 ounces fresh Brussels sprouts (about 12 large)

2 tablespoons extra virgin olive oil

1 tablespoon water

$\frac{1}{2}$ teaspoon ground black pepper

$\frac{1}{2}$ teaspoon salt

$\frac{1}{3}$ cup pine nuts

1 teaspoon crushed garlic

$\frac{1}{3}$ cup grated Parmesan cheese

NUTRITION FACTS (PER SERVING)

Calories: 376

Protein: 15 g

Cholesterol: 7 mg

Carbohydrates: 46 g

Fat: 18.5 g

Sodium: 433 mg

Fiber: 9 g

Saturated fat: 3 g

Calcium: 120 mg

PENNE WITH BROCCOLI, SHRIMP & SUN-DRIED TOMATOES

Yield: 5 Servings

• • • • • • • • • •

8 ounces uncooked whole grain penne pasta

4 cups fresh broccoli florets

3 tablespoons extra virgin olive oil

$^2/_3$ cup sliced leek (white and light green parts only), or 1 medium yellow onion cut into thin wedges

2 teaspoons crushed garlic

1 cup dry white wine

1 pound shrimp, peeled and deveined

$^1/_4$ cup chopped sun-dried tomatoes

$^1/_2$ teaspoon salt

$^1/_2$ teaspoon ground black pepper

2 tablespoons grated Parmesan cheese

2 tablespoons finely chopped fresh basil, or 2 teaspoons dried

1. Cook the pasta according to package directions. Two minutes before the pasta is done, add the broccoli and cook until the broccoli is crisp-tender and the pasta is al dente. Drain the pasta and broccoli, reserving $^1/_4$ cup of the cooking liquid. Set aside.

2. In a large nonstick skillet, combine the olive oil and leek. Cover and cook over medium heat for about 5 minutes, or until the leek softens. Add the garlic and cook for 30 seconds, or until it begins to turn color and smells fragrant. Add the wine and bring to a boil. Lower the heat to a simmer. Cover and cook for 3 minutes.

3. Add the shrimp, sun-dried tomatoes, salt, and black pepper to the skillet, and adjust the heat to maintain a simmer. Cook uncovered for 5 minutes, or until the shrimp turn opaque and are cooked through, stirring occasionally.

4. Add the pasta and broccoli to the skillet and cook for about 2 minutes to heat through. Add a little of the reserved cooking liquid if the mixture seems too dry. Remove from the heat and toss in the Parmesan. Sprinkle with the basil and serve immediately.

NUTRITION FACTS (PER 2-CUP SERVING)

Calories: 381	Carbohydrates: 37 g	Fiber: 7.3 g
Protein: 28 g	Fat: 11.3 g	Saturated fat: 2 g
Cholesterol: 139 mg	Sodium: 437 mg	Calcium: 144 mg

SPAGHETTI SQUASH WITH BRAISED WHITE BEANS

1. Preheat the oven to 375°F. Cut the squash in half lengthwise and scoop out the seeds. Coat a large baking sheet with cooking spray and lay the squash halves, cut side down, on the sheet. Bake for about 40 minutes, or until easily pierced with a fork.

2. Coat a large nonstick skillet with cooking spray and add the mushrooms and onion. Cover and cook over medium heat for about 5 minutes, or until tender. If necessary, cook uncovered for a couple of minutes to evaporate any liquid and allow the mushrooms to brown lightly.

3. Add the garlic and cook for 30 seconds. Add the tomatoes, beans, basil, salt, black pepper, and olive oil. Cover and bring to a boil. Reduce the heat to a simmer and cook for 10 minutes, stirring occasionally. Cook uncovered for 3 to 5 minutes to thicken the tomatoes to a sauce consistency.

4. Use a fork to separate the squash into strings. For each serving, place 1 cup squash on a serving plate and top with a quarter of the bean mixture (about $7/8$ cup). Sprinkle with $1/2$ tablespoon Parmesan cheese. Serve immediately.

Yield: 4 Servings

• • • • • • • • • •

1 medium spaghetti squash (about 2 pounds)

3 cups sliced baby portobello or white button mushrooms

$3/4$ cup chopped yellow onion

2 teaspoons crushed garlic

14.5-ounce can unsalted diced tomatoes, or 3 cups fresh chopped tomatoes

15-ounce can reduced-sodium cannellini or white beans, drained but not rinsed

2 teaspoons dried basil

$3/4$ teaspoon salt

$1/2$ teaspoon ground black pepper

1 tablespoon extra virgin olive oil

2 tablespoons grated Parmesan cheese

NUTRITION FACTS (PER SERVING)

Calories: 215	Carbohydrate: 34 g	Fiber: 9.1 g
Protein: 10 g	Fat: 5.7 g	Saturated fat: 1.2 g
Cholesterol: 3 mg	Sodium: 560 mg	Calcium: 120 mg

FOR A CHANGE . . .

Subsitute Zucchini Noodles (page 187) or polenta for the spaghetti squash.

Shrimp Croquettes with Corn & Avocado Salsa

Yield: 4 Servings

• • • • • • • • • • •

$2/_3$ cup uncooked white quinoa

12 ounces shrimp, peeled and deveined

$2/_3$ cup finely chopped scallions

$1/_4$ teaspoon salt

$1/_4$ teaspoon ground black pepper

Olive oil cooking spray

SALSA

1 cup frozen (thawed) or fresh-cooked whole kernel corn

1 cup diced avocado

$1/_4$ cup finely chopped fresh cilantro

$1/_4$ cup thinly sliced scallions

2 teaspoons finely chopped fresh or pickled jalapeño peppers, or to taste

2 teaspoons lime juice

$1/_8$ teaspoon salt

1. Cook the quinoa according to package directions. Let cool before proceeding with the recipe.

2. In a medium-sized bowl, combine all the salsa ingredients. Toss to mix. Set aside.

3. In a food processor, combine the cooked quinoa, shrimp, scallions, salt, and black pepper. Pulse for a few seconds at at time until the shrimp is coarsely chopped and the ingredients are well mixed. Shape into 8 patties, each about 3 inches in diameter.

4. Coat a large nonstick skillet with the cooking spray and preheat over medium heat. Add 4 patties to the skillet and spray the tops lightly with the cooking spray. Cook for 2 to 3 minutes on each side, or until lightly browned and cooked through. Remove the patties and set aside to keep warm. Wipe the skillet with a paper towel, coat it again with cooking spray, and cook the remaining 4 patties. Serve hot, topping each serving with a quarter of the salsa.

Nutrition Facts (Per 2 Patties with Salsa)

Calories: 260	Carbohydrates: 30 g	Fiber: 5.6 g
Protein: 18 g	Fat: 8.1 g	Saturated fat: 1.1 g
Cholesterol: 107 mg	Sodium: 436 mg	Calcium: 83 mg

SEARED FISH TACOS

1. In a small bowl, combine all the salsa ingredients and toss to mix. Set aside.

2. In a small bowl, combine the chili powder, cumin, black pepper, garlic powder, and salt. Stir to mix. Sprinkle the spice mix over both sides of the fish fillets.

3. Coat a large nonstick skillet with olive oil cooking spray and preheat over medium-high heat. Add the fish to the skillet, and spray the tops lightly with the cooking spray. Cook for about 3 minutes on each side, or until the fish is cooked through. Remove from the heat and set aside.

4. Stack all 8 tortillas and wrap them in aluminum foil. Place them in a 350°F oven for 10 minutes, or wrap stacks of 4 tortillas in a damp paper towels and microwave them for about 30 seconds. Leave wrapped until ready to serve.

5. Fill each tortilla with an eighth of the fish, $1/4$ cup lettuce, 1 slice avocado, 2 tablespoons salsa, and 2 teaspoons cheese. Serve immediately.

NUTRITION FACTS (PER 2 TACOS)

Calories: 274	Carbohydrate: 23 g	Fiber: 6.5 g
Protein: 28 g	Fat: 8.6 g	Saturated fat: 2.1 g
Cholesterol: 49 mg	Sodium: 386 mg	Calcium: 258 mg

FOR A CHANGE . . .

Substitute shrimp for the fish fillets. Toss the shrimp in the herb mixture and cook for about a minute on each side until opaque and cooked through.

Yield: 4 Servings

• • • • • • • • • •

1 teaspoon chili powder

1 teaspoon ground cumin

$1/2$ teaspoon ground black pepper

$1/2$ teaspoon garlic powder

$1/4$ teaspoon salt

1 pound whitefish fillets, such as grouper, flounder, or cod

Olive oil cooking spray

8 corn or whole wheat flour tortillas (5- to 6-inch rounds)

2 cups shredded romaine lettuce

1 medium avocado, cut into 8 wedges

$1/3$ cup shredded reduced-fat Mexican blend cheese or crumbled queso fresco

SALSA

1 cup chopped fresh tomato

$1/3$ cup chopped red onion

2 teaspoons seeded and finely chopped pickled jalapeño peppers

1 teaspoon juice from the jar of jalapeño peppers

$1/8$ teaspoon salt

$1/8$ teaspoon ground black pepper

$1/3$ cup chopped fresh cilantro

EGGPLANT PARMESAN

Yield: 4 Servings

• • • • • • • •

1 medium eggplant (about 1 1/4 pounds)

3 egg whites, or 1 egg plus 1 egg white

1/2 cup finely ground dried breadcrumbs

1/3 cup grated Parmesan cheese

1/2 teaspoon ground black pepper

Olive oil cooking spray

2 1/2 cups ready-made marinara sauce, heated

1 cup shredded reduced-fat mozzarella cheese

1. Preheat the oven to 400°F. Trim off the ends of the eggplant and slice the eggplant into 12 rounds, each about 1/2-inch thick. Set aside.

2. Pour the eggs into a medium-sized bowl and whisk until smooth. In a shallow bowl, combine the breadcrumbs, Parmesan cheese, and black pepper. Stir to mix. Set aside.

3. Dip the eggplant rounds first in the egg and then in the breadcrumb mixture, turning to coat both sides. Coat 2 large baking sheets with olive oil cooking spray and place the eggplant rounds on the sheets, spacing them 1 inch apart. Sprinkle any unused breadcrumb mixture over the eggplant rounds and spray the tops with the cooking spray. Bake for 10 minutes, turn the rounds with a spatula, and bake for 5 to 7 minutes more, or until nicely browned and tender.

4. Coat a 9-x-13-inch baking pan with olive oil cooking spray and place the eggplant rounds in the pan, slightly overlapping as needed to make them fit. Pour the hot marinara sauce over the eggplant rounds and top with the mozzarella cheese. Bake for 5 minutes, or until the cheese is melted. Serve hot.

NUTRITION FACTS (PER 3 ROUNDS)

Calories: 290	Carbohydrates: 34 g	Fiber: 8.2 g
Protein: 19 g	Fat: 9.6 g	Saturated fat: 4.7 g
Cholesterol: 23 mg	Sodium: 789 mg	Calcium: 363 mg

ROASTED RATATOUILLE

1. Preheat the oven to 450°F.

2. Coat a 12-x-16-inch roasting pan or the bottom of a large broiler pan with cooking spray and add the vegetables and garlic. Sprinkle with the thyme, salt, black pepper, and balsamic vinegar. Toss to mix. Spray the top of the vegetable mixture lightly with the cooking spray.

3. Bake uncovered for 25 to 35 minutes, stirring after 10 minutes, and every 5 to 8 minutes thereafter. Cook until the vegetables are tender and nicely browned. Remove from the oven and toss in the olive oil.

4. While the vegetables are cooking, place the beans in a 1-quart saucepan. Cover and cook over medium heat for about 8 minutes to heat through. Drain off the liquid, return to the pot, and set aside to keep warm.

5. For each serving, spread $^1/_2$ cup beans over the bottom of a shallow serving bowl. Top with a quarter of the ratatouille (about $^3/_4$ cup), 1 tablespoon parsley, and 1 tablespoon cheese.

NUTRITION FACTS (PER SERVING)

Calories: 291	Carbohydrates: 43 g	Fiber: 12 g
Protein: 14.2 g	Fat: 8.7 g	Saturated fat: 2.2 g
Cholesterol: 3 mg	Sodium: 611 mg	Calcium: 176 mg

FOR A CHANGE . . .

Substitute 2 cups cooked brown rice or polenta for the beans. For a brunch dish, omit the beans and top each serving of ratatouille with a poached egg.

Yield: 4 Servings

• • • • • • • • • •

1 pound plum tomatoes, sliced lengthwise into $^3/_4$-inch wedges (about 7 medium)

3 cups diced unpeeled eggplant ($^3/_4$-inch cubes)

2 medium zucchini, halved lengthwise and sliced $^3/_4$-inch thick (2 cups)

2 medium yellow onions, cut into $^3/_4$-inch wedges

1 cup chopped red or yellow bell pepper ($^3/_4$-inch pieces)

6 cloves garlic, cut into thin slivers

1 teaspoon dried thyme

$^1/_2$ teaspoon salt

$^1/_2$ teaspoon ground black pepper

1 tablespoon balsamic vinegar

Olive oil cooking spray

2 tablespoons extra virgin olive oil

19-ounce can reduced-sodium cannellini or white beans (2 cups), undrained

$^1/_4$ cup finely chopped fresh parsley

$^1/_4$ cup crumbled reduced-fat feta cheese

CRISPY TOSTADAS

Yield: 4 Servings

8 thin corn tortillas
(5-inch rounds)

Olive oil cooking spray

15-ounce can reduced-sodium
pinto or black beans, undrained
and mashed with a fork

$1/3$ cup chunky-style salsa

$1/2$ teaspoon chili powder

$1/2$ teaspoon ground cumin

TOPPINGS

1 cup chopped fresh tomato

2 tablespoons finely chopped
pickled jalapeño peppers

$1/2$ cup thinly sliced scallions

2 cups shredded romaine lettuce

1 medium avocado, finely chopped

$1/2$ cup shredded reduced-fat
Mexican blend cheese or
crumbled queso fresco

1. Preheat the oven to 400°F. Coat 2 large baking sheets with cooking spray and lay the tortillas in a single layer on the sheets. Spray the tops of the tortillas lightly with the cooking spray. Bake for 4 minutes, turn the tortillas, and bake for 3 to 4 minutes more, or until lightly browned and crisp. Remove from the oven and set aside.

2. Coat a medium-sized skillet with cooking spray and add the beans, salsa, chili powder, and cumin over medium heat. Bring to a boil. Cook uncovered for about 6 minutes, or until the consistency of refried beans, stirring frequently. Cover to keep warm and set aside.

3. For each tostada, place a tortilla on a work surface and spread with scant $1/4$ cup of the warm bean mixture. Top with 2 tablespoons tomato, $3/4$ teaspoon jalapeño peppers, 1 tablespoon scallions, $1/4$ cup lettuce, $1 1/2$ tablespoons avocado, and 1 tablespoon cheese. Serve immediately.

NUTRITION FACTS (PER 2 TOSTADAS)

Calories: 291	Carbohydrate: 41 g	Fiber: 12.4 g
Protein: 14 g	Fat: 9.9 g	Saturated fat: 2.6 g
Cholesterol: 10 mg	Sodium: 471 mg	Calcium: 301 mg

HELPFUL HINT

Be sure to use *thin* corn tortillas for the shells, otherwise they may turn out chewy instead of crispy. To save time, you can purchase ready-made baked tostada shells.

FIESTA RICE BOWL

1. In a small bowl, combine all of the salsa ingredients and toss to mix. Set aside.

2. In a medium-sized nonstick skillet, combine the beans, tomatoes, chili powder, and cumin. Cover and cook over medium heat for about 5 minutes, or until the tomatoes break down. Cook uncovered for about 3 minutes to thicken the sauce.

3. For each serving, spread $1/2$ cup brown rice over the bottom of a shallow bowl and top with a quarter (scant $1/2$ cup) of the beans. Arrange a quarter of the avocado, corn, and salsa around the beans. Sprinkle $1/2$ cup lettuce and 2 tablespoons cheese over the top. Serve immediately.

NUTRITION FACTS (PER SERVING)

Calories: 362   Carbohydrate: 56 g   Fiber: 13.3 g

Protein: 16 g   Fat: 10.2 g   Saturated fat: 2.8 g

Cholesterol: 10 mg   Sodium: 398 mg   Calcium: 155 mg

FOR A CHANGE . . .

For extra flavor, when making the rice, substitute vegetable broth or light coconut milk (no more than 5 g fat per cup) for the water.

Yield: 4 Servings

15-ounce can reduced-sodium black beans, undrained

$1/2$ cup chopped fresh tomatoes

$1/2$ teaspoon chili powder

$1/2$ teaspoon ground cumin

2 cups hot cooked brown rice

1 cup diced avocado (about 1 large)

1 cup frozen (thawed) or fresh-cooked whole kernel corn

2 cups shredded romaine lettuce

$1/2$ cup reduced-fat Mexican blend cheese or crumbled queso fresco

SALSA

$1 1/2$ cups chopped fresh tomato

$1/2$ cup chopped red onion

$1/2$ cup chopped fresh cilantro

2 teaspoons finely chopped pickled jalapeño peppers

2 teaspoons juice from the jar of jalapeño peppers

$1/8$ teaspoon salt

9

Delightful Salads
& Side Dishes

Side dishes add balance and flair to meals. When done right, they can substantially boost your fiber intake, too. Fruit and vegetables naturally contain fiber, so salads and vegetable side dishes naturally fit a high-fiber lifestyle. As for grain-based sides such as pilafs or pasta, a simple switch to whole grains instantly adds fiber. Including a vegetable, fruit, or whole grain side dish at each meal can easily provide over 10 grams of fiber over the course of a day. And high-fiber side dishes are a must if your main dish is a piece of meat, poultry, or fish, none of which contains fiber.

This chapter features an array of fiber-rich side dishes that are also packed with nutrients and flavor. You'll be delighted to find that these low-fuss side dishes can deliver both taste and nutrition at every meal.

CRUNCHY-NUTTY CARROT SALAD

1. Cook the farro or wheat berries according to package directions. Chill before proceeding with the recipe.

2. In a large bowl, combine the cooked farro or wheat berries, carrots, scallions, and pecans. Toss to mix. Set aside.

3. In a small bowl, combine all the dressing ingredients. Whisk to mix. Pour the dressing over the salad and toss to mix. Let sit for 10 minutes before serving, or cover and chill until ready to serve.

NUTRITION FACTS (PER $^3/_4$-CUP SERVING)

Calories: 171	Carbohydrates: 16 g	Fiber: 4 g
Protein: 3.2 g	Fat: 11.6 g	Saturated fat: 1.2 g
Cholesterol: 0 mg	Sodium: 137 mg	Calcium: 34 mg

HELPFUL HINT

When cooking grains such as farro, wheat berries, or spelt, consider preparing a little extra for later use. Store the cooked grain in freezer bags, squeezing out as much air as possible, and place it in the freezer. It should retain its quality for up to six months. Farro, wheat berries, and spelt increase in size by about $2^1/_2$-fold when cooked, so if a recipe calls for 1 cup uncooked grain, use $2^1/_2$ cups moderately packed cooked grain.

BRUSSELS SPROUT SLAW WITH CARROTS & PECANS

1. Rinse the Brussels sprouts and trim away any tough outer leaves. Slice the Brussels sprouts thinly, discarding the tough stem ends. There should be 3 cups of loosely packed shreds.

2. In a large bowl, combine the Brussels sprouts, carrots, scallions, and pecans. Toss to mix. Set aside.

3. In a small bowl, combine all the dressing ingredients. Stir to mix. Pour the dressing over the salad. Toss to mix.

4. Let sit for 20 minutes, or cover and chill until ready to serve. Toss in the blue cheese just before serving if desired.

NUTRITION FACTS (PER ⅔-CUP SERVING)

Calories: 124	Carbohydrates: 8 g	Fiber: 3 g
Protein: 2 g	Fat: 10 g	Saturated fat: 1.2 g
Cholesterol: 0 mg	Sodium: 200 mg	Calcium: 34 mg

Yield: 4 Servings

8 ounces fresh Brussels sprouts (about 2 cups)

¾ cup julienned carrots

½ cup thinly sliced scallions

¼ cup chopped pecans

1½ tablespoons crumbled reduced-fat blue cheese (optional)

DRESSING

1½ tablespoons extra virgin olive oil

1½ tablespoons orange juice

2 teaspoons balsamic vinegar

1 teaspoon Dijon mustard

¼ teaspoon crushed garlic

¼ teaspoon salt

¼ teaspoon ground black pepper

FABULOUS FIBER FACT

In addition to providing fiber, plant foods offer many essential nutrients. For instance, Brussels sprouts are a rich source of vitamin K, vitamin C, and folate. They also provide sulfur-containing compounds that support the body's detoxification process.

BULGUR WHEAT SALAD WITH ZUCCHINI, TOMATOES & BASIL

Yield: 6 Servings

• • • • • • • • • •

1 cup uncooked bulgur wheat

1 1/2 cups diced zucchini (about 1/4-inch dice)

1 cup chopped, seeded plum tomatoes

1/2 cup sliced scallions

1/4 cup finely chopped fresh basil

1/4 cup chopped black olives

1/4 cup crumbled reduced-fat feta cheese

DRESSING

2 tablespoons extra virgin olive oil

2 tablespoons lemon juice

1/2 teaspoon salt

1/4 teaspoon ground black pepper

1. Prepare the bulgur wheat according to package directions, and set aside.

2. In a large bowl, combine the prepared bulgur wheat, zucchini, tomatoes, scallions, basil, and olives. Toss to mix. Set aside.

3. In a small bowl, combine all the dressing ingredients. Stir to mix. Pour the dressing over the salad. Toss to mix. Let sit for 20 minutes before serving, or cover and chill until ready to serve. If you are going to chill the salad, add the tomatoes 30 to 60 minutes before serving. Toss in the feta cheese just before serving.

NUTRITION FACTS (PER 7/8-CUP SERVING)

Calories: 163	Carbohydrates: 23 g	Fiber: 4.2 g
Protein: 5 g	Fat: 6.4 g	Saturated fat: 1.3 g
Cholesterol: 2 mg	Sodium: 297 mg	Calcium: 31 mg

FOR A CHANGE . . .

Substitute whole wheat orzo or farro for the bulgar wheat.

Quinoa Salad with Black Beans, Corn & Tomatoes

1. Cook the quinoa according to package directions. Chill before proceeding with the recipe.

2. In a large bowl, combine the cooked quinoa, black beans, corn, tomatoes, scallions, and cilantro. Toss to mix. Set aside.

3. In a small bowl, combine all the dressing ingredients. Stir to mix. Pour the dressing over the salad. Toss to mix. Let sit for 15 minutes before serving, or cover and chill until ready to serve. If you are going to chill the salad, add the tomatoes 30 to 60 minutes before serving.

Nutrition Facts (Per ¾-Cup Serving)

Calories: 147	Carbohydrates: 22 g	Fiber: 4.7 g
Protein: 5.7 g	Fat: 4.6 g	Saturated fat: 0.6 g
Cholesterol: 0 mg	Sodium: 267 mg	Calcium: 26 mg

Yield: 8 Servings

$2/3$ cup uncooked white quinoa

15-ounce can reduced-sodium black beans, drained and rinsed

1 cup frozen (thawed) or fresh-cooked whole-kernel corn

1 cup chopped, seeded plum tomatoes

$3/4$ cup thinly sliced scallions

$1/4$ cup finely chopped fresh cilantro

DRESSING

2 tablespoons extra virgin olive oil

1 tablespoon lime juice

1 tablespoon white wine vinegar

$1/2$ teaspoon salt

$1/2$ teaspoon ground black pepper

FABULOUS FIBER FACT

Legumes (dried beans, peas, and lentils) provide more fiber than any other food group—up to 20 grams per cup. Some of the fiber in legumes helps to lower blood cholesterol levels, some improves regularity, and some nourishes good bacteria in the gut.

MIDDLE EASTERN GARBANZO BEAN SALAD

Yield: 6 Servings

· · · · · · · · · ·

15-ounce can reduced-sodium garbanzo beans, drained

1 cup chopped seeded plum tomatoes

1 cup chopped peeled and seeded cucumber

$1/2$ cup chopped fresh parsley

$1/2$ cup thinly sliced scallions

DRESSING

2 tablespoons extra virgin olive oil

2 tablespoons lemon juice

1 teaspoon crushed garlic

$1/2$ teaspoon salt

$1/4$ teaspoon ground black pepper

1. In a large bowl, combine the beans, tomatoes, cucumber, parsley, and scallions. Toss to mix. Set aside.

2. In a small bowl, combine all the dressing ingredients. Stir to mix. Pour the dressing over the salad. Toss to mix. Let sit for 10 minutes, or cover and chill until ready to serve. If you are going to chill the salad, add the tomatoes 30 to 60 minutes before serving.

NUTRITION FACTS (PER $2/3$-CUP SERVING)

Calories: 120	Carbohydrates: 14 g	Fiber: 4 g
Protein: 4.3 g	Fat: 5.7 g	Saturated fat: 0.8 g
Cholesterol: 0 mg	Sodium: 249 mg	Calcium: 39 mg

HELPFUL HINT

To avoid the sodium in canned beans, look for lower-sodium options, or cook dried beans at home. When you cook your own beans, you also avoid BPA (bisphenol A), a chemical found in the lining of some cans. One cup of dried beans yields 3 cups cooked, about what you would get in two 15-ounce cans.

ORZO SALAD WITH SPINACH & ARTICHOKES

1. Prepare the orzo according to package directions. Let cool before proceeding with the recipe.

2. In a large bowl, combine the orzo, spinach, artichoke hearts, olives, and onion. Sprinkle with the black pepper and salt. Drizzle with 3 table-spoons of the reserved artichoke marinade and toss to mix.

3. Cover and chill for at least 30 minutes before serving. If desired, toss in the feta cheese just before serving.

NUTRITION FACTS (PER $^3/_4$-CUP SERVING)

Calories: 137	Carbohydrates: 21 g	Fiber: 4.2 g
Protein: 3.8 g	Fat: 4.4 g	Saturated fat: 0.2 g
Cholesterol: 0 mg	Sodium: 247 mg	Calcium: 26 mg

Yield: 7 Servings

1 cup uncooked whole wheat orzo

2 cups thinly sliced fresh spinach, moderately packed

1 cup chopped marinated artichoke hearts, drained (reserve the marinade)

$^1/_2$ cup pitted black olives, cut lengthwise into slivers

$^1/_2$ cup chopped red onion

$^1/_4$ teaspoon ground black pepper

$^1/_8$ teaspoon salt

3 tablespoons crumbled reduced-fat feta cheese (optional)

FABULOUS FIBER FACT

Any pasta or grain dish can be made both richer in fiber and more filling through the addition of veggies. Simply add lots of non-starchy vegetables, such as spinach, kale, broccoli, carrots, artichoke hearts, zucchini, and tomatoes. This will allow you to enjoy satisfying portions without an excess of carbohydrates or calories.

KALE-QUINOA SALAD

Yield: 4 Servings

. . . .

$^1/_4$ cup uncooked red or tricolor quinoa

6 cups moderately packed baby kale, or thinly sliced large kale leaves with the tough stems removed

I cup thinly sliced quarter-moons cucumber

I cup quartered grape tomatoes

4 slices red onion, cut into quarter-rings

$^1/_4$ cup pumpkin seeds

DRESSING

I $^1/_2$ tablespoons extra virgin olive oil

I $^1/_2$ tablespoons lemon juice

$^3/_4$ teaspoon crushed garlic

Scant $^1/_2$ teaspoon salt

Scant $^1/_2$ teaspoon ground black pepper

1. Cook the quinoa according to package directions. Let cool before proceeding with the recipe.

2. In a large bowl, combine the quinoa, kale, cucumber, tomatoes, onion, and pumpkin seeds. Toss to mix. Set aside.

3. In a small bowl, combine all the dressing ingredients. Stir to mix. Pour the dressing over the salad. Toss to mix.

4. Divide the salad equally among 4 salad plates. Serve immediately.

NUTRITION FACTS (PER 2-CUP SERVING)

Calories: 168	Carbohydrates: 16 g	Fiber: 3.6 g
Protein: 6 g	Fat: 10.1 g	Saturated fat: 1.5 g
Cholesterol: 0 mg	Sodium: 240 mg	Calcium: 69 mg

FABULOUS FIBER FACT

Nuts and seeds are the ultimate "good fats," providing healthy oils in a natural unprocessed package. Nuts and seeds also supply fiber and protein along with a wide range of phytonutrients, vitamins, and minerals.

COLORFUL KALE SALAD

1. Remove and discard the tough stems from the kale leaves. Thinly slice the leaves to make 6 cups loosely packed kale.

2. Remove any tough or discolored outer leaves from the Brussels sprouts. Thinly slice the sprouts and discard the tough stem ends. There should be 1 cup loosely packed shreds.

3. In a large bowl, combine the kale, Brussels sprouts, cabbage or carrots, walnuts, dried cranberries, and if using, the cheese. Toss to mix. Set aside.

4. In a small bowl, combine all the dressing ingredients. Stir to mix. Pour the dressing over the salad. Toss to mix.

5. Divide the salad equally among 4 salad plates. Serve immediately.

NUTRITION FACTS (PER 1¾-CUP SERVING)

Calories: 197	Carbohydrates: 19 g	Fiber: 3.5 g
Protein: 3 g	Fat: 13.6 g	Saturated fat: 1.6 g
Cholesterol: 0 mg	Sodium: 170 mg	Calcium: 73 mg

FOR A CHANGE . . .

Substitute balsamic vinegar for the lemon juice in the dressing.

Yield: 4 Servings

1 small bunch kale (about 8 ounces)

6 medium-sized fresh Brussels sprouts

1 cup shredded red cabbage or julienned carrots

$1/3$ cup chopped walnuts

$1/4$ cup dried cranberries

$1/2$ cup coarsely shredded reduced-fat white cheddar or Gouda cheese (optional)

DRESSING

2 tablespoons extra virgin olive oil

$1 1/2$ tablespoons lemon juice

1 tablespoon orange juice

2 teaspoons honey

$1/4$ teaspoon salt

$1/4$ teaspoon ground black pepper

ARUGULA SALAD WITH CHICKPEAS, PEPPERS & ONIONS

Yield: 4 Servings

• • • • • • • • • • •

1 large red bell pepper, seeded and sliced into half-rings ($1/4$-inch thick)

1 medium yellow onion, sliced into half-rings ($1/4$-inch thick)

Olive oil cooking spray

6 cups fresh arugula leaves

1 cup garbanzo beans (chickpeas), rinsed and drained (reduced-sodium if canned)

$1/4$ cup plus 2 tablespoons chopped Kalamata olives or black olives

$1/2$ cup diced fresh mozzarella cheese

DRESSING

2 tablespoons extra virgin olive oil

2 tablespoons balsamic vinegar

1 teaspoon Dijon mustard

$1/2$ teaspoon ground black pepper

$1/4$ teaspoon salt

1. Preheat the oven to broil. Coat a large baking sheet with olive oil cooking spray and add the bell pepper and onion. Spray the vegetables lightly with the cooking spray. Broil for 10 minutes, or until tender and nicely browned, stirring after 6 minutes. Remove from the oven and set aside for 5 minutes to cool slightly.

2. In a small bowl, combine all the dressing ingredients. Whisk to mix. Set aside.

3. In a large bowl, combine the arugula, bell pepper, and onion. Pour the dressing over the salad. Toss to mix.

4. Divide the salad equally among 4 salad plates. Top each serving with $1/4$ cup garbanzo beans, $1 1/2$ tablespoons olives, and 2 tablespoons mozzarella cheese. Serve immediately.

NUTRITION FACTS (PER SERVING)

Calories: 230	Carbohydrates: 21 g	Fiber: 5.4 g
Protein: 8 g	Fat: 12.8 g	Saturated fat: 2.6 g
Cholesterol: 10 mg	Sodium: 357 mg	Calcium: 179 mg

FOR A CHANGE . . .

Substitute spinach or mixed baby greens for the arugula.

ARUGULA & ASIAN PEAR SALAD

1. In a small bowl, combine all the dressing ingredients. Whisk to mix. Set aside.

2. Peel the pears and use a mandolin or vegetable peeler to cut them into very thin slices, discarding the cores. Alternatively, use a julienne slicer to cut into thin strips.

3. In a large bowl, combine the pears and arugula. Pour the dressing over the salad. Toss gently to mix.

4. Divide the salad equally among 4 salad plates. Top each serving with 1 tablespoon walnuts and 1 tablespoon cheese. Serve immediately.

NUTRITION FACTS (PER SERVING)

Calories: 190	Carbohydrates: 14 g	Fiber: 5.2 g
Protein: 3.7 g	Fat: 14.2 g	Saturated fat: 2.8 g
Cholesterol: 6 mg	Sodium: 193 mg	Calcium: 95 mg

Yield: 4 Servings

3 medium Asian pears

8 cups baby arugula leaves

$1/4$ cup chopped walnuts or pecans

$1/4$ cup crumbled reduced-fat goat cheese or blue cheese

DRESSING

2 tablespoons extra virgin olive oil

1 tablespoon white wine vinegar

1 tablespoon orange juice

$1/2$ teaspoon finely chopped fresh thyme, or $1/8$ teaspoon dried thyme

$1/4$ teaspoon salt

$1/4$ teaspoon ground black pepper

FABULOUS FIBER FACT

To get a healthy intake of fiber consistently, fill at least half your plate with vegetables and fruits, choose whole grains over refined versions, and eat legumes often.

ESCAROLE SALAD WITH APPLES & WALNUTS

Yield: 4 Servings

8 cups torn fresh escarole or romaine lettuce

I medium red-skinned apple, unpeeled, quartered, cored, and very thinly sliced

$1/3$ cup chopped walnuts

$1/4$ cup crumbled reduced-fat blue cheese or goat cheese

DRESSING

2 tablespoons extra virgin olive oil

I tablespoon white wine vinegar

I tablespoon orange juice

I teaspoon Dijon mustard

$1/4$ teaspoon salt

$1/4$ teaspoon ground black pepper

1. In a large bowl, combine all the dressing ingredients. Whisk to mix. Add the escarole, apple, and walnuts. Toss to mix.

2. Divide the salad equally among 4 salad plates. Top each serving with 1 tablespoon cheese. Serve immediately.

NUTRITION FACTS (PER SERVING)

Calories: 197	Carbohydrates: 14 g	Fiber: 5.1 g
Protein: 5 g	Fat: 14.8 g	Saturated fat: 2.6 g
Cholesterol: 4 mg	Sodium: 294 mg	Calcium: 105 mg

FOR A CHANGE . . .

Substitute $2/3$ cup mandarin orange sections plus $2/3$ cup halved seedless red grapes for the apple, and substitute sliced almonds for the walnuts.

FABULOUS FIBER FACT

Pectin—a fiber found in many fruits, including apples, citrus fruits, and berries—has been found to reduce cholesterol levels. Commercially made pectin, which is extracted from citrus peels and apples, is used to thicken jams and some other foods, such as yogurt.

SUMMER BERRY SALAD

1. Place the salad greens in a large bowl. Set aside. In a small bowl, combine all the dressing ingredients. Whisk to mix. Pour the dressing over the salad. Toss to mix.

2. Divide the salad equally among 4 salad plates. Top each serving with a quarter of the berries, nuts, and cheese. Serve immediately.

NUTRITION FACTS (PER SERVING)

Calories: 180	Carbohydrates: 11 g	Fiber: 4.3 g
Protein: 4 g	Fat: 14.6 g	Saturated fat: 2.8 g
Cholesterol: 4 mg	Sodium: 275 mg	Calcium: 58 mg

Yield: 4 Servings

• • • • • • • • • • •

8 cups mixed baby salad greens

1 cup sliced fresh strawberries

1 cup fresh blackberries
or blueberries

$1/3$ cup chopped pecans, walnuts,
or sliced almonds

$1/3$ cup crumbled reduced-fat feta,
blue, or goat cheese

DRESSING

2 tablespoons extra virgin
olive oil

1 tablespoon balsamic vinegar

1 tablespoon orange juice

$1/2$ teaspoon Dijon mustard

$1/4$ teaspoon salt

$1/4$ teaspoon ground
black pepper

FABULOUS FIBER FACT

A high-fiber diet fights heart disease by promoting a healthy weight, moderating blood sugar, reducing blood cholesterol and triglyceride levels, and facilitating lower blood pressure. Fiber-rich plants also provide many nutrients that reduce inflammation and foster a healthy heart and blood vessels.

GUACAMOLE SALAD

Yield: 4 Servings

• • • • • • • • • •

1 1/4 cups chopped tomato

1/4 cup finely chopped red onion

1/4 cup finely chopped fresh cilantro

2 teaspoons finely chopped pickled jalapeño peppers

1/4 teaspoon salt, divided

2 medium avocados, peeled, seeded, and diced

1 teaspoon lime juice

6 cups shredded romaine lettuce

1/4 cup plus 2 tablespoons shredded reduced-fat Monterey Jack cheese or crumbled queso fresco (optional)

1. In a small bowl, combine the tomato, onion, cilantro, jalapeño peppers, and 1/8 teaspoon salt. Toss to mix. Set aside.

2. In a medium-sized bowl, combine the avocado, lime juice, and remaining salt. Mash the avocado, leaving it slightly chunky. Set aside.

3. Place 1 1/2 cups lettuce on each of 4 salad plates. Mound a quarter of the guacamole in the center of each serving. Arrange a quarter of the tomato mixture around the guacamole. Sprinkle each serving with 1 1/2 tablespoons cheese if desired. Serve immediately.

NUTRITION FACTS (PER SERVING)

Calories: 140	Carbohydrates: 12 g	Fiber: 7 g
Protein: 2.9 g	Fat: 10.9 g	Saturated fat: 1.5 g
Cholesterol: 0 mg	Sodium: 163 mg	Calcium: 39 mg

FABULOUS FIBER FACT

Avocados are a delicious way to give recipes a fiber boost. Just half of a medium avocado provides nearly 5 grams of fiber as well as good amounts of the B vitamins, vitamins E and K, copper, and phytonutrients.

SOUTHWESTERN CHOPPED SALAD

1. In a large bowl, combine the lettuce, corn, black beans, tomatoes, and scallions. Set aside.

2. Combine all the dressing ingredients in a blender. Blend until smooth. Pour the dressing over the salad and toss to mix.

3. Divide the salad equally among 4 serving plates. Serve immediately.

NUTRITIONAL FACTS (PER SERVING)

Calories: 175	Carbohydrates: 23 g	Fiber: 7.8 g
Protein: 6.6 g	Fat: 7.9 g	Saturated fat: 1.2 g
Cholesterol: 0 mg	Sodium: 238 mg	Calcium: 43 mg

Yield: 4 Servings

• • • • • • • • •

4 cups shredded romaine lettuce

I cup frozen (thawed) or fresh-cooked whole-kernel corn

I cup cooked black beans, rinsed and drained (reduced-sodium if canned)

I cup diced grape tomatoes

$^1/_3$ cup sliced scallions

DRESSING

$^1/_2$ cup chopped avocado

$^1/_2$ cup chopped fresh cilantro

I tablespoon extra virgin olive oil

I tablespoon lime juice

I$^1/_2$ teaspoons white wine vinegar

$^1/_4$ teaspoon salt

$^1/_4$ teaspoon ground black pepper

Two-Bean Salad with Basil & Tomatoes

1. Steam the green beans for about 5 minutes, or just until tender.

2. In a large bowl, combine the steamed green beans, cannellini beans, grape tomatoes, and basil. Toss to mix.

3. In a small bowl, combine all the dressing ingredients. Whisk to mix. Pour the dressing over the bean mixture. Toss gently to mix.

4. Cover and refrigerate the salad for at least 1 hour before serving. Toss in the cheese just before serving if desired.

Nutrition Facts (Per 3/4-Cup Serving)

Calories: 102	Carbohydrates: 13 g	Fiber: 4.2 g
Protein: 4 g	Fat: 4.5 g	Saturated fat: 0.6 g
Cholesterol: 0 mg	Sodium: 122 mg	Calcium: 46 mg

FABULOUS FIBER FACT

Fermentable, or prebiotic, fiber is so-called because it is fermented and used as a source of nourishment by "good" bacteria in the gut. Many foods, including fruits, vegetables, legumes, oats, barley, and garlic, naturally contain prebiotic fiber.

GARLIC BAKED ARTICHOKES

1. Preheat the oven to 425°F. Slice $1/2$ inch off the tops of the artichokes. Use scissors to snip off the sharp leaf tips. Slice each artichoke in half lengthwise. Immediately rub the sliced sides of the artichokes with the lemon (to prevent browning), or lightly brush them with lemon juice.

2. Using a paring knife, cut out the purple leaves and hairy fibers at the centers of the artichoke halves to form depressions (take care not to trim out the heart, which is adjacent to the fibers). Place the artichoke halves sliced side up in a 9-x-13-inch baking pan.

3. Fill the depressions in each artichoke half with garlic, using 1 to 2 cloves per artichoke half. Pour the water or broth into the bottom of the pan. Cover the pan with foil and bake for about 45 minutes, or until the artichokes are tender when pierced at the base with a toothpick.

4. In a small bowl, combine all the dressing ingredients except the tarragon. Whisk until smooth, and then stir in the tarragon. Serve the artichokes warm or at room temperature. Drizzle each artichoke half with $1^1/2$ teaspoons of the dressing just before serving.

Yield: 4 Servings

4 large artichokes (about 8 ounces each)

1 lemon, cut in half, or 1 tablespoon lemon juice

1 head garlic, separated into cloves and peeled

$3/4$ cup water or vegetable broth

DRESSING

2 tablespoons lemon juice

2 tablespoons extra virgin olive oil

$1/2$ teaspoon Dijon mustard

$1/4$ teaspoon salt

$1/4$ teaspoon ground black pepper

1 tablespoon finely chopped fresh tarragon, or 1 teaspoon dried

NUTRITION FACTS (PER SERVING)

Calories: 131	Carbohydrates: 16 g	Fiber: 7.1 g
Protein: 4.6 g	Fat: 7 g	Saturated fat: 1 g
Cholesterol: 0 mg	Sodium: 266 mg	Calcium: 68 mg

HELPFUL HINT

To eat the artichokes, remove the leaves one at a time and pull them through slightly clenched teeth to strip off the tender flesh at the base. (Discard the fibrous remainder of the leaves.) Continue until all the leaves have been removed and you are down to the heart. Remove any hairy fibers covering the heart. Cut the remaining heart into bite-sized pieces and eat.

ASPARAGUS WITH ALMONDS

Yield: 2 Servings

• • • • • • • •

10 ounces asparagus spears

1 1/2 teaspoons margarine or butter

2 tablespoons sliced almonds

1/8 teaspoon salt

1/8 teaspoon ground black pepper

1. Rinse the asparagus and pat dry with paper towels. Snap off the tough stem ends and discard them.

2. Coat a large nonstick skillet with cooking spray and add the asparagus. Cover and cook over medium-high heat for 2 minutes. Lower the heat to medium and cook for 3 minutes more, or until crisp-tender, shaking the pan occasionally. Add a little water during cooking if needed, but only enough to prevent scorching.

3. Add the margarine or butter and almonds to the skillet. Cook for 30 seconds to melt the margarine; then shake the skillet to coat the asparagus. Sprinkle with the salt and black pepper. Serve immediately.

NUTRITION FACTS (PER SERVING)

Calories: 76	Carbohydrates: 6 g	Fiber: 3.1 g
Protein: 3.7 g	Fat: 5.2 g	Saturated fat: 0.9 g
Cholesterol: 0 mg	Sodium: 170 mg	Calcium: 42 mg

GREEN BEANS WITH GINGER & GARLIC

Yield: 4 Servings

• • • • • • • •

1 pound fresh green beans, trimmed

1/4 cup water

1 tablespoon finely grated fresh ginger root

1 teaspoon crushed garlic

1/4 teaspoon salt

2 teaspoons canola oil

1 1/2 teaspoons sesame seeds

1. In a large skillet, combine the green beans and water. Cover and cook over medium-high heat for 6 to 8 minutes, or until the beans are crisp-tender, stirring occasionally. Add a little more water if needed, but only enough to prevent scorching. If any liquid is left in the skillet, remove the lid and let it evaporate before proceeding.

2. Add the ginger, garlic, salt, canola oil, and sesame seeds. Lower the heat to medium. Toss the mixture over medium heat for 1 minute. Serve immediately.

NUTRITION FACTS (PER SERVING)

Calories: 59	Carbohydrates: 8 g	Fiber: 3 g
Protein: 2 g	Fat: 3.1 g	Saturated fat: 0.3 g
Cholesterol: 0 mg	Sodium: 152 mg	Calcium: 39 mg

HELPFUL HINT

To save time and money, store ginger root in the freezer. Ginger is easier to grate when frozen and keeps well for several months. First, wash the root and pat it dry with a paper towel. There is no need to peel it if you will be finely grating it for recipes. Wrap the root tightly in plastic wrap or place it in a small freezer bag and squeeze out as much air as possible. When you need ginger root, grate the frozen root with a microplane or box grater and return the unused portion to the freezer.

GARDEN PILAF

1. Cook the grain according to package directions. Set aside.

2. In a large nonstick skillet, combine the olive oil, broccoli, and carrot. Cover and cook over medium heat for about 4 minutes, or just until the vegetables are tender. Add a little water if needed, but only enough to prevent scorching. Add the garlic and cook for 30 seconds, or until the garlic begins to smell fragrant.

3. Add the cooked grain, salt, and black pepper. Toss gently for 1 minute to heat through. Serve immediately.

Yield: 4 Servings
• • • • • • •

$^3/_4$ cup uncooked farro, barley, or brown rice

1 tablespoon plus 1 teaspoon extra virgin olive oil

2 cups chopped broccoli florets ($^1/_4$-inch pieces)

1 medium carrot, julienned (about $^3/_4$ cup)

$^3/_4$ teaspoon crushed garlic

$^1/_4$ teaspoon salt

$^1/_4$ teaspoon ground black pepper

NUTRITION FACTS (PER $^7/_8$-CUP SERVING)

Calories: 180	Carbohydrates: 28 g	Fiber: 5.3 g
Protein 5.6 g	Fat: 5.4 g	Saturated fat: 0.7 g
Cholesterol 0 mg	Sodium 177 mg	Calcium: 32 mg

SPICY SWEET POTATO FRIES

1. Preheat the oven to 400°F.

2. Peel the potatoes and cut them into $1/2$-inch-thick fries. In a large bowl, combine the potatoes, olive oil, chili powder, and salt. Toss to coat.

3. Coat a large baking sheet with cooking spray. Arrange the potatoes in a single layer on the sheet. Bake for 12 minutes, turn, and bake for about 5 minutes more, or until browned and tender. Serve hot.

Yield: 2 Servings
. . . .

2 medium sweet potatoes (about 6 ounces each)

$1 1/2$ teaspoons olive oil or canola oil

1 teaspoon chili powder

$1/4$ teaspoon salt

NUTRITION FACTS (PER SERVING)

Calories: 152	Carbohydrates: 28 g	Fiber: 4.6 g
Protein: 2.3 g	Fat: 3.8 g	Saturated fat: 0.3 g
Cholesterol: 0 mg	Sodium: 310 mg	Calcium: 45 mg

PILAF WITH SPINACH, MUSHROOMS & PEAS

1. Cook the grain according to package directions. Set aside.

2. In a large nonstick skillet, combine the olive oil, mushrooms, and onion. Cover and cook over medium heat for about 4 minutes, or until the vegetables are tender, stirring occasionally.

3. Add the peas and garlic to the skillet. Cover and cook for 1 minute, or until the peas thaw. Add the spinach and cook uncovered for 2 minutes, or until the spinach wilts.

4. Toss in the cooked grain, salt, and black pepper. Toss gently for 1 minute to heat through. Serve hot.

Yield: 4 Servings
. . . .

$3/4$ cup uncooked farro, barley, or brown rice

1 tablespoon plus 1 teaspoon extra virgin olive oil

$1 1/2$ cups sliced white button or baby portobello mushrooms

$1/3$ cup chopped yellow onion

$3/4$ cup frozen green peas

$1/2$ teaspoon crushed garlic

2 cups (packed) chopped fresh spinach

$1/4$ teaspoon salt

$1/8$ teaspoon ground black pepper

NUTRITION FACTS (PER $7/8$-CUP SERVING)

Calories: 188	Carbohydrates: 29 g	Fiber: 5.3 g
Protein: 6.7 g	Fat: 5.4 g	Saturated fat: 0.7 g
Cholesterol: 0 mg	Sodium: 186 mg	Calcium: 25 mg

For a Change . . .

For a hearty breakfast dish, top the pilaf with a poached egg.

Brussels Sprouts with Parmesan & Garlic Breadcrumbs

1. Tear the bread into pieces, place the pieces in a food processor, and process into breadcrumbs. There should be about $1/3$ cup crumbs.

2. In a large nonstick skillet, combine 1 teaspoon olive oil and the garlic. Cook over medium heat for about 30 seconds, or just until the garlic begins to smell fragrant, stirring frequently. Add the breadcrumbs and cook for about 1 minute, or until lightly browned, stirring frequently. Transfer the mixture to a small bowl and set aside.

3. Remove any tough or discolored leaves from the Brussels sprouts. Slice the Brussels sprouts $1/4$-inch thick. Discard the tough stem ends. Separate the Brussels sprouts into shreds. There should be 6 cups loosely packed shreds.

4. Add 1 tablespoon olive oil to the skillet. Add the Brussels sprouts, black pepper, salt, and water. Cover and cook over medium heat for about 5 minutes, or until crisp-tender, stirring occasionally. Add a little more water if needed, but only enough to prevent scorching.

5. Remove the skillet from the heat and toss in the breadcrumbs, cheese, and walnuts. Serve immediately.

Yield: 4 Servings

$1/2$ slice firm whole wheat bread

1 tablespoon plus 1 teaspoon extra virgin olive oil, divided

$3/4$ teaspoon crushed garlic

1 pound fresh Brussels sprouts (about 4 cups)

$1/4$ teaspoon ground black pepper

$1/8$ teaspoon salt

2 tablespoons water

2 tablespoons grated Parmesan cheese

3 tablespoons chopped walnuts (optional)

Nutrition Facts (Per $3/4$-Cup Serving)

Calories: 98

Protein: 4.4 g

Cholesterol: 2 mg

Carbohydrates: 10 g

Fat: 5.5 g

Sodium: 142 mg

Fiber: 3.6 g

Saturated fat: 1.1 g

Calcium: 65 mg

ACORN SQUASH EXTRAORDINAIRE

Yield: 4 Servings

• • • • • • • • • • •

1 large acorn squash (1 1/4 pounds)

Olive oil cooking spray

1/4 teaspoon salt

1/4 teaspoon ground
black pepper

6 cups sliced fresh spinach

1/4 cup chopped dried figs

1/4 cup chopped pecans

1/4 cup crumbled goat cheese

DRESSING

1 tablespoon plus 1 teaspoon extra
virgin olive oil

1 tablespoon white wine vinegar

1 teaspoon honey

1 teaspoon frozen (thawed)
orange juice concentrate

1/8 teaspoon salt

1/8 teaspoon ground
black pepper

1. Preheat the oven to 400°F.

2. Cut the squash into 4 wedges. Remove and discard the seeds. Line a large baking sheet with aluminum foil and spray with cooking spray. Place the squash wedges on the sheet, skin side down. (If necessary, trim a small slice from the bottom of each wedge for stability.) Spray each wedge lightly with cooking spray and sprinkle with a pinch of salt and black pepper. Bake for about 25 minutes, or until tender.

3. In a small bowl, combine all the dressing ingredients. Stir to mix. Set aside.

4. Coat a large nonstick skillet with cooking spray and add the spinach. Cook over medium heat for about 2 minutes, or just until wilted.

5. For each serving, place a squash wedge on a serving plate. Top with a quarter of the spinach and drizzle with about 2 teaspoons dressing. Top with 1 tablespoon figs, 1 tablespoon pecans, and 1 tablespoon goat cheese. Serve immediately.

NUTRITION FACTS (PER SERVING)

Calories: 192	Carbohydrates: 22 g	Fiber: 4.2 g
Protein: 4.5 g	Fat: 11.4 g	Saturated fat: 2.2 g
Cholesterol: 3 mg	Sodium: 284 mg	Calcium: 112 mg

ZUCCHINI NOODLES

1. Using a julienne vegetable slicer, shred the zucchini into long thin "noodles." Shred only the skin and firm outer portions of the zucchini, stopping when you reach the seeded portion.

2. Coat a large nonstick skillet with cooking spray and preheat over medium-high heat until a drop of water sizzles when added. Add the zucchini noodles and cook for about 5 minutes, or until crisp-tender, tossing occasionally.

3. Add the garlic, salt, and black pepper to the skillet. Cook for 30 seconds, or until the garlic begins to smell fragrant. Toss in the olive oil and dill or parsley if desired. Serve immediately as a side dish, or top with spaghetti sauce and meatballs as an entrée.

NUTRITION FACTS (PER $\frac{7}{8}$-CUP SERVING)

Calories: 31	Carbohydrates: 6 g	Fiber: 2.4 g
Protein: 2.1 g	Fat: 0.6 g	Saturated fat: 0.1 g
Cholesterol: 0 mg	Sodium: 159 mg	Calcium: 30 mg

Yield: 4 Servings

• • • • • • • • • •

4 medium zucchini
(about 8 ounces each)

1 $\frac{1}{2}$ to 2 teaspoons crushed garlic

$\frac{1}{4}$ teaspoon salt

$\frac{1}{4}$ teaspoon ground
black pepper

2 teaspoons extra virgin
olive oil (optional)

1 tablespoon finely chopped fresh
dill, or 2 tablespoons finely
chopped fresh parsley (optional)

HELPFUL HINT

Reserve the seeded center portions of the zucchini for later use. They can be diced and added to salads.

Spicy Black-Eyed Peas

Yield: 6 Servings

- - - - - - - - - - -

1 1/2 cups water

1 1/4 cups chopped fresh tomatoes

2 tablespoons extra virgin olive oil

1 cup chopped yellow onion

3/4 cup finely chopped green bell pepper

3/4 cup finely chopped celery

2 teaspoons crushed garlic

1 teaspoon ground cumin

1 teaspoon smoked paprika

3/4 teaspoon salt

1 tablespoon finely chopped pickled jalapeño peppers

3 cups frozen or fresh black-eyed peas (15 ounces)

1 tablespoon liquid from the jar of jalapeño peppers

1. In a blender, combine the water and tomatoes. Purée until smooth. Set aside.

2. Pour the olive oil into a 2-quart pot. Add the onion, bell pepper, and celery. Cover and cook over medium heat for about 6 minutes, or until tender, stirring occasionally. Add a little water if needed to prevent scorching. Add the garlic and cook for 30 seconds.

3. Add the cumin, paprika, salt, jalapeño peppers, black-eyed peas, and blended tomato mixture to the saucepan and bring to a boil. Lower the heat to a simmer. Cover and cook without stirring for 30 minutes, or until the black-eyed peas are tender. Stir in the jalapeño pepper liquid. If necessary, increase the heat to medium and cook uncovered for a couple of minutes to thicken the sauce a bit. Serve hot.

NUTRITION FACTS (PER 2/3-CUP SERVING)

Calories: 185	Carbohydrate: 28 g	Fiber: 7 g
Protein: 9 g	Fat: 5.2 g	Saturated fat: 0.7 g
Cholesterol: 0 mg	Sodium: 324 mg	Calcium: 40 mg

10

Sweets & Treats

A taste of something sweet is one of life's simple pleasures. The good news is that there are plenty of ways to sneak some fiber and nutrition into many of your favorite sweet treats. With that said, it is important to be smart about our sweet indulgences. Fruit is by far the best choice for satisfying a sweet tooth. Freshly picked in-season fruit is so luscious that it requires no added sugar. A small piece of dark chocolate or a few chocolate-covered nuts can also do the job.

When you want something more elaborate, enjoy one of the treats presented in this chapter. These recipes feature naturally sweet fruits along with other wholesome ingredients such as yogurt, nuts, seeds, and whole grains. They also minimize added sugars and fats, making them a good choice when you want a treat that is low in calories but high in satisfaction.

BERRIES WITH VANILLA CUSTARD SAUCE

Yield: 4 Servings
• • • • • • • •

3 large egg yolks

3 tablespoons sugar

1 1/2 teaspoons cornstarch

1 1/2 teaspoons vanilla extract

1 cup whole milk

3 cups mixed fresh berries such as raspberries, blueberries, and sliced strawberries

3 tablespoons Glazed Almonds (page 191) or sliced almonds (optional)

1. Place the egg yolks, sugar, cornstarch, and vanilla in a 1-quart heat-proof bowl and whisk to mix well. Set aside.

2. Pour the milk into a 1-quart saucepan and place over medium heat. Cook, stirring frequently, until the milk is steamy and starts to boil. Slowly pour the hot milk into the egg mixture, whisking constantly.

3. Pour the milk-egg mixture back into the pot and place over medium heat. Cook, stirring constantly, for 5 to 8 minutes, or until the mixture thickens to the consistency of buttermilk. Do not allow the mixture to boil; reduce the heat if necessary. Remove from the heat and let sit for 5 minutes, stirring a couple of times. Transfer to a covered container and refrigerate for several hours or overnight. (The sauce will thicken a bit more during this time.)

4. Place 3/4 cup berries in each of four 8-ounce wine glasses or dessert dishes. Top each with a quarter of the sauce (about 1/4 cup). Add a sprinkling of the almonds to each if desired, and serve immediately.

NUTRITION FACTS (PER SERVING)

Calories: 165	Carbohydrates: 25 g	Fiber: 3.7 g
Protein: 4.8 g	Fat: 5.8 g	Saturated fat: 2.4 g
Cholesterol: 144 mg	Sodium: 34 mg	Calcium: 101 mg

HELPFUL HINT

To reduce the sugar content, use a low-calorie sweetener instead of sugar. You will save 36 calories and 9 grams carbohydrate per serving.

GLAZED ALMONDS

1. In a large nonstick skillet, combine the sugar, water, and salt. Cook over medium heat for 1 or 2 minutes, or until the mixture comes to a boil and the sugar dissolves, stirring frequently.

2. Stir in the almonds. Cook for about 5 minutes, or until the mixture is completely dry and the almonds are lightly browned, stirring frequently.

3. Spread the almonds evenly on a nonstick 9-x-13-inch baking sheet. Use a fork to separate any pieces that may be sticking together. Cool to room temperature and then transfer to an airtight container. To maintain freshness, store in the refrigerator or freezer.

Yield: 1 $\frac{1}{4}$ Cups

$\frac{1}{4}$ cup sugar

2 tablespoons water

Pinch salt

1 cup sliced almonds

NUTRITION FACTS (PER TABLESPOON)

Calories: 36	Carbohydrates: 3.5 g	Fiber: 0.6 g
Protein: 1 g	Fat: 2.3 g	Saturated fat: 0.2 g
Cholesterol: 0 mg	Sodium: 7 mg	Calcium: 12 mg

BERRIES WITH YOGURT, HONEY & WALNUTS

1. Place $\frac{1}{4}$ cup berries in each of four 8-ounce wine glasses.

2. Top each with $1\frac{1}{2}$ tablespoons yogurt, 1 teaspoon honey, and $1\frac{1}{2}$ teaspoons walnuts. Repeat the layers and serve immediately.

Yield: 4 Servings

2 cups fresh blackberries, raspberries, or blueberries

$\frac{3}{4}$ cup vanilla Greek-style yogurt (2-percent or 4-percent fat)

2 tablespoons plus 2 teaspoons honey

$\frac{1}{4}$ cup chopped walnuts

NUTRITION FACTS (PER SERVING)

Calories: 127	Carbohydrates: 20 g	Fiber: 4.2 g
Protein: 5.7 g	Fat: 3.9 g	Saturated fat: 1.2 g
Cholesterol: 6 mg	Sodium: 26 mg	Calcium: 74 mg

BERRIES & CREAM PARFAITS

Yield: 4 Servings

• • • • • • • •

2 cups fresh raspberries, blackberries, or blueberries

1/2 cup plain light sour cream or Greek-style yogurt (2-percent or 4-percent fat)

2 tablespoons plus 2 teaspoons light brown sugar

1. Place 1/4 cup berries in each of four 8-ounce wine glass.

2. Top each with 1 tablespoon sour cream and 1 teaspoon brown sugar. Repeat the layers and serve immediately.

NUTRITION FACTS (PER SERVING)

Calories: 107	Carbohydrates: 18 g	Fiber: 4 g
Protein: 3 g	Fat: 2.9 g	Saturated fat: 2 g
Cholesterol: 10 mg	Sodium: 18 mg	Calcium: 63 mg

FOR A CHANGE . . .

Substitute seedless red grapes or diced fresh pineapple for the berries.

COCONUT CHIA PUDDING

Yield: 4 Servings

• • • • • • • •

1 cup coconut milk

2 tablespoons honey or sugar

1/2 teaspoon vanilla extract

1/4 cup chia seeds

1. Place the coconut milk, honey or sugar, and vanilla in a small bowl. Stir until the honey or sugar is dissolved. Stir in the chia seeds.

2. Cover and refrigerate for several hours or overnight, stirring occasionally, until the mixture thickens to a pudding-like texture.

3. Serve each portion in a small decorative glass such as a 4-ounce cordial glass, or layer with fresh fruit in an 8-ounce wine glass.

NUTRITION FACTS (PER 1/3-CUP SERVING)

Calories: 103	Carbohydrates: 14 g	Fiber: 5.3 g
Protein: 3 g	Fat: 5.6 g	Saturated fat: 1.5 g
Cholesterol: 0 mg	Sodium: 0 mg	Calcium: 86 mg

HELPFUL HINT

Select coconut milk that has 4 to 5 grams fat per cup. This can be found in the dairy case of most grocery stores.

FOR A CHANGE . . .

To make chocolate chia pudding, add $1^1/_2$ tablespoons cocoa powder to the coconut milk mixture.

REFRESHING FRUIT POPSICLES

1. In a blender, combine the berries, juice concentrate, and sugar. Blend until smooth. Let sit for 5 minutes to allow the sugar to dissolve, and then blend for an additional 30 seconds.

2. Divide the mixture equally among twelve 3-ounce popsicle molds. Freeze until firm. If desired, remove the popsicles from the molds and transfer them to a freezer bag for storage.

NUTRITION FACTS (PER POPSICLE)

Calories: 63	Carbohydrates: 15 g	Fiber: 2.8 g
Protein: 0.7 g	Fat: 0.4 g	Saturated fat: 0 g
Cholesterol: 0 mg	Sodium: 2 mg	Calcium: 17 mg

Yield: 12 Popsicles

• • • • • • •

3 cups sliced fresh or frozen (thawed) strawberries

3 cups fresh or frozen (thawed) raspberries or blueberries

$^1/_4$ cup plus 2 tablespoons frozen grape, pomegranate, or cranberry juice concentrate

$^1/_4$ cup sugar

FOR A CHANGE . . .

Substitute red or purple grapes for the raspberries or blueberries.

HELPFUL HINT

To reduce the sugar content, use a low-calorie sweetener instead of sugar. You will save 15 calories and 5 grams carbohydrate per serving. Depending on the fruit, you may be able to omit the sweetener entirely.

RUSTIC APPLE TART

Yield: 6 Servings
• • • • • • •

3 cups sliced apples (see the inset on page 197)

2 to 3 tablespoons sugar

$^1/_2$ teaspoon ground cinnamon

$^1/_4$ teaspoon ground nutmeg

4 teaspoons water, divided

3 tablespoons raisins

2 teaspoons cornstarch

CRUST

$^1/_2$ cup plus 2 tablespoons (2.65 ounces) whole wheat pastry flour (see inset on page 72)

$^1/_2$ cup quick-cooking oats

2 tablespoons sugar

$^1/_4$ teaspoon baking powder

$^1/_4$ cup margarine or butter (11 g fat per tablespoon), melted

2 teaspoons water, or as needed

1. Preheat the oven to 375°F.

2. In a 2-quart saucepan, combine the apples, sugar, cinnamon, nutmeg, and 2 teaspoons water. Toss to mix. Cover and cook over medium heat, stirring occasionally, for about 5 minutes, or until the apples start to release their juices and are crisp-tender. Stir in the raisins.

3. In a small bowl, combine the cornstarch and 2 teaspoons water, and stir to mix. Add to the apple mixture while stirring constantly for about 30 seconds, or until the juices thicken. Remove the saucepan from the heat and set aside uncovered.

4. To prepare the crust, place the flour, oats, sugar, and baking powder in a large bowl and stir to mix. Stir in the melted margarine or butter. If needed, stir in enough water to make the dough moist enough to hold together and shape into a ball.

5. Place the dough on a 15-inch square of parchment paper and pat into a 6-inch disk. Cover the disk with a 12-inch sheet of waxed paper and use a rolling pin to roll it into a 10-inch circle. Peel off and discard the waxed paper. Slide the parchment paper and crust onto a large baking sheet.

6. Pile the fruit mixture onto the center of the dough, leaving a 2-inch border on all sides. Use a spatula to lift the border of the crust and fold over the edges of the filling, pleating the crust as necessary. Bake uncovered for about 25 minutes, or until the crust is lightly browned. Remove from the oven and let sit for at least 20 minutes before cutting into wedges and serving.

NUTRITION FACTS (PER SERVING)

Calories: 205	Carbohydrates: 34 g	Fiber: 3.8 g
Protein: 2 g	Fat: 7.5 g	Saturated fat: 2.8 g
Cholesterol: 0 mg	Sodium: 62 mg	Calcium: 13 mg

BROWN SUGAR BAKED APPLES

1. Preheat the oven to 350°F.

2. Slice a 1-inch strip of peel from the top of each apple. If necessary, trim a small section from the bottom of each apple to make it sit upright. Use a melon baller to scoop the cores from the apples, creating a well in the center of each apple, stopping about $1/2$ inch from the bottom.

3. In a small bowl, combine the nuts, raisins, brown sugar, and cinnamon. Stir to mix. Add the margarine. Stir to mix. Stuff a quarter of the nut mixture into the center of each apple.

4. Place the apples in an 8-x-8-inch baking dish. Pour the juice into the bottom of the dish. Bake uncovered for about 40 minutes, or until the apples are tender when pierced with a sharp knife. Drizzle with the pan juices every 15 minutes. Let sit for at least 15 minutes before serving warm.

Yield: 4 Servings

4 medium apples (see the inset on page 197)

$1/4$ cup chopped walnuts, pecans, or almonds

$1/4$ cup raisins or dried cranberries, cherries, figs, or dates

3 tablespoons brown sugar

$1/2$ teaspoon ground cinnamon

I tablespoon plus I teaspoon reduced-fat margarine or light butter (5 g fat per tablespoon)

$1/3$ cup orange or apple juice

NUTRITION FACTS (PER SERVING)

Calories: 184	Carbohydrates: 33 g	Fiber: 3.5 g
Protein: 2 g	Fat: 6.9 g	Saturated fat: 1.3 g
Cholesterol: 0 mg	Sodium: 32 mg	Calcium: 29 mg

HELPFUL HINT

To reduce the sugar content, use a low-calorie sweetener instead of brown sugar. You will save 34 calories and 8 grams carbohydrate per serving.

TRIPLE BERRY PANNA COTTA

Yield: 6 Servings
• • • • • • •

$^1/_2$ cup plus 2 tablespoons pomegranate juice, divided

$1^1/_4$ teaspoons unflavored gelatin

3 tablespoons sugar

2 cups vanilla Greek-style yogurt (4-percent milk fat)

TOPPINGS

$1^1/_2$ cups fresh raspberries

$^3/_4$ cup sliced fresh strawberries

1 tablespoon sugar

$^1/_4$ cup Glazed Almonds (page 191) or sliced almonds

1. Place $^1/_4$ cup of the juice in a 1-quart heatproof bowl. Sprinkle the gelatin over the top and set aside for 2 minutes.

2. In a $1^1/_2$-quart saucepan, bring the remaining juice to a boil over medium heat, or microwave at high power for about 30 seconds to bring to a boil. Add the heated juice to the gelatin mixture. Whisk for 1 minute, or until the gelatin is completely dissolved. Add the sugar. Whisk for 1 minute, or until completely dissolved. Set aside for 10 minutes.

3. Add the yogurt to the juice mixture. Whisk until smooth. Spray the bottoms of six 6-ounce custard cups lightly with cooking spray. Divide the mixture equally among the cups. Cover and chill for at least 8 hours, or until set.

4. To prepare the topping, combine the berries and sugar in a 1-quart bowl and toss to mix. Set aside for 10 minutes.

5. For each serving, run a knife around the edges of a panna cotta and invert onto a dessert plate. Top with $^1/_3$ cup of the berry mixture and 2 teaspoons of almonds. Serve immediately.

NUTRITION FACTS (PER SERVING)

Calories: 168	Carbohydrates: 26 g	Fiber: 3 g
Protein: 8 g	Fat: 4.6 g	Saturated fat: 1.7 g
Cholesterol: 10 mg	Sodium: 46 mg	Calcium: 107 mg

HELPFUL HINT

To reduce the sugar content, use a low-calorie sweetener instead of sugar in the panna cotta and fruit topping. You will save 30 calories and 8 grams carbohydrate per serving.

SUMMER FRUIT CRISP

1. Preheat the oven to 375°F.

2. In a large bowl, combine the fruit, sugar, cinnamon, ginger, orange juice, and cornstarch. Toss to mix.

3. Coat a 9-inch deep-dish pie pan with cooking spray and spread the fruit mixture evenly in the dish. Cover the pan with aluminum foil and bake for 20 minutes, or until the fruit is heated through and starts to soften.

4. While the fruit cooks, prepare the topping. In a medium-sized bowl, combine the oats, flour, brown sugar, and cinnamon. Stir to mix. Add the margarine or butter. Stir until the mixture is evenly mixed, moist, and crumbly. If the mixture seems too dry, add a little more margarine or butter. Stir in the nuts.

5. Sprinkle the topping over the fruit. Bake uncovered for about 20 minutes, or until the edges are bubbly and the topping is golden brown. Let sit for at least 20 minutes before serving.

NUTRITION FACTS (PER $\frac{1}{2}$-CUP SERVING)

Calories: 179	Carbohydrates: 29 g	Fiber: 3 g
Protein: 2.9 g	Fat: 6.7 g	Saturated fat: 1 g
Cholesterol: 0 mg	Sodium: 23 mg	Calcium: 25 mg

FOR A CHANGE . . .

Substitute pears or apples for the peaches, plums, or nectarines.

Yield: 8 Servings

• • • • • • • •

4 cups pitted and sliced fresh peaches, plums, or nectarines

3 to 4 tablespoons sugar

$\frac{1}{2}$ teaspoon ground cinnamon

$\frac{1}{4}$ teaspoon ground ginger

2 tablespoons orange juice

1 $\frac{1}{2}$ teaspoons cornstarch

TOPPING

$\frac{1}{2}$ cup quick-cooking oats

$\frac{1}{4}$ cup whole wheat pastry flour or spelt flour

$\frac{1}{3}$ cup light brown sugar

$\frac{1}{2}$ teaspoon ground cinnamon

2 tablespoons soft tub-style reduced-fat margarine or light butter (5 g fat per tablespoon)

$\frac{1}{2}$ cup chopped walnuts or pecans

The Best Apples for Baking

When making recipes such as baked apples, tarts, pies, or crisps, it's important to choose a variety of apple that holds its shape throughout cooking. Cortland, Granny Smith, Honeycrisp, Jonathan, Winesap, and Rome are some varieties that are recommended for cooking and baking. Experiment to find the flavors you like best. Some bakers like to combine more than one variety for a more complex flavor and a nice balance of sweet and tart.

CHERRY-ALMOND CRISP

Yield: 8 Servings

• • • • • • • •

4 cups frozen or fresh pitted sweet cherries (20 ounces)

2 tablespoons sugar

3 tablespoons orange juice, divided

$^1/_4$ cup dried cherries

2 teaspoons cornstarch

TOPPING

$^1/_2$ cup quick-cooking oats

$^1/_4$ cup whole wheat pastry flour or spelt flour

$^1/_3$ cup light brown sugar

$^1/_4$ teaspoon ground cinnamon

2 tablespoons soft tub-style reduced-fat margarine or light butter (5 g fat per tablespoon)

$^1/_2$ cup sliced almonds

1. Preheat the oven to 375°F.

2. In a 2-quart saucepan, combine the fruit, sugar, and 2 tablespoons orange juice. Toss to mix. Cover and cook over medium heat for about 7 minutes, or until the cherries release their juices and the mixture comes to a boil. Stir in the dried cherries.

3. In a small bowl, combine the cornstarch and 1 tablespoon orange juice. Stir to dissolve the cornstarch. Add the mixture to the cherries while stirring constantly. Cook and stir for about 30 seconds, or until thickened. Coat a 9-inch pie pan with cooking spray and spread the fruit mixture evenly in the dish. Set aside.

4. To prepare the topping, combine the oats, flour, brown sugar, and cinnamon in a medium-sized bowl. Stir to mix. Add the margarine or butter. Stir until the mixture is evenly mixed, moist, and crumbly. If the mixture seems too dry, add a little more margarine or butter. Stir in the almonds.

5. Sprinkle the topping over the fruit. Bake uncovered for about 20 minutes, or until the edges are bubbly and the topping is golden brown. Let sit for at least 20 minutes before serving.

NUTRITION FACTS (PER $^1/_2$-CUP SERVING)

Calories: 183	Carbohydrates: 35 g	Fiber: 3.4 g
Protein: 3 g	Fat: 4.7 g	Saturated fat: 0.7 g
Cholesterol: 0 mg	Sodium: 23 mg	Calcium: 34 mg

FOR A CHANGE . . .

Substitute blueberries for the cherries.

SPICED PEAR SAUCE

1. Place all of the ingredients in a 2-quart saucepan and stir to mix.

2. Cover and cook over medium heat for about 5 minutes, or until the pears start to release their juices and the mixture comes to a boil. Lower the heat to a simmer and cook covered for about 20 minutes, or until soft, stirring occasionally.

3. Using an immersion blender, purée the sauce to the desired consistency. Alternatively, transfer the sauce to a standing blender and blend at low speed until the desired consistency is reached. (Remove the center piece of the blender lid to allow steam to escape, placing a clean towel over the opening to prevent splatters while blending.) If necessary, simmer uncovered for a few minutes to reduce in volume to 2 cups.

4. Let sit for 20 minutes. Serve warm, or transfer to a covered container and refrigerate for up to 3 days before serving.

Yield: 4 Servings

. . . .

4 cups peeled and chopped fresh pears

$1/3$ cup orange juice

$1 1/2$ tablespoons sugar

$3/4$ teaspoon ground cinnamon

$1/2$ teaspoon ground ginger

NUTRITION FACTS (PER $1/2$-CUP SERVING)

Calories: 124

Protein: 0.7 g

Cholesterol: 0 mg

Carbohydrates: 33 g

Fat: 0.2 g

Sodium: 2 mg

Fiber: 5 g

Saturated fat: 0 g

Calcium: 20 mg

HELPFUL HINT

To reduce the sugar content, use a low-calorie sweetener instead of sugar. You will save 18 calories and 5 grams carbohydrate per serving.

CITRUS-GLAZED PEARS

Yield: 4 Servings

• • • • • • •

2 medium unpeeled pears (firm but ripe)

$^1/_4$ cup orange juice

2 tablespoons water

3 tablespoons orange marmalade

1 tablespoon margarine or butter (9 g to 11 g fat per tablespoon)

$^3/_4$ teaspoon finely grated fresh ginger root, or $^1/_4$ teaspoon ground ginger

2 tablespoons Glazed Almonds (page 191) or sliced almonds

1. Cut the pears in half lengthwise and scoop out the fibrous cores. In a 10-inch nonstick skillet, combine the orange juice and water. Arrange the pears cut side down over the juice mixture.

2. Bring to a boil over medium-high heat; then lower the heat to a simmer. Cover and cook for 8 to 10 minutes, or until the pears are easily pierced with a sharp knife. Add a little water during cooking if needed to maintain about $^1/_4$ cup liquid in the skillet. Remove the pear halves and place each, cut side up, in a dessert dish.

3. Add the marmalade, margarine or butter, and ginger to the liquid in the skillet. Stir to mix. Cook uncovered over medium heat for about 2 minutes, or until the mixture is syrupy and reduced in volume to $^1/_3$ cup, stirring frequently. Spoon a quarter of the sauce over each pear half. Top each serving with $1^1/_2$ teaspoons almonds. Serve immediately.

NUTRITION FACTS (PER SERVING)

Calories: 125	Carbohydrates: 25 g	Fiber: 3.8 g
Protein: 1 g	Fat: 3.5 g	Saturated fat: 0.7 g
Cholesterol: 0 mg	Sodium: 31 mg	Calcium: 12 mg

HELPFUL HINT

Keep cans of frozen juice concentrate in the freezer for cooking and baking. This way you can reconstitute only the amount you need for your recipe. Most juice concentrates are reconstituted with water in a 3-to-1 ratio. So, if you need $^1/_4$ cup juice, mix 1 tablespoon juice concentrate with 3 tablespoons water.

FABULOUS FRUIT GELATO

1. In a small bowl, combine the sugar and yogurt. Stir to mix, and set aside for 5 minutes to allow the sugar to dissolve.

2. Place the frozen fruit in a food processor. Process for 2 minutes, or until finely ground with a granita-like appearance. Add the yogurt mixture and process for 1 or 2 minutes, or until creamy, light, and smooth, scraping down the sides as needed.

3. Divide the mixture equally among four 8-ounce dessert dishes or wine glasses. Serve immediately.

Yield: 4 Servings

• • • • • • •

$^1/_3$ cup sugar

1 cup vanilla nonfat or low-fat Greek-style yogurt

4 cups coarsely chopped frozen fruit such as strawberries, cherries, peaches, plums, kiwi, or pineapple

NUTRITION FACTS (PER $^3/_4$-CUP SERVING)

Calories: 129	Carbohydrates: 28 g	Fiber: 3 g
Protein: 4.8 g	Fat: 0.5 g	Saturated fat: 0.1 g
Cholesterol: 1 mg	Sodium: 17 mg	Calcium: 66 mg

FOR A CHANGE . . .

Add $^1/_2$ cup chopped walnuts or sliced almonds to the food processor along with the yogurt.

HELPFUL HINT

To reduce the sugar content, use a low-calorie sweetener instead of sugar. You will save 60 calories and 15 grams carbohydrate per serving.

CRUNCHY GRANOLA BARK

Yield: 24 Pieces

• • • • • • • •

1 cup plus 2 tablespoons quick-cooking oats

$^1/_2$ cup chopped pecans

$^1/_4$ cup sliced almonds

$^1/_4$ cup chopped dark chocolate, or $^1/_4$ cup semisweet chocolate chips

$^1/_4$ cup dark raisins

$^1/_4$ cup unsweetened grated coconut

3 tablespoons dried cranberries

3 tablespoons raw pumpkin seeds

1 tablespoon hulled raw sesame seeds

1 tablespoon chia seeds

$^1/_4$ cup plus 2 tablespoons maple syrup

$2^1/_2$ tablespoons canola oil

1 teaspoon vanilla extract

$^1/_4$ cup sugar, divided

1. Preheat the oven to 250°F. Line an 11-x-17-inch rimmed baking sheet with parchment paper or aluminum foil and coat lightly with cooking spray. Set aside.

2. In a large bowl, combine the first 10 ingredients (oats through chia seeds). Toss to combine. Set aside.

3. In a small bowl, combine the maple syrup, oil, vanilla extract, and 3 tablespoons sugar. Whisk to mix. Pour the maple syrup mixture over the oat mixture. Stir until the dry ingredients are evenly moist. Turn the granola onto the prepared pan and press firmly into an 8-x-12-inch rectangle to about $^1/_4$-inch thickness. Sprinkle the remaining 1 tablespoon sugar over the top.

4. Bake for about 60 minutes, or until lightly browned and firm to the touch. (The bark will become crisper as it cools.) Remove the baking sheet from the oven and place it on a wire rack. Let the bark cool on the sheet to room temperature. Break the bark into pieces, each about $1^1/_2$ by $2^1/_2$ inches. (Do not attempt to cut the bark with a knife, as it will shatter.) Store in an airtight container.

NUTRITION FACTS (PER PIECE)

Calories: 102	Carbohydrates: 12 g	Fiber: 1.5 g
Protein: 1.7 g	Fat: 6.1 g	Saturated fat: 1.4 g
Cholesterol: 0 mg	Sodium: 2 mg	Calcium: 15 mg

WHOLE GRAIN BANANA-NUT BREAD

1. In a large bowl, combine the whole wheat pastry flour, coconut flour or oats, brown sugar, baking powder, baking soda, and nutmeg or cardamom. Stir to mix. Use the back of a spoon to press out any lumps in the baking powder. Set aside.

2. In a medium bowl, combine the banana, egg, oil, and vanilla extract. Stir to mix. Add the banana mixture to the flour mixture. Stir until the dry ingredients are moistened. Set the batter aside for 10 minutes. While the batter sits, preheat the oven to 325°F.

3. Coat a 9-x-5-inch loaf pan with cooking spray. Fold the nuts into the batter. Spread the batter evenly in the pan. Bake for about 45 minutes, or until a wooden toothpick inserted in the center of the loaf comes out clean.

4. Remove the bread from the oven and cool on a wire rack for 20 minutes. Remove the bread from the pan and place on the wire rack to cool thoroughly before slicing.

NUTRITION FACTS (PER SLICE)

Calories: 169	Carbohydrates: 24 g	Fiber: 3 g
Protein: 2.7 g	Fat: 7.1 g	Saturated fat: 0.8 g
Cholesterol: 0 mg	Sodium: 55 mg	Calcium: 43 mg

FOR A CHANGE . . .

Substitute unsweetened applesauce, puréed fresh figs, or puréed fresh strawberries for the mashed banana.

Yield: 16 Slices

• • • • • • •

$1\frac{1}{2}$ cups whole wheat pastry flour

$\frac{1}{4}$ cup coconut flour, or $\frac{1}{2}$ cup quick-cooking oats

$\frac{3}{4}$ cup light brown sugar

1 teaspoon baking powder

$\frac{1}{4}$ teaspoon baking soda

$\frac{1}{2}$ teaspoon ground nutmeg or cardamom

$1\frac{1}{4}$ cups very ripe mashed banana (about $2\frac{1}{2}$ large)

2 large egg whites, or 1 large egg, beaten

$\frac{1}{4}$ cup canola oil

1 teaspoon vanilla extract

$\frac{2}{3}$ cup chopped walnuts or pecans

PUMPKIN-PECAN BREAD

Yield: 16 Slices
• • • • • •

1 3/4 cups whole wheat pastry flour

1/3 cup quick-cooking oats

3/4 cup light brown sugar

1 teaspoon baking powder

1/2 teaspoon baking soda

1 1/2 teaspoons pumpkin pie spice

3/4 cup canned or cooked mashed pumpkin

1/2 cup apple or orange juice

2 egg whites, or 1 large egg, beaten

1/4 cup canola oil

1 teaspoon vanilla extract

3/4 cup chopped pecans

1/2 cup golden raisins or chopped dates

1. Preheat the oven to 325°F. In a large bowl, combine the flour, oats, brown sugar, baking powder, baking soda, and pumpkin pie spice. Stir to mix.

2. In a medium bowl, combine the pumpkin, juice, egg, oil, and vanilla extract. Stir to mix. Add the pumpkin mixture to the flour mixture. Stir until the dry ingredients are moistened.

3. Coat a 9-x-5-inch loaf pan with cooking spray. Fold the pecans and raisins or dates into the batter. Spread the batter evenly in the pan. Bake for about 45 minutes, or until a wooden toothpick inserted in the center of the loaf comes out clean.

4. Remove the bread from the oven and cool on a wire rack for 20 minutes. Remove the bread from the pan and place on the wire rack to cool thoroughly before slicing.

NUTRITION FACTS (PER SLICE)

Calories: 177	Carbohydrates: 27 g	Fiber: 2.8 g
Protein: 2.6 g	Fat: 7.6 g	Saturated fat: 0.7 g
Cholesterol: 0 mg	Sodium: 73 mg	Calcium: 44 mg

HELPFUL HINT

If you don't have any pumpkin pie spice on hand, substitute 1 teaspoon ground cinnamon, 1/4 teaspoon ground ginger, and 1/4 teaspoon ground nutmeg or cloves.

Metric Conversion Tables

COMMON LIQUID CONVERSIONS

Measurement	=	Milliliters
1/4 teaspoon	=	1.25 milliliters
1/2 teaspoon	=	2.50 milliliters
3/4 teaspoon	=	3.75 milliliters
1 teaspoon	=	5.00 milliliters
1 1/4 teaspoons	=	6.25 milliliters
1 1/2 teaspoons	=	7.50 milliliters
1 3/4 teaspoons	=	8.75 milliliters
2 teaspoons	=	10.0 milliliters
1 tablespoon	=	15.0 milliliters
2 tablespoons	=	30.0 milliliters

Measurement	=	Milliliters
1/4 cup	=	0.06 liters
1/2 cup	=	0.12 liters
3/4 cup	=	0.18 liters
1 cup	=	0.24 liters
1 1/4 cups	=	0.30 liters
1 1/2 cups	=	0.36 liters
2 cups	=	0.48 liters
2 1/2 cups	=	0.60 liters
3 cups	=	0.72 liters
3 1/2 cups	=	0.84 liters
4 cups	=	0.96 liters
4 1/2 cups	=	1.08 liters
5 cups	=	1.20 liters
5 1/2 cups	=	1.32 liters

CONVERTING FAHRENHEIT TO CELSIUS

Fahrenheit	=	Celsius
200–205	=	95
220–225	=	105
245–250	=	120
275	=	135
300–305	=	150
325–330	=	165
345–350	=	175
370–375	=	190
400–405	=	205
425–430	=	220
445–450	=	230
470–475	=	245
500	=	260

CONVERSION FORMULAS

LIQUID		
When You Know	Multiply By	To Determine
teaspoons	5.0	milliliters
tablespoons	15.0	milliliters
fluid ounces	30.0	milliliters
cups	0.24	liters
pints	0.47	liters
quarts	0.95	liters

WEIGHT		
When You Know	Multiply By	To Determine
ounces	28.0	grams
pounds	0.45	kilograms

Resources

This book encourages wholesome, natural foods as the first and foremost way for you to meet your fiber needs. Virtually everything you need to enjoy a high-fiber lifestyle can be easily found in your local supermarket or natural foods store. In some cases, you may want or need to utilize fiber supplements. (See page 16.) As you put your high-fiber eating plan into action, you may have questions about certain foods, or simply want to learn more about them. This section provides information and links to manufacturers and websites that may be helpful.

You may have questions not only about diet but also about your underlying health issues. This section also provides information on a variety of organizations that can help you learn more about nutrition and diet, as well as the health conditions that may benefit from a high-fiber lifestyle. Keep in mind, however, that certain resources may be supported, at least in part, by commercial interests, and that this fact should be considered when interpreting information or advice. Potential conflicts of interest may be found by looking at an organization's board of directors or by searching company websites for industry partners, industry memberships, advertisers, and sponsors.

FOOD-RELATED RESOURCES

AmeriFlax
2718 Gateway Avenue, Suite 301
Bismarck, ND 58503
Phone: 701-663-9799
Website: www.ameriflax.com
AmeriFlax promotes the use of US-grown flax and is also involved in research and educational programs on the subject. The AmeriFlax website provides nutrition information about flax along with recipes and tips for incorporating flax in your diet.

Arrowhead Mills
The Hain Celestial Group, Inc.
4600 Sleepytime Drive
Boulder, CO 80301

Phone: 800-434-4246
Website: www.arrowheadmills.com
Arrowhead Mills sells a variety of foods, including whole grains, whole grain flours, seeds, nut butters, cereals, and pulses. The company website features product information and recipes. Arrowhead Mills foods are available in natural foods stores and grocery stores nationwide, as well as online.

The Bean Institute
Website: http://beaninstitute.com
The Bean Institute represents dry bean growers in North Dakota and Minnesota. Its website provides nutrition, health, and culinary information and resources for consumers and home cooks, nutrition and health educators, culinary and food service professionals, and school nutrition professionals.

Bob's Red Mill Natural Foods

13521 SE Pheasant Court
Milwaukie, OR 97222
Phone: 800-349-2173
Website: www.bobsredmill.com

Bob's Red Mill Natural Foods produces an extensive line of whole grains, flours, baking mixes, seeds, pulses, and more. Its website features nutritional information, methods of preparation, and recipes for its products. Bob's Red Mill has products available in natural foods stores and grocery stores, as well as online.

Canadian Lentils

Phone: 306-668-3668
Website: www.lentils.ca

Canadian Lentils is an organization that promotes lentil consumption. Its website offers information on different types of lentils, basic methods of lentil preparation, nutritional and health-related facts about lentils, lentil recipes, and more.

FishWatch

Website: www.fishwatch.gov

Fishwatch is maintained by the National Oceanic and Atmospheric Administration (NOAA) Fisheries. The site provides information about the sustainability of U.S. seafood, including both wild and farmed species.

Flax Council of Canada

465-167 Lombard Avenue
Winnipeg, Manitoba R3B 0T6 Canada
Phone: 204-982-2115
Email: flax@flaxcouncil.ca
Website: www.flaxcouncil.ca

This organization promotes Canadian flax and flax products. It also supports flax-related research and educational programs. Its website offers information on the nutritional qualities of flax as well as recipes and tips for incorporating flax into your diet.

Fruits & Veggies—More Matters

7465 Lancaster Pike
Suite J, 2nd Floor
Hockessin, DE 19707

Phone: 302-235-2329
Website: www.fruitsandveggiesmorematters.org

Fruits & Veggies More Matters is a health initiative focused on helping Americans increase fruit and vegetable consumption for better health. This program is spearheaded by the Produce for Better Health Foundation (PBH) in partnership with the Centers for Disease Control & Prevention (CDC). The website offers nutrition tips; information about choosing, storing, and preparing fruits and vegetables; and a large selection of recipes.

Hodgson Mill

1100 Stevens Avenue
Effingham, IL 62401
Phone: 800-525-0177
Email: customerservice@hodgsonmill.com
Website: www.hodgsonmill.com

Hodgson Mill produces a number of different whole grain foods, including many flours, cereals, and pastas. Its products are available in natural foods stores and grocery stores nationwide, as well as online. Its website also offers recipes for whole grains.

King Arthur

Phone: 800-827-6836
Website: www.kingarthurflour.com

King Arthur offers a selection of whole grain flours, nut flours, and baking ingredients. The company's products may be found in grocery stores nationwide and can be purchased through its website, which also provides tips and recipes for whole grain baking.

Monterey Bay Aquarium Seafood Watch

886 Cannery Row
Monterey, CA 93940
Website: www.seafoodwatch.org

The Monterey Bay Aquarium Seafood Watch program helps consumers and businesses choose seafood that's fished or farmed in ways that protect sea life and habitats, now and for future generations. Recommendations indicate which seafood items are "Best Choices" or "Good Alternatives," and which ones to "Avoid."

National Barley Foods Council

2702 W. Sunset Boulevard
Spokane, WA 99224
Phone: 509-456-2481
Email: mary@wagrains.org
Website: www.barleyfoods.org

The National Barley Foods Council (NBFC) promotes awareness, education, research, and usage of barley on behalf of the US barley industry. The NBFC website features health and nutrition information about barley, tips for using barley and barley products, and recipes.

Natural Resources Defense Council

40 West 20th Street, 11th Floor
New York, NY 10011
Phone: 212-727-2700
Website: www.nrdc.org
Seafood Buying Guide: www.nrdc.org/stories/smart-seafood-buying-guide

The NRDC works in many areas to safeguard the earth—its people, its plants and animals, and the natural systems on which all life depends. The site offers tips for reducing exposure to pesticides and other chemicals in foods and for choosing foods that are environmentally sustainable. The NRDC's Smart Seafood Buying Guide lets you know which fish have the least mercury and which have moderate, high, or very high mercury levels.

Oldways Whole Grains Council

266 Beacon Street, Suite 1
Boston, MA 02116
Phone: 617-421-5500
Website: http://old.oldwayspt.org/

Oldways Whole Grains Council is a consumer advocacy group working to increase the consumption of whole grains for better health. Its website features information on the health benefits of whole grains, cooking tips, recipes, whole grain options when eating out, links to manufacturers of whole grain products, and more.

Pulse Canada

1212-220 Portage Avenue
Winnipeg, Manitoba R3C 0A5 Canada
Phone: 204-925-4455
Email: office@pulsecanada.com

Website: www.pulsecanada.com

Pulse Canada represents growers, processors, and traders of pulse (dried bean, pea, and lentil) crops in Canada. Its website offers nutritional and health information on pulses along with cooking tips, recipes, and more.

US Dry Bean Council

PO Box 1026
Pierre, SD 57501
Phone: 605-494-0280
Website: www.usdrybeans.com

The US Dry Bean Council (USDBC) is dedicated to promoting the bean trade in the United States and educating people about the health benefits and versatility of beans. The USDBC website offers information on the nutritional value of beans, cooking tips, recipes, and many ideas for adding beans to your diet.

USA Dry Pea & Lentil Council

2780 W. Pullman Road
Moscow, ID 83843
Phone: 208-882-3023
Email: info@usapulses.org
Website: www.usapulses.org

USADPLC promotes the interests of growers, processors, warehouse workers, and sellers of dry peas, lentils, and garbanzo beans in the United States. Its website features nutritional information on pulses along with cooking tips, recipes, videos, and more.

HEALTH-RELATED RESOURCES

Academy of Nutrition and Dietetics

120 South Riverside Plaza, Suite 2190
Chicago, IL 60606-6995
Phone: 800-877-1600
Website: www.eatright.org

The world's largest organization of food and nutrition professionals, the Academy of Nutrition and Dietetics offers information on healthy eating, weight loss, managing various diseases and conditions, and much more on its website. If you are looking for a registered dietitian in your area, click on "Find an Expert" on the home page to perform a search.

American Diabetes Association
2451 Crystal Drive, Suite 900
Arlington, VA 22202
Phone: 800-342-2383
Website: www.diabetes.org

This national organization seeks to improve the lives of people affected by diabetes. The American Diabetes Association (ADA) website features information on treating and preventing diabetes, including tips on how to manage the disease through diet and fitness.

American Heart Association
7272 Greenville Avenue
Dallas, TX 75231
Phone: 800-242-8721
Email: review.personal.info@heart.org
Website: www.heart.org

The American Heart Association (AHA) seeks to reduce the risk and incidence of heart disease, stroke, obesity, and diabetes. The association's website provides links to information about disorders of the heart and cardiovascular system, as well as tips for a heart-healthy diet and lifestyle.

American Institute for Cancer Research
1759 R Street NW
Washington, DC 20009
Phone: 800-843-8114
Email: aicrweb@aicr.org
Website: www.aicr.org

The American Institute for Cancer Research (AICR) supports research on the roles of nutrition, physical activity, and weight in cancer risk. Its website provides tips for cancer prevention as well as information for cancer patients and their families.

Dietary Guidelines for Americans
USDA Center for Nutrition Policy and Promotion
3101 Park Center Drive, 10th Floor
Alexandria, VA 22302-1594
Website: www.cnpp.usda.gov/dietary-guidelines
Every five years, the United States Department of Agriculture (USDA) and the US Department of Health and Human Services (HHS) review, update, and release the Dietary Guidelines for Americans. These guidelines contain nutritional

and dietary guidance for the general public and are the foundation for federal nutrition programs. The current guidelines, as well as public comment on the report, can be accessed online.

Environmental Working Group
Website: www.ewg.org

EWG's mission is to empower people to live healthier lives in a healthier environment. Its website offers the "Dirty Dozen" and "Clean Fifteen" lists that highlight pesticide levels in foods so that you can make informed purchases of produce. Go to the website to find updated versions of these lists as well as other helpful information.

Harvard T.H. Chan School of Public Health—The Nutrition Source
677 Huntington Avenue
Boston, MA 02115
Phone: 617-495-1000
Website: www.hsph.harvard.edu/nutritionsource

The Department of Nutrition at the Harvard T.H. Chan School of Public Health maintains an online resource known as "The Nutrition Source," which provides timely information on diet and nutrition. This resource does not accept commercial sponsorship or advertising, and it does not endorse any particular products. Through this website, you will find tips for healthy eating, disease prevention, and weight management, among other health-related matters.

International Scientific Association for Probiotics and Prebiotics
3230 Arena Boulevard, #245-172
Sacramento, CA 95834
Email: info@isappscience.org
Website: www.isapp.net

ISAPP is an association of academic and industrial scientists involved in research and education on probiotics and prebiotics. The ISAPP website provides information on pro- and prebiotics as well as guidelines for choosing these products.

MedlinePlus
Website: www.nlm.nih.gov/medlineplus

Provided by the National Institutes of Health (NIH), MedlinePlus is produced by the US National Library of Medicine. This online resource is meant for patients and their families and friends, and offers links to information about a wide variety of diseases, conditions, treatments, medications, supplements, wellness issues, and much more.

National Institute of Diabetes and Digestive and Kidney Diseases

Health Information Center
Phone: 800-860-8747
Email: healthinfo@niddk.nih.gov
Website: www.niddk.nih.gov

The National Institute of Diabetes and Digestive and Kidney Diseases (NIDDK) conducts and supports research on a broad spectrum of metabolic diseases, including diabetes, obesity, digestive problems such as constipation and diverticular disease, kidney disease, liver disease, and more. The NIDDK website provides information on relevant health and disease topics and offers material on prevention and treatment strategies as well as other resources.

USDA National Organic Program

1400 Independence Avenue, SW
Room 2642-South, Ag Stop 0268
Washington, DC 20250-0268
Phone: 202-720-3252
Website: www.ams.usda.gov/about-ams/programs-offices/national-organic-program

Housed within the Agricultural Marketing Service of the United States Department of Agriculture (USDA), the National Organic Program (NOP) develops regulations and guidance on organic standards for agricultural products. Its website provides information on organic labeling, the USDA organic seal, and organic rules and regulations.

Index